The Community
in Urban Society

Second Edition

Larry Lyon
Baylor University

Robyn Driskell
Baylor University

WAVELAND

PRESS, INC.

Long Grove, Illinois

For information about this book, contact:
    Waveland Press, Inc.
    4180 IL Route 83, Suite 101
    Long Grove, IL 60047-9580
    (847) 634-0081
    info@waveland.com
    www.waveland.com

10-digit ISBN 1-57766-741-7
13-digit ISBN 978-1-57766-741-4

Printed in the United States of America

7   6   5   4   3   2

To Roland Warren

and

Charles Bonjean

Contents

SECTION II
Community and the Quality of Life   91

SECTION III
Studying the Community   141

Preface

The community is one of the most important and interesting fields in social science, but in some ways it is a field that doesn't exist. It is difficult to say exactly where community research and theory merge into urban sociology, rural development, regional studies, formal organizations, or any number of other related fields of inquiry. It's even difficult to say precisely what a community is. Yet no field was more instrumental than community studies in influencing the early development of sociology. When Robert Park and his colleagues at the University of Chicago established the academic legitimacy of sociology, the community was their primary unit of analysis. Accordingly, few fields cover more important philosophical, epistemological, or practical concerns than community sociology. The community is that special place where theory and the "real" world come together. And further, we believe that no field holds greater promise for those with a reformist bent. You can't save the world, but you can improve a community! We try to communicate these exceptional aspects of community sociology in this book.

One of the best books on community sociology since Ferdinand Tönnies's *Gemeinschaft und Gesselschaft* was Roland Warren's *The American Community*. In fact, Warren's decision not to produce a fourth edition of his classic theoretical text played a significant role in the decision to write the first edition this book. Our book is more of a text than *The American Community*. *The Community in Urban Society* (*CUS*) is probably more akin to Warren's earlier and less well-known *Studying Your Community*. The second edition of *CUS* includes several methodological chapters absent from *The American Community* and other community texts. These methodological chapters produced considerable differences of opinion among the initial reviewers of this manuscript. Some felt that methodological issues should be reserved for research books, while others believed as we do that community research is sufficiently different from other research areas to deserve special and separate treatment. And until a book devoted to community research methods is published, we believe these methodological chapters are necessary because our best opportunities to do something practical as "professional sociologists" often come from our community research skills. The community is more

xiii

than an abstract object of theoretical inquiry; it is also a place where we live and a place that we can study and improve. That is what this text is about.

This book also reflects our belief that knowledge should not be presented apart from the events that produced it. There is a lot of "sociology of sociology" in *The Community in Urban Society.* Local conditions change. New research techniques emerge. "Knowledge" about the community is inherently transitory. An understanding of why we approach the community as we do, and of how new conditions require new approaches, is necessary in studying a phenomenon as dynamic and "slippery" as the community.

Larry Lyon
Robyn Driskell

BASIC APPROACHES TO THE COMMUNITY

In spite of, and perhaps even because of, the early primacy of the "city" and the "community" as focal points for social science theory and research, considerable disagreement still exists over answers to such basic questions as: What is a community? How does a community differ from a city? How have communities changed, and why? What are the best ways to conceptualize and study communities? In the first six chapters we examine the most prominent answers to these questions and, in the process, examine some of the seminal thinkers of the nineteenth and twentieth centuries: Ferdinand Tönnies, Karl Marx, Max Weber, Émile Durkheim, Georg Simmel, Robert Park, and Talcott Parsons.

The community, more than the city, has long been an intellectual will-o'-the-wisp, always intriguing but often just beyond our conceptual grasp. As we will see in the first chapter, the community, with its lack of formal organization and absence of political boundaries, presents special problems for analysis and even for definition. In these initial chapters the community is defined in a number of ways, with different definitions leading to different approaches which in turn result in different views of the community. Of course, conceptual disagreements are hardly unique to the study of community; they are common throughout the social sciences. In these sciences a direct and positive relationship often exists between a phenomenon's importance and the level of controversy over how it is to be defined and studied. Thus, the fact that the first chapter of this text considers many definitions of community and the next four chapters outline four different approaches to the community is a testament to the importance this concept has had in the intellectual development of the social sciences generally and of sociology specifically.

The final chapter in this section reconsiders the four major approaches and develops a theme that is followed throughout the book—a pragmatic eclecticism arguing that since no single approach to community works best in all situations, we should use the one that works best for the situation at hand. In addition to reflecting the authors' own bias in this area, it allows new students of community to be exposed to all the predominant approaches in the field.

1

The Concept of Community

This chapter introduces community sociology by first examining the various definitions of community, explaining why community has been such an important but nebulous concept, and adopting a general definition of community for use throughout the book. Then, it outlines the origins of community theory and research and finally charts community sociology's rise, decline, and revival. In this chapter we consider only the most important developments in community sociology, and even those only briefly. However, this summary sets an agenda for the entire book, so that the concepts briefly mentioned here appear in more detail in subsequent chapters.

Definitions of Community

Community is a word with many—some say too many—meanings. Even if most of these definitions are related somehow to a set of common concepts, such broad variation in usage can be exasperating. If a course title includes this term (e.g., Community Sociology, Utopian Communities, Community Studies, Community Development), what can be expected in the subject matter? Would a course in community politics be different from one in urban politics? Is a community a city? Is it a group? Do you live in a community? Would you want to?

Most of us probably think of a small- to medium-size town when conjuring up a mental image of community—a town with white picket fences and white smiling faces (from TVLand reruns, Andy Griffith's Mayberry will do nicely).[1] As we will soon see, such an image fits well with many definitions of community. The term often does imply a small-town nostalgia in which neighborly, homogeneous people care about and help one another. Sometimes, however, a community is defined in a way that includes a modern-day ethnic neighborhood in a large city (Suttles 1972), a large corporation (Minar and Greer 1969), an informal professional group such as the "scientific community" (Kuhn 1962), individuals connected on the Internet (Driskell and Lyon 2002), or even a philosophical and psychological commitment to communal lifestyles (Etzioni 1996b).

3

Why So Many Definitions?

Whenever a word has several meanings it seems subjective, perhaps better suited for the subtleties of philosophy than for the rigorous precision required of scientific terms. Yet, in the social sciences the most important concepts are often among the most imprecise. In economics, inflation can be defined in a number of ways, with the most popular measure—the Consumer Price Index—under continual attack for either overestimating or underestimating inflation. Psychologists disagree on the definition of basic concepts such as personality, neurosis, and psychosis, and what was once a personality disorder can become a lifestyle. Even though a concept such as intelligence can be measured precisely through standardized tests, its meaning is still elusive; witness the charges over racial bias and new measures such as "emotional intelligence." Similarly, in sociology considerable controversy exists as to the meaning of a term such as social class. Sometimes it is used as an inclusive concept, referring to an aggregate social position that includes education, occupation, and family background. At other times it refers only to economic ranking. Still, there are probably no concepts in the social sciences more basic, more important, or more useful than the ones we have mentioned.

In fact, in the social sciences an inverse relationship seems to exist between the importance of a concept and the precision with which it is defined. Because basic concepts such as those mentioned above are important to almost all social scientists, and because scientists vary in their personal and professional viewpoints, basic concepts are interpreted differently. For example, a liberal heterodox economist will be as concerned with supply and demand as a free-market neoclassical economist, but he or she may make very different assumptions about the meaning and relationship of those concepts. Similar examples include physiological and environmental psychologists and their distinct understandings of the causes for behavior, or political scientists and sociologists and their definition of power. Thus, the competing and sometimes contradictory definitions of community indicate the degree to which the concept is important to a large number of social scientists representing diverse approaches and areas of interest. Bearing this in mind, we now turn to the task of defining community.

Defining Community

One of the first American sociologists to define community was Robert Park. As we shall see later in this chapter, Park and his colleagues in the Sociology Department at the University of Chicago were instrumental in establishing community as a central concept in American sociology, but for now it is sufficient simply to examine his early attempt to define community:

> The essential characteristics of a community, so conceived, are those of:
> (1) a population territorially organized, (2) more or less completely rooted in the soil it occupies, (3) its individual units living in a relationship of mutual interdependence. . . . (Park 1936, 3)

This initial attempt at defining community was not the only definition to appear. In fact, the number of various definitions that developed after Park's is astounding, even for a concept as central to early American sociology as community.

Building on Park's definition. Less than twenty years after Park's attempt, George Hillery, Jr. (1955) found no fewer than ninety-four separate definitions of community in the sociological literature. Hillery encountered definitions of community as a group, a process, a social system, a geographic place, a consciousness of kind, a totality of attitudes, a common lifestyle, the possession of common ends, local self-sufficiency, and on and on. The only area of complete agreement was the rather obvious point that communities are made up of people. Such variation is an extreme example of the conceptual imprecision discussed at the beginning of this chapter. Fortunately, however, there were some areas of partial agreement. Hillery found that sixty-nine of his ninety-four community definitions contained the common elements of area, common ties, and social interaction. From these three elements, then, it should be possible to construct a definition that reflects the most common uses of the term.

If we defined a community as *people in a specific area who share common ties and interact with one another*, we would have a definition that largely agrees with most of the definitions Hillery analyzed. Interestingly, we would also have a definition very much like Robert Park's initial concept. The large number of competing definitions Hillery found indicates the central importance of community to American sociology during the 1930s and 1940s. The fact that most definitions included area, common ties, and social interaction suggests that Park's early definition had considerable influence on subsequent community analysis.

The implications of imprecision. Even if we settle on a definition of community as being a territorially organized population with common ties and social interaction, considerable imprecision remains. The type and degree of these three elements remain nebulous. The area of the community might be a politically defined municipal boundary, an economically defined zone of metropolitan dominance, or a socially defined neighborhood. Likewise, the basis of the common ties or bonds (family, ethnicity, propinquity, social class, religion), as well as the amount and quality of social interaction, can vary. So, we are still left with a definition broad enough to include a sprawling, multi-county metropolis, an ethnic neighborhood, or a largely rural village.[2] In short, a community can encompass many different kinds of human organizations.

This flexibility gives community sociology a breadth not found in either urban or rural sociology in that the study of community is not quite so compartmentalized as these neighboring subfields. Additionally, the focus on common bonds and social interaction provides a continuing concern for the quality of life, a concern that is not always as apparent in other fields.

Although some sociologists view the broad and sometimes competing definitions of community as a problem that requires more specific definitions (e.g., Hillery 1963; Freilich 1963; Rossi 1972; Brint 2001),[3] another, and perhaps more accurate, view is that the multiple definitions of community indicate the importance of the term to sociology. As Albert Hunter (1975, 538) eloquently noted, "The very looseness of the concept [community] is valuable in providing a common whetstone on which to sharpen the cutting edge of competing ideas." And the presence of such competition is more a sign of a dynamic, significant sociological concept rather than a problem requiring a narrower, "scientific" definition.

In sum, to study community is to study people who are in and identify with a particular place and to give special attention to the type, quality, and bases of their interaction. Such a broad definition includes much of the subject matter of sociology, so it is not surprising that community theory and research have played a major role in the development of American sociology.

The Origins of Community Theory: Tönnies's *Gemeinschaft* and *Gesellschaft*

If it is possible to mark the beginning of community sociology, it is probably in 1887, with the publication of Ferdinand Tönnies's book, *Gemeinschaft und Gesellschaft* (usually translated as *Community and Society*). Tönnies contrasted the types of human relationships typically appearing in extended families or rural villages (*gemeinschaft*) with those found in modern, capitalist states (*gesellschaft*). *Gemeinschaft*-like relationships are based on a natural will (*wesenwille*) that includes sentiment, tradition, and common bonds as governing forces. The basis for this natural will is in either the family or the "soil" (i.e., living and working in a common place). *Gemeinschaft* is characterized by a strong identification with the community, emotionalism, traditionalism, and holistic conceptions of other members of the community (i.e., viewing another as a total person rather than only as a segment of his collective status, or viewing a person as significant in her own right rather than as a means to an end).

In contrast, *gesellschaft*-like relationships are based on a rational will (*kurwille*) that includes, of course, rationality, as well as individualism and emotional disengagement as key elements. The basis for this rational will is urban, industrial capitalism. *Gesellschaft* is characterized by little or no identification with the community, affective neutrality, legalism, and segmented conceptions of other members of the community. In short, *gesellschaft is* the opposite of *gemeinschaft*.

According to Tönnies, *gemeinschaft* and *gesellschaft* are both ideal types. That is, there is no place one can find totally *gemeinschaft*- or *gesellschaft*-dominated relations. Rather, they are hypothetical, extreme constructs, existing for the purpose of comparison with the real world. A community in which all authority is traditional, where all interactions are completely holistic and emotion rules totally over logic, has never existed. A society in which all authority is based on law, where people are always only a means to an end and logic has completely displaced emotion, also does not exist. Instead, all human organizations are somewhere between the two extremes. Tönnies, in his comparison of *wesenwille and kurwille,* explains that

> between these two extremes all real volition takes place. The consideration that most volition and action resembles or is inclined toward either one or the other makes it possible to establish the concepts of natural will and rational will, which concepts are rightly applied only in this sense. We call them normal concepts. What they represent are ideal types, and they serve as standards by which reality may be recognized and described. (Tönnies 1887, 248)

By comparing our own relationships to these two ideal types, we view ourselves more clearly and can chart movement toward one type or the other.

Tönnies, in common with many of his contemporary sociologists (e.g., Durkheim and Weber), held that European social relationships were becoming more *gesellschaft*-like. Likewise, in America community sociologists were particularly concerned with the type and quality of human relationships as our society seemed to become progressively more oriented toward *gesellschaft*. In fact, concern with the loss of *gemeinschaft*-like relationships in an increasingly *gesellschaft*-dominated society is one of the basic and continuing themes in community sociology. It is also a principal concern in this book. As Tönnies's ideas took root in American sociology, however, numerous revisions and extensions occurred.

The Rise of Community Theory and Research in American Sociology

The concept of community was so central to early American sociology that the following outline of the development of community theory and research is in many ways an outline of American sociology as well. First, we show how community theory (in the form of Tönnies's *gemeinschaft/gesellschaft* typology) was the foundation for many of the most prominent theories in American sociology. Then, we consider the role the community played in the pioneering research and theory developed at the University of Chicago. We briefly analyze the popularity and influence of the classic holistic community studies on both American sociology and society and, as a final example of the early predominance of community theory and research in American sociology, we examine the tremendous outpouring of research into community power.

Typological Theory and the Lost Community

Although Max Weber pioneered the methodology of ideal types, Tönnies's use of contrasting, opposite ideal types arguably became the most common and useful analytic tool in American sociology. We can find this concept reflected in many of the most important American theoretical efforts. Early typologies (e.g., Cooley's primary/secondary groups, MacIver's communal/associational relations, Odum's folk/state distinction, Sorokin's familistic/contractual relationships, and Redfield's folk/urban continuum) were among the foremost theoretical efforts of American sociology, and each of these explanations of social change can be traced to the seminal ideas of Tönnies. More recent and equally important efforts, such as Howard Becker's sacred/secular continuum and Talcott Parsons's pattern variables, are also related to the *gemeinschaft*/*gesellschaft* typology. In the 1950s and 1960s, the movement from *gemeinschaft* to *gesellschaft* was the source of considerable concern regarding the loss of and the quest for community (e.g., Nisbet 1953; Stein 1960). More recently, the typology provides an initial starting point and intellectual template for postindustrial and postmodern sociology.

We explore many of these models in chapter 2 and examine the ways in which they build on Tönnies's ideas, but for now it is sufficient to recognize that the same theoretical concepts that marked the beginning of community sociology also provided the framework for many of the major advances in social theory.

The Chicago School

To a substantial degree, sociology became an accepted part of American academia through the efforts of Robert Park and his colleagues at the University of Chicago. Park, the chairman of the sociology department, was joined by Ernest Burgess, Louis Wirth, Roderick McKenzie, Frederick Thrasher, Nels Anderson, Harvey Zorbaugh, Paul Cressey, Clifford Shaw, and Walter Reckless in authoring the now classic studies of the urbanization process in Chicago. The theoretical basis for their research was borrowed from the already established and accepted science of biology. Employing ecological concepts such as competition, symbiosis, evolution, and dominance that were originally used to explain the interrelationships in the plant and animal kingdoms, they demonstrated that the scientific methods developed in biology could successfully explain the structure and dynamics of American cities. As a result, they were able to establish sociology as an academically and scientifically legitimate discipline. Thus, sociology won out over many other new disciplines that were also competing for academic acceptance (Hawley 1968, 329; Martindale 1981, 94–95).

The community played a major role in the Chicago school's ecological analysis. The first introductory sociology textbook was produced at the University of Chicago (Small and Vincent 1894), and it devoted more pages to community than any other subject. At that time, the community—whether it was a Jewish ghetto, an upper-class neighborhood, or the entire city of Chicago—was the most important single object of sociological inquiry.

Tönnies's concept of increasingly *gesellschaft*-like relationships can be seen throughout the human ecology emphasis of the Chicago school. The most famous example is in Louis Wirth's "Urbanism as a Way of Life" (1938). In this article, Wirth explains how three ecological variables—population size, density, and heterogeneity—combine to produce a more *gesell-schaft*-like lifestyle. Wirth was not the only Chicago sociologist to deal with movement toward *gesellschaft*-like relationships. Some of the best-known portraits of the weakened social integration and accompanying disorganization that beset Chicago during the rapid urbanization of the 1920s can be found in Anderson's *The Hobo* (1923), Thrasher's *The Gang* (1927), Zorbaugh's *Gold Coast and Slum* (1929), Wirth's *The Ghetto* (1928), Shaw's *The Jackroller, A Delinquent Boy's Own Story* (1930), and Cressey's *The Taxi Dance Hall* (1932).

Holistic Studies: The Lynds' Research in Middletown

While the ecological version of community sociology was flourishing at Chicago, Robert and Helen Lynd were pioneering another form of community research: holistic studies that described the various parts of the community and explained their interrelationships. Originally, the Lynds did not set out to study an entire community. Rather, their goal was to study only the religious beliefs and practices in a medium-sized American city. However, they soon realized that religion did not stand in isolation from other local institutions. To understand religion they found it necessary to uncover the relationships between local religious beliefs and practices and other social phenomena in the community. Thus, the Lynds' book describing and explaining life in *Middletown* (Muncie, Indiana) includes not only a chapter on "Engaging in Religious Practices" but chapters entitled "Getting a Living," "Making a Home," and "Using Leisure" as well.

Middletown, published in 1929, was both a literary and sociological phenomenon. It became a best seller with a wide general audience (a rare event for a sociology book). For sociologists, it became a classic community study. Colin Bell and Howard Newby (1972, 82) describe *Middletown* quite accurately as "a magnificent and imaginative leap forward" that "provided a model for sociological advances." It is the best known, the most widely cited, and probably the most influential community study ever published.

A primary reason for its significance and acceptance lay in the rich, relatively objective description of small-town life. Muncie (with a population of approximately thirty-five thousand residents) is described in very much the same way as an anthropologist would detail the activities of a preindustrial village. The research methods were decidedly eclectic, including participant observation, content analysis of historical records, and closed-ended and open-ended questionnaires. *Middletown* describes the various activities and beliefs of Muncie residents in copious detail (e.g., the time different groups arise in the morning, the amount of time spent on household chores, gender roles, parents' aspirations for their children, political and religious values); but, of equal importance, the Lynds also attempted to explain *why* Muncie is the way it is. For example, they explained how religious and political values supported business interests and why residents could claim that there were no class differences in Muncie when the Lynds' own research revealed class difference so pervasive as to affect virtually every aspect of life.

The publication of *Middletown* began a long series of holistic community studies, not the least of which was the Lynds' sequel, *Middletown in Transition* (1937). In their return to Muncie the Lynds analyzed the local effects of the Great Depression. They found that the Depression had enabled one family, the X family, to monopolize the economic means of production, which enabled them to control the entire community. In an often-cited interview, a Muncie resident reports that

> if I'm out of work I go to the X plant; if I need money I go to the X Bank, and if they don't like me I don't get it; my children go to the X college; when I get sick I go to the X hospital; I buy a building lot or house in an X subdivision; my wife goes downtown to buy clothes at the X department store; if my dog strays away he is put in the X pound; I buy X milk; I drink X beer, vote for X political parties, and get help from X charities; my boy goes to the X YMCA and my girl to their YWCA; I listen to the word of God in X subsidized churches; if I'm a Mason, I go to the X Masonic Temple; I read the news from the X morning newspaper; and, if I am rich enough, I travel via the X airport. (Lynd and Lynd 1937, 4)

The Lynds' description of unequally distributed local power and influence was in some ways the forerunner of another type of community research—one that in terms of sheer quantity ranks about as high as any set of research efforts in sociology: community power research.

Community Power

The exposé of the X family notwithstanding, serious, extended study of community power began with the publication of Floyd Hunter's *Community Power Structure* in 1953. Hunter was originally involved in community planning and development in Atlanta. However, he became frustrated with the inability of his Community Planning Council as well as other local entities to produce meaningful social change. Consequently, he attempted to learn how power was distributed in Atlanta and to discover the "real" leaders. If these leaders could be identified, he reasoned, then appropriate communication with or pressure on these leaders might be able to produce significant local change.

Using a variety of methods, most of which were based on face-to-face interviews with strategically placed people in Atlanta, Hunter uncovered a group of forty community influentials. Most of them were businessmen with no official position in local government (only four were government personnel), yet they met with one another frequently to determine the future of Atlanta. In short, Hunter concluded, democracy was not operating as it should. The elected officials of the community had relatively little influence on important, supposedly public, decisions.

Naturally, Hunter's findings were controversial. Political scientists were especially skeptical, not only of Hunter's findings but of his research methods as well. Robert Dahl's *Who Governs?* (1961), a study of decision making in New Haven, set the tone for the polemic that followed. Dahl avoided the interview techniques used by Hunter that asked for the names of powerful people. Rather, he focused on actual decisions that had been made in the community, identified conflicting positions and their supporters, and determined whose views prevailed. Equally significant to the differences in research methods, the findings of *Who Governs?* were in many ways the exact opposite of those of *Community Power Structure.* Dahl found a pluralistic democracy in New Haven with an elected official, the mayor, playing the pivotal role in most major community decisions.

The quantity of research and debate that followed these two books on community power was remarkable. Hundreds of articles and books describing the power distribution of one community or another and voluminous exchanges between pluralists and elitists were published. And now, as a result of that research and debate, it is possible to measure, at least to a degree, the distribution of power in a community and thereby determine who does and does not govern. And most recently and perhaps appropriately, community power research is returning to the holistic approaches that first uncovered the X family in Middletown.

The Decline of Community and the Rise of the Mass Society

The preceding discussions indicate just how prominent a place the community has held as a subject of inquiry in American sociology. Yet, despite the heuristic value of Tönnies's seminal ideas on subsequent social theory, despite the dominance of community in the most prominent sociology department, despite the appeal of holistic studies to both social scientists and the general public, and despite the tremendous outpouring of scientific research following the first community power studies, these community-based activities all but came to a halt in the 1950s and 1960s.

The Decline of Community Theory and Research

By 1970, Tönnies's ideas had become less relevant for community analysis. Bell and Newby began their book *Community Studies* (1972) with the only partially whimsical question, "Who reads Ferdinand Tönnies today?" The answer, at least in the late 1960s and early 1970s, was hardly anyone. The most influential application of Tönnies's ideas was provided by the pattern variables of Talcott Parsons (Parsons and Shils 1951), but Parsons's analysis was seldom directed toward the territorial community; it focused rather on the entire society.

Similarly, the significance of the community as a research site began to fade. Ecological models of urban or community growth (e.g., Burgess's early concentric zone model and the subsequent modifications discussed in chapter 2) were criticized when urban ecologists encountered city after city that were exceptions to the rules. Additionally, considerable ecological research began to be directed at census tracts and other units more precisely defined than the community. Many ecologists even suggested dropping the nebulous, philo-sophical term "community" and substituting more neutral or specific con-cepts such as place, neighborhood, suburb, region, tract, or metropolitan area.

Holistic studies of the *Middletown* genre became rare, with Arthur Vidich and Joseph Bensman's *Small Town in Mass Society* (1958) being one of the last widely cited research efforts. Holistic approaches were not well suited to large cities, and the relevance of small-town research became questionable. Vidich and Bensman even concluded that events in the larger, mass society that lay beyond the local community were more important in their effects on Springdale (the small town they studied) than events in Springdale itself.

Community power research suffered a similar demise. By the 1970s, very few communities were being studied in order to uncover the distribution of power. Although most of the methodological debate had subsided with a gen-eral agreement that combinational techniques featuring multiple approaches to measuring power were best, many began to question whether it was neces-sary to measure the distribution of local power. The chief problem was that knowledge of community power seemed to be largely irrelevant in explaining and predicting community events (e.g., Lyon 1977). Again, the most com-mon explanation of this lack of relevance was that events beyond the local community had more influence on local phenomena than the distribution of local power.

On all fronts, then, the tides of community theory and research began to subside in the 1950s and 1960s. After 1957, the American Sociological Associa-tion no longer included community sections in its annual meetings. The com-munity fell from the highest pinnacles of sociological concern to the low levels reserved for historical curiosities, such as regional studies, rural sociology, or the sociology of religion.[4] When we occasionally referred to or read community theory and research, it was to see only where sociology had been. The commu-nity appeared to have very limited relevance to contemporary sociology.

There are numerous reasons for the decline of interest in various types of community theory and research. Some are unique to their own areas and unrelated to the causes of the decline in other types of community analysis. However, one major trend in American society in general and American soci-ology in particular can be seen as a substantial contributor to the decline of community sociology in *all* areas: the analysis of America as a mass society.

The Rise of the Mass Society

A mass society is a standardized, homogeneous society devoid of major ethnic and class divisions and, most importantly for the community, devoid of substantial regional and local variation.[5] Because of mass media, standard-ized public education, and residential mobility, the intercommunity variation in norms, values, and behavior has been reduced to a remarkable degree. The territorial community, then, is of little scientific importance in a mass society. Residents of New York, New Haven, New Orleans, and New Deal, Texas (population 732) will be much more alike than they are different. They watch the same TV shows and movies, read the same magazines and syndicated columnists, study the same textbooks in the same grades, and travel from one city to the next with ease. Under such circumstances, the logical site of scientific inquiry is the national society, not the local community.[6]

In the 1960s, theories about the structure and dynamics of *societies* became common. Similar theories about *communities* were no longer in vogue. Research based on national samples replaced studies of single communities. Decisions reached in corporate headquarters and state and national capitals far beyond the local community precluded the relevance of community power. In short, the rise of interest in the mass society was matched by the concomitant decline in analysis of the community.

The Revival of Community as a Topic of Sociological Inquiry: Bellah, Putnam, and Tönnies

At this point, students reading this book as a text may well conclude that they made a serious mistake by registering for a course in a dead or, at best, dying field. Fortunately (for both students and teacher), community sociology has experienced a revival. The community and urban sociology section of the American Sociological Association was reconstituted in 1973.[7] By 2009 it had grown to nearly 700 members, ranking in size with other large and established sections such as "theoretical sociology," "deviance," and "sex and gender." Ecologists are again developing models of community structure (Abu-Lughod 1999) and growth and sprawl (Bullard, Johnson, and Torres 2000). Holistic community studies made a comeback, led by a third visit to Middletown (Anderson 1999; Caplow et al. 1982). New community studies are being conducted with advanced techniques (e.g., computer-aided social network analysis methods) and new communities are being built (e.g., New Urbanism). And perhaps most important, a public discussion of our lost levels of community has been renewed by Robert Bellah's *Habits of the Heart* (1996) and Robert Putnam's *Bowling Alone* (2000).

Robert Bellah described the excesses of individualism that can lead to isolation and alienation in his best-selling work, *Habits of the Heart* (1996). According to Bellah, many of the ills of today's society result from too great an emphasis on individualism and too weak a commitment to the community. As individualism, selfishness, and greed in America have grown, our civic commitment and our sense of responsibility to society have declined. Participation in the community will reduce alienation and "enable people to belong and contribute to the larger society" (Bellah 1996, xxxiii). Bellah's widely heeded call for the renewal of civic membership is often based on the beloved community of yesterday.

More recently, Robert Putnam's *Bowling Alone* (2000) gained academic and popular recognition even greater than *Habits of the Heart*. Putnam sides with Bellah and ominously notes that we are "bowling alone" in that more

Americans are bowling today than ever before, but bowling in organized leagues has fallen in the last decade. He claims that a decline in the traditions of civic engagement is weakening our society and sense of community and, unlike Bellah, he backs up his claim with empirical data. Putnam documents the noticeable absence of Americans' involvement in voluntary associations and the reduced patterns of political participation. The trend is disengagement from membership in fraternal organizations, religious affiliations, labor unions, and voluntary associations such as women's societies, school service groups, Boy Scouts, and the Red Cross.

If all this were not enough to document a revival of interest in the community, perhaps the surest sign is that some sociologists may even be reading Tönnies again! Or at least they are rediscovering his concepts of *gemeinschaft* and *gesellschaft* as keys to understanding the community in American society (Martin 2004; Brint 2001; Etzioni 1994b).

In the twenty-first century, a more balanced view of the community in a global, urbanized American society is being developed. While the community is obviously no longer a self-contained, self-sufficient, homogeneous village, neither has it become an impotent group of unrelated, alienated, anonymous residents with little or no local ties. The modern American community is linked with the larger society in so many ways that to study it without acknowledgment and analysis of these links is fruitless, but the practice of ignoring the local community because of these abundant links is equally sterile. Today, community sociology is attempting to rediscover the need for social interaction and common bonds and to understand the interface between the global network, mass society and the local community. As a theoretical base for exploring this interaction, we consider the most common approaches to conceptualizing the community in urban society, beginning with the typological approach in chapter 2.

NOTES

[1] Since Mayberry, programming that focuses on homogeneous residential communities is rare. Note that the more recent TV shows involve a situation comedy with a group of *Friends* meeting at the Central Perk coffee house, or several individuals meeting at a local bar "where everybody knows your name" (*Cheers*). Today, *Cheers* has been replaced on TV by *How I Met Your Mother* friends who meet at MacLaren's Bar. All of these are "third places" (Oldenburg 2001) that emerge in response to the loss of residential community.

[2] Although community remains a broad concept, certain uses of the term are eliminated by this definition. For example, a scientific community could not exist under these conditions. Scientists may interact on occasion and they may share certain values, but there is no specified territory, no place. Scientists may be analyzed more specifically and probably more effectively as a subculture rather than as a community. Similarly, a corporation is not a population living in a specific area and is better described as a formal organization (see Brint 2001). Recent debates of online communities in cyberspace (Wellman 2001) are presented in chapter 7 of this volume.

[3] As examples, see Hillery's (1968) use of "vill" as a more specific term and Bernard's (1973) distinction between "community" as a psychological concept and "the community" as a geographic entity. A similar distinction with new terminology is the current use of place vs. space.

[4] Just as with the community, the fields mentioned here have experienced a measure of renewal after an extended period of decline. The sociology of religion probably resembles the community most closely in both the high level of initial importance and the strength of its recovery.

[5] In some ways mass society is the forerunner of today's theories on globalization. Just as globalization moves emphasis away from the nation-state, mass society moved emphasis away from the local community.

[6] As with the concept of community, as the idea of America as a mass society gained prominence, the definitions of mass society became more numerous. William Kornhauser (1959) and Edward Shils (1972) played pioneering roles in its development. Maurice Stein (1960) initially explained the effect of the mass society on the community while Robert Nisbet (1953), David Riesman (1953), and Robert Putnam (2000) analyzed its effects on individuals (see also chapter 7).

[7] The fact that the ASA section is now named "Community and Urban" rather than simply "Community," as it originally was, indicates both a decline in the significance of community since its heyday in the 1930s and a move of sociology and society to a more urban focus.

chapter two

The Typological Approach
Community on a Rural/Urban Continuum

The typological approach is the most fundamental of all approaches to the community. It is also among the most important in all of sociology. Robert Nisbet makes the case for the importance of the typological approach in *The Sociological Tradition* (1966, 71):

> Nowhere has sociology's contribution to modern social thought been more fertile, more often borrowed from by other social sciences, especially with reference to the contemporary study of undeveloped nations, than in the typological use of the idea of community. Through this typology, the momentous historical transition of nineteenth-century society from its largely communal and medieval character to its modern industrialized and politicized form has been taken from the single context of European history in which it arose and made into a more general framework of analysis applicable to analogous transitions in other ages and other areas of the world.

In addition to examining some of the major contributions to community sociology, this chapter includes many of the seminal ideas in social science as well.

Classic Typologies

As we examine some of the key concepts in social science, we will be reviewing the contributions of the pioneers in social science as well: Weber, Durkheim, Simmel, Redfield, Wirth, and especially Ferdinand Tönnies.

Ferdinand Tönnies (1855–1936):
Gemeinschaft und Gesellschaft

At the relatively young age of thirty-two, German philosopher and sociologist Ferdinand Tönnies published *Gemeinschaft und Gesellschaft* (1887) and

17

provided the foundation for virtually all the subsequent developments in the typological approach. His theory of movement from a *gemeinschaft* lifestyle based on *wesenwille* to a *gesellschaft* lifestyle based on *kurwille* is outlined in the preceding chapter, allowing us to focus on the implications of his work here.

Certainly much of the significance of Tönnies's typological approach lies in the use of contrasting ideal types on opposite ends of a continuum. Yet, Pitirim Sorokin (1963) points out that the use of polar extremes hardly originated with Tönnies. Earlier polar types can be found in the analyses of Confucius, Plato, Aristotle, St. Augustine, and Ibn Khaldun. Similarly, Max Weber is usually credited with fully developing the ideal type as a useful theoretical and empirical construct. Why, then, is Tönnies seen as the founder of the typological approach?

Tönnies, unlike predecessors such as Confucius or Khaldun, was able to observe and analyze the *gesellschaft*-producing effects of the industrial revolution on the *gemeinschaft*-like medieval nations of Europe. Thus, he was able to construct a model of social change with implications for industrializing/ industrialized societies that is of continued relevance. Further, Tönnies, more than Weber, explicitly demonstrated the utility of *polar* ideal types for comparison with real-world phenomena. It is Tönnies, then, who almost immediately influenced the subsequent typological approaches of Weber, Durkheim, and Simmel and later indirectly influenced the analysis of Louis Wirth, Robert Redfield, Howard P. Becker, and Talcott Parsons.

Max Weber (1864–1920): Rationalization

Weber's contributions to sociology, political science, and economics are manifold, but for our purposes we focus primarily on his contributions to the typological approach; here we find remarkable similarities with the earlier analysis of Tönnies. In Weber's classics *The Protestant Ethic and the Spirit of Capitalism* (originally published in 1904–5), *Economy and Society* (originally published in 1921 but written between 1910 and 1914), and *Sociology of Religion* (originally published in 1920–21), we find Tönnies's theme of a communal, medieval Europe being transformed into an individualistic, capitalistic Europe. Weber refers to the transformation as the result of increasing "rationalization," but the phenomena being described are virtually identical to moving from *gemeinschaft* to *gesellschaft*. For example, Weber's distinctions between rational actions based on "efficiency" and the "amount of return" (*zweckrational*) and the more *gemeinschaft*-like actions based on values (*wertrational*), emotion (*affektuell*), or tradition (*traditionell*) are similar to Tönnies's original typology.

These four types of action are ideal types that Weber compared to actual occurrences of behavior, and he concluded, much like Tönnies, that Europe was becoming increasingly *zweckrational*. For example, his study of religion focused on the growing rationalization of religious life from magic into "book religion." In law, he found the personalized justice of traditional or charismatic leaders replaced by rationally enacted, codified laws from objective, legal–rational rulers. In music, he contrasted the spontaneous music of Asia and Africa with the standardized music of a European symphony. In sum, Weber's cross-cultural and historical analysis led him to conclude that the trend of world history was toward increasing rationalism, or in Tönnies's terms, toward increasing *gesellschaft*.

Émile Durkheim (1858–1917): Mechanical and Organic Solidarity

Much like Weber, the French sociologist Émile Durkheim influenced the social sciences in ways far beyond his writing on community typologies. Still, one of his most enduring contributions is to be found in his distinction between *gemeinschaft*-like mechanical solidarity and *gesellschaft*-like organic solidarity.

In *The Division of Labor in Society* (1893), Durkheim described the dissolution of medieval social ties based on similarity. Medieval Europe was a homogeneous society. Values concerning politics, economics, family, and religion were almost universally accepted. Likewise, lifestyles showed little variation from village to village and from generation to generation. Society, Durkheim explained, was held together by a mechanical solidarity in which everyone was alike with little social or economic differentiation. However, an industrial revolution in England and a political revolution in France destroyed the basis for mechanical solidarity. Violently different ideas about politics, economics, and religion developed, and different lifestyles (based on an infinitely more complex division of labor) became common. What, Durkheim asked, is the "glue" for the new *gesellschaft*-like Europe? What is the new basis for social solidarity? His answer was an organic solidarity based on mutual interdependence. That is, individuals work together for the common good because they must. Self-sufficiency is no longer possible in a *gesellschaft*-like society.

Although Durkheim reasoned that organic solidarity is now necessary at the societal level, he believed it to be psychologically inadequate at the individual level. The theme of his classic work *Suicide* (1897) was the need for associational memberships to offset the loss of the communal, group identifications common to mechanical solidarity. In *Suicide* we find not only an analysis of problems associated with movement from *gemeinschaft* to *gesellschaft* but also a proposed solution to the "quest for community" problem so central to community sociology. Durkheim demonstrates that close, personal group relationships in families or religious worship can provide some of the psychological integration (i.e., *gemeinschaft*-like community) necessary in a society based on organic solidarity.

Georg Simmel (1858–1918): "The Metropolis and Mental Life"

The German philosopher and sociologist Georg Simmel is responsible for some of the richest, most insightful analysis of urban life ever written. In an often-reprinted lecture delivered in the winter of 1902–3, he describes "The Metropolis and Mental Life"(1983), exploring the relationship between the urban environment and the psychic experience of the inhabitants by focusing on their uniquely urban experiences, attitudes, and behaviors. In so doing, he practices a social psychology that shows how a multitude of characteristics (e.g., intellectuality, emphasis on a precise time schedule, and a belief in causality, individuality and most notably a blasé attitude) are part of an urban or *gesellschaft* lifestyle. For Simmel, a key to understanding the *gesellschaft*-like psychology predominant in the great metropolises of Europe was to consider the role of a money economy:

> The metropolis has always been the seat of the money economy. Here the multiplicity and concentration of economic exchange gives an importance to the means of exchange which the scantiness of rural commerce would not have allowed. Money economy and the dominance of the intellect are intrinsically connected. They share a matter-of-fact attitude in dealing with men and with things; and, in this attitude, a formal justice is often coupled with an inconsiderate hardness. . . . By being the equivalent to all the manifold things in one and the same way, money becomes the most frightful leveler. For money expresses all qualitative differences of things in terms of "how much?" Money, with all its colorlessness and indifference, becomes the common denominator of all values; irreparably it hollows out the core of things, their individuality, their specific value, and their incomparability. All things float with equal specific gravity in the constantly moving stream of money. (Simmel 1902–3, "The Metropolis and Mental Life," quoted from Wolff 1978, 411)

A plumber, then, who charges $100 per hour to repair your faucet is more than twice as valuable as a teacher who receives $40 per hour for instructing your child, but that plumber is only one tenth as valuable as a surgeon who repairs your heart at $1000 per hour. A Picasso painting that sells for $1 million is ten times better than a Rembrandt that may go for $100,000, and so on. Simmel's imagery in this lecture for describing the urban, *gesellschaft* lifestyle is unsurpassed. The same can be said for his insightful analysis. For example, he explains that while

> metropolitan man is "free" in a spiritualized and refined sense, in contrast to the pettiness and prejudices which hem in the small-town man . . . [i]t is obviously only the obverse of this freedom if, under certain circumstances, one nowhere feels as lonely and lost as in the metropolitan crowd. (Simmel 1902–3, "The Metropolis and Mental Life," quoted from Wolff 1978, p. 418)

Although Simmel's European contemporaries were the founding fathers of modern sociology, even Tönnies's, Weber's, and Durkheim's descriptions do not match his rich imagery. Further, their primary focus was more at the societal level than on local phenomena. It is, rather, in the American sociologist Louis Wirth that we find typological analysis in the tradition of Georg Simmel.

Louis Wirth (1897–1952): "Urbanism as a Way of Life"

Wirth was a student of urban ecologist Robert Park (who had been a student of Simmel's) in the sociology department at the University of Chicago. Although the ecological approach to community is treated separately in this book, Wirth's classic article "Urbanism as a Way of Life" is considered here because it remains American sociology's definitive statement of *gesellschaft*. Wirth notes many of the same characteristics as Simmel—the blasé attitude, time schedules, individuality—but differs considerably from his European predecessor in accounting for their origin. While Simmel focused mainly on a money economy and only to a lesser extent on population size, Wirth (1938, 18) maintained that three population characteristics cause the distinctive urban lifestyle and that

> on the basis of three variables, number, density of settlement, the degree of heterogeneity of the urban population, it appears possible to explain the characteristics of urban life and to account for the differences between cities of various sizes and types.

If his proposition were wholly true, this book could be considerably shorter and community life much easier to understand. Still, his article was the impetus for an outpouring of research evaluating the causes of *gesellschaft*, and we consider that research later in this chapter. For now it is sufficient to summarize what is possibly the most cited, most influential article ever written in American sociology.

Wirth reasoned that large population *size* would necessarily result in *gesellschaft* characteristics such as a more specialized division of labor and more impersonal, segmented relations. He explained how the increased population *density* of the city requires a greater tolerance of individual differences but nevertheless results in more "competition," "exploitation," and "disorder." That, in turn, leads to more "formal controls" on behavior. Finally, the higher levels of urban *heterogeneity* were seen as producing a more complex stratification system, a money economy, more stereotyping, and categorical thinking. In other words, Wirth employed the spatial-population variables predominant in the ecological analysis of the Chicago School to account for the differences between *gemeinschaft* and *gesellschaft* described in the classic European works of Tönnies, Weber, Durkheim, and Simmel. And although later tests of his theory often found it wanting, the initial field research of the anthropologist Robert Redfield provided strong support for Wirth's ideas.

Robert Redfield (1897–1958): "The Folk Society"

Also a student of Robert Park at the University of Chicago, Robert Redfield published his now-famous study of four Mexican communities only three years after Wirth's "Urbanism as a Way of Life" article appeared in the *American Journal of Sociology*. In *The Folk Culture of Yucatan* (1941), Redfield found that the smaller, the more isolated, the more homogeneous the community, the more *gemeinschaft*-like the lifestyle. Based on his research in the Yucatan peninsula and other studies, Redfield later published the *AJS*'s *gemeinschaft* companion piece to the *gesellschaft* "Urbanism as a Way of Life." Redfield's article, "The Folk Society," described the ideal *gemeinschaft* type: "small, isolated, nonliterate and homogeneous with a strong sense of group solidarity" (Redfield 1947, 293). It has only a minimal division of labor, based largely on sex role differentiation and a shared means of production. He describes the ideal folk community as economically self-contained, with no dependence on the larger surrounding society. Culturally, it is traditional and uncritical and is based on religion and kinship. In contrast, he describes the prototypical urban, industrialized civilization as large, heterogeneous, and secular with impersonal relationships.

When Redfield's "The Folk Society" is combined with Wirth's "Urbanism as a Way of Life," we have a rural/urban continuum with the polar types defined in considerable detail. Any actual community or society can be placed at some point between the two opposite types and then compared with other actual cases to determine existing levels of *gemeinschaft* or *gesellschaft*. By the 1950s, then, the rural/urban continuum was in place as a major approach to community theory and research. There were, however, subsequent innovations in this approach that transformed it into something quite different from the original *gemeinschaft*/*gesellschaft* perspective.

Innovations in the Typological Approach

In the 1950s, Howard P. Becker and Talcott Parsons used the typological approach to establish themselves as major (and in Parsons's case, *the* major) social theorists of post–World War II American sociology. While their work is clearly in the *gemeinschaft*/*gesellschaft* tradition, both made several key modifications in the approach of Tönnies and other theorists who built upon his perspective.

Howard P. Becker (1899–1960): Sacred/Secular

Howard Becker's sacred/secular continuum (1957) is clearly built upon the works of Tönnies and Weber, but there are some notable differences. Unlike Tönnies, Becker sometimes discusses movement away from the *gesellschaft*-secular end of the continuum and toward greater sacredness.[1] Also, unlike Weber, Becker refers to his polar types as constructed types rather than ideal types. Partially, this change was due to his belief that "ideal" is too value-laden and therefore too susceptible to misleading connotations. More important, however, was his insistence that the characteristics of the type be based on an actual "culture case study" rather than a purely mental construct.[2] For Becker, an example of a constructed type would be Redfield's folk society—an extreme case for comparison with real-world phenomena, but with characteristics derived from his empirical fieldwork in the Yucatan peninsula.

Becker's key distinction between the sacred and secular is the reluctance to (sacred) or readiness for (secular) change. In an extremely sacred society, for example, martyrdom to preserve religious values would be a common response to an attempted change in orthodoxy. Conversely, in a highly secular society, one might find a scientist risking life or limb in pursuit of new knowledge. In fact, these kinds of sacrificial activities would be empirical references for his constructed types.

Becker maintained that societies were within the extremes, possessing both sacred and secular values. Further, he moved away from the evolutionary view of growing *gesellschaft*-like secularization. He argued that skipping stages and reversing movement were possible and that when a society reached extreme secularization, charismatic leadership can often lead to a sudden reversal to extreme sacralization. Becker refined typological theory in a way that made it more compatible with historical events, but at the same time he reduced its predictive and explanatory power. No longer could simple predictions be made about an increasingly *gesellschaft*-like society, and no longer could social change be explained by an evolutionary model.

Talcott Parsons (1902–1979): Pattern Variables

Without serious qualification, it can be argued that the zenith of the typological approach was reached in 1951 with the publication of Talcott Parsons's and Edward Shils's *Toward a General Theory of Action*. Building on Tönnies's *gemeinschaft/gesellschaft* types, they developed what became, perhaps, the most widely cited aspect of Parsons's influential structural-functional theory—the four pattern variables of social action:

- *affectivity/affective neutrality*—referring to whether gratification is immediate or deferred;
- *diffuseness/specificity*—referring to whether relationships are holistic and cover a large number of situations (e.g., mother-child) or narrow and constrained to only a single basis for interaction (e.g., bureaucrat-client);
- *particularism/universalism*—referring to whether special standards are applied to special groups (e.g., neighbors, kin, strangers) or whether the same standards are applied to all (e.g., citizens); and
- *quality/performance* (originally designated as ascription/achievement)—referring to whether an object is based on what it is (e.g., an antique clock), or what it does (e.g., tells time with less precision than a low-priced Timex).

Parsons believed that although a social structure (e.g., a society, a community, or an interpersonal relationship) may seem to be typically *gemeinschaft* or *gesellschaft,* closer inspection would reveal a mixture that varied along the four polar types of the pattern variables. For example, Parsons argued that while a modern physician's relations to patients would be *gesellschaft* when compared to the more affective, particularistic treatment of a tribal medicine man, "by virtue of the canon that 'the welfare of the patient' should come ahead of the self-interest of the doctor, this was clearly one of *gemeinschaft*" (Parsons and Smelser 1956, 34). Thus, the pattern variables can be viewed as a multidimensional refinement of Tönnies's original polar types.

As we shall see later in this chapter, the pattern variables can be used to estimate the magnitude of the "loss of community" phenomenon. However, Parsons was not particularly interested in the local community. Rather, he felt his pattern variables applied to all forms of social actions and usually adopted a micro-interpersonal unit of analysis or a macro focus on entire societies that in either case bypassed the community.

The Third Type: Global, Post-Modern, Post-*Gesellschaft* Societies[3]

There is a still emerging but increasingly accepted theoretical position stating that modern industrial societies have moved beyond the elements of *gesellschaft* and are entering an entirely new basis for social relationships. Various names for this new stage have been offered: "The Third Wave" (Toffler 1980), "The Informational City" (Castells 1991), "The Global City" (Sassen 2001), "Edge City" (Garreau 1992), "Cyberspace Communities" (Rheingold 1993), "Postmodern Urbanism" (Ellin 1996), and "Edgeless Cities" (Lang 2003). C. Wright Mills, in *The Sociological Imagination* (1959, 165–166), was among the first sociologists to see the beginning of a postmodern period:

> We are at the ending of what is called The Modern Age. Just as Antiquity was followed by several centuries of Oriental ascendancy, which Westerners provincially called The Dark Ages, so now The Modern Age is being succeeded by a Post-Modern period.

The claims of distinctiveness for this new type are often quite extensive. Michael Dear (2000, 157) sees us entering

> a postmodern urban process in which the urban periphery organizes the center within the context of a globalizing capitalism. The postmodern urban process remains resolutely capitalist, but the nature of that enterprise is changing in very significant ways, especially through (for instance) the telecommunications revolution, the changing nature of work, and globalization . . . we understand that a radical break is occurring . . . Contemporary urbanism is a consequence of how local and inter-local flows of material and information (including symbols) intersect in a rapidly-converging globally-integrated economy driven by the imperatives of flexism. Landscapes and peoples are homogenized to facilitate large-scale production and consumption. Highly mobile capital and commodity flows outmaneuver geographically fixed labor markets, communities, and nation states, and cause a globally bifurcated polarization.

An interesting aspect of the recent debates on the postmodern society is the notion of a "radical break" from both the past and *gemeinschaft*-like relationships. Still, the most pertinent question for those who argue for a post-*gesellschaft* typology is precisely what Dear takes as given: Have we already entered into a new social order based on relationships *fundamentally* different from the *gesellschaft* condition described by Tönnies over one hundred years earlier? There is no clear consensus in the research about the nature of the radical break or the specific characteristics that define this new postmodern society. Some analysts have declared our current society to be the same business as usual, only a more rapid, supermodern society with technologically advanced forms of communications. Ted Relph (1987, 265) does not feel that these changes in society merit a move into a postmodern era.

> For all the dramatic modifications that have been made to urban landscapes over the last 100 years I begin to suspect that the only fundamental social advances have been to do with sanitation. All the other changes—skyscrapers, renewal, suburban subdivisions, expressways, heritage districts—amount to little more than fantastic imagineering and spectacular window dressing.

Douglas Kellner (1989, 12) considers the postmodernization to be a fad that will soon pass.

> The postmodern moment had arrived and perplexed intellectuals, artists, and cultural entrepreneurs wondered whether they should get on the bandwagon and join the carnival, or sit on the sidelines until the new fad disappeared into the whirl of cultural fashion.

While the hyperspeed of change and types of technological interaction have impacted communities throughout the globe, is it sufficient for us to speak of a radical break to a postmodern society? If electronic communication via e-mail, the Internet, and text messaging replaces the written word, that would not, in itself, constitute a new "wave," "stage," or "type." Rather, we would want to know if this new form of communication significantly changed social interactions. Will a computer-linked social network replace the associations that replaced informal neighboring? Will people begin to view one another, their communities, or their societies in substantially different ways? Between *gemeinschaft* and *gesellschaft,* the answer is reasonably clear and affirmative. Between *gesellschaft* and post-*gesellschaft*, a clear consensus opinion has not formed.

For now, we would do well to remember that much *gemeinschaft*-like community remains even in our industrialized mass society. Even if a third "wave" is upon us, we would expect considerable *gesellschaft* to remain in a post-*gesellschaft* society with some of the desire for *gemeinschaft* driven by pervasive *gesellschaft*. The transformation into this third type may not be as sweeping as its proponents claim.

Why Was There Movement toward *Gesellschaft*?

Although there is near unanimity concerning both the distinctiveness of *gesellschaft* from *gemeinschaft* and the general trend toward a more *gesellschaft*-

like society, there is little agreement on why *gesellschaft* is distinctive and why there is movement toward the *gesellschaft* end of the continuum.[4] We begin by investigating the popular causal variable of the classic typologists—capitalism.

Capitalism: A Marxist Explanation

If capitalism is the key causal variable, then the presence of capitalism as a new economic system would be the major cause of the distinctive *gesellschaft* lifestyle. Simmel's focus on the role of a money economy comes to mind here.[5] Similarly, the spread of capitalism and its advancement into successive stages of economic development would account for the movement toward more *gesellschaft*-like societies. In this regard, the explanation is within the province of a Marxist approach to the community. In *The German Ideology* Marx and Engels (1846) show how capitalism propels the Industrial Revolution through the development of new factory-based towns. This begins the breakdown of the medieval-*gemeinschaft* lifestyle and its replacement with the alienation of *gesellschaft*:

> Within the capitalist system all methods for raising the social productiveness of labor are brought about at the cost of the individual laborer; all means for the development of production transform themselves into means of domination over, and exploitation of, the producers; they mutilate the laborer into a fragment of a man, degrade him to the level of an appendage of a machine, destroy every remnant of charm in his work, and turn it into a hated toil; they estrange him from the intellectual potentialities of the labor process in the same proportion as science is incorporated in it as an independent power; they distort the conditions under which he works, subject him during the labor process to a despotism the more hateful for its meanness, they drag his wife and child beneath the wheels of the juggernaut of capital. (Marx 1867, *Capital*, quoted from Nisbet 1966, 291)

Thus, capitalism "sows the seeds of its own destruction" by clustering together the alienated workers in these new urban centers.

Although capitalism has yet to destroy itself, we find today a major approach to the problems of urban, *gesellschaft*-like societies based on the proposition that capitalism is the key causal variable. The conflict approach will be considered shortly, but for now it is sufficient to note that when it overlaps with the typological approach, it does so by offering capitalism as the driving force behind the movement to *gesellschaft*.

Population Characteristics: An Ecological Explanation

Just as the conflict approach overlaps community typologies on the question of why there is movement toward *gesellschaft*, the ecological approach overlaps here also. Although Simmel provided the initial ecological arguments for an increasing population size leading to *gesellschaft* relations (see Kamolnick 2001), it is in Wirth's "Urbanism as a Way of Life" that population characteristics are most clearly linked to lifestyle.

The research testing Wirth's propositions about population size, density, and heterogeneity is now legion. And as is often the case when there is a large body of research, the results are somewhat contradictory. Still, most of the empirical evidence is at odds with Wirth's theory. *Gemeinschaft* patterns have been found in large centers of dense, heterogeneous populations such as Boston (Gans 1962), Tokyo (Bestor 1989), Chicago (Anderson 1990), New York (Abu-Lughod 1999), and Santa Barbara (Molotch, Freudenburg, and Paulsen 2000). And, conversely, rural areas possessing small, diffuse, homogeneous populations have shown distinctively *gesellschaft* characteristics. For example, Oscar Lewis (1951) studied the same Mexican village of Tepoztlan originally referred to by Redfield as extremely *gemeinschaft*. He found not *gemeinschaft*-like harmony and consensus, but rather a "pervading quality of fear, envy and distrust in interpersonal relations" (Lewis 1951, 429). In short, studies of the effect of population size (Fischer 1995), density (Gans 1962; Wellman and Leighton 1979), and heterogeneity (Sjoberg 1965; Suttles 1968; Wilson 1985) have often failed to find the causal relationships with lifestyles posited in Wirth's "Urbanism as a Way of Life." And yet, more rural areas do prove to have more *gesellschaft* lifestyles when compared to more urban areas (Beggs, Haines, and Hurlbert 1996.

Industrialization: A Technological Explanation

One of the most thorough refutations of Wirth's theory also supplied some of the most compelling evidence for industrialization as the key causal variable in movement toward *gesellschaft*. Gideon Sjoberg's *The Preindustrial City* (1965) analyzed the ecological and social conditions in preindustrial cities of medieval Europe and other parts of the world. He reported two major findings:

1. Urban centers existing prior to an industrial revolution exhibit certain common characteristics such as nonrational economics, an ascriptive class system, extended families, and restricted formal education.

2. Modern industrial cities differ significantly from preindustrial cities in that industrialization requires rational, centralized, extracommunity economics; a class system based on achievement; a small, flexible family; and mass education.

Sjoberg, then, has found that while preindustrial cities may have had relatively large, dense and heterogeneous populations, they were decidedly *gemeinschaft*-like. It is only after an industrial revolution that more *gesellschaft*-like characteristics appear. His technological explanation of movement toward *gesellschaft* is opposed to Wirth's ecological explanation, and subsequent cross-cultural survey research has substantiated Sjoberg's thesis. Alex Inkeles and David H. Smith (1974) administered surveys in Argentina, Chile, India, Israel, Nigeria, and Bangladesh and found a wide range of *gesellschaft* characteristics associated with working in factories. Seventy-six percent of the factory workers in these nations exhibited *gesellschaft* personality traits, compared to only two percent of the respondents with no factory or other formal organization experience. Research in "moral development" (Kohlberg 1984; Giddens 1991; Etzioni 1996b) shows similar results—namely, that children living in industrialized societies progress more rapidly and develop a more complex attitude toward morality than children in nonindustrial societies.

Still, it would be incorrect to infer from this research that industrialization alone can explain the emergence of *gesellschaft* characteristics. The moral development research, for example, also shows rural/urban differences beyond levels of societal industrialization (White, Bushnell, and Regnemer 1978), and even Sjoberg (1965) rejects a wholly technological explanation of society.

More Recent Research: The Validity of the Typological Approach and Multiple, Interrelated Causation

A considerable body of empirical research has been inspired by the typological approach to community. Some of it is directed toward assessing the validity of the typological approach.

Are there really community or society types? Do communities or societies actually vary along the dimensions suggested by the typological theorists? Early research suggested an affirmative answer. Joseph McKinney and Charles Loomis (1958) tested Parsons's typological approach in two communities in Costa Rica. They found that social patterns in these two communities could be accounted for with a typological continuum and that "Tönnies' analysis of *gemeinschaft* and *gesellschaft* and the related work of other theorists attacking similar problems is still relevant" (McKinney and Loomis 1958, 574). A much larger sample from the Human Relations Area File provided similar conclusions. Linton Freeman and Robert Winch (1957) applied Guttman scalogram analysis to eight *gemeinschaft/gesellschaft*-type variables (e.g., barter and exchange versus a money economy) in forty-eight societies and found that six of the variables did indeed vary in a systematic unidimensional pattern similar to that posited by the typological approach.

Multiple causes for movement. Still, most of the typological research has been directed at accounting for the movement from *gemeinschaft* to *gesellschaft*. Some has been field research similar to Redfield's, but usually more indirect, survey-type methods have been applied. An influential example of this type of research is John Kasarda's and Morris Janowitz's (1974) survey of over two thousand residents in one hundred communities throughout England. They found that the social class of the residents, their age, and especially their length of residence in the community have more of an influence on the presence of *gemeinschaft* characteristics (such as having numerous friends and relatives in the community) than population size and density. A conclusion from their survey is that the degree to which *gemeinschaft* or *gesellschaft* characteristics exist is due to a number of different variables, some ecological, some cultural. Paula Dressel and Harold Nix (1982) studied 19 US communities with similar findings, but they did conclude that the continuum was particularly useful in explaining variation in community politics and development. Other researchers (Kasarda and Crenshaw 1991; Fischer 1995) have made similar cases for the complexity of accounting for movement toward *gesellschaft*, but now there is some question concerning whether this complexity is worth unraveling.

Evaluating the Typological Approach: Is That All There Is?

When Tönnies, Weber, Simmel, and Durkheim described the distinctions between *gemeinschaft* and *gesellschaft*, a giant step was taken for sociological analysis generally and community analysis particularly. But since then, how far has the typological approach progressed? Roland Warren (1983, 78) noted with some distress that "we content ourselves with referring, often with malice, to the alleged old *gemeinschaft*-like community, and tell each other ponderously that modern industrial communities are more *gesellschaft*-like. Is this the last word? I hope not!" We would all hope not because if this is the last word, then it is a word uttered initially by Tönnies; and we would have added nothing of substance to it since 1887! And with all due respect to the modifications and specifications made by luminaries such as Becker and Parsons, what is there to the typological approach beyond the now obvious movement from *gemeinschaft* to *gesellschaft*? One disappointing but common response to the query is: That is indeed all there is to the typological approach.

That's All There Is.

This stance was initially and forcefully taken by Richard Dewey (1960) in his influential article, "The Rural–Urban Continuum: Real but Relatively Unimportant." Dewey maintains that the large number of descriptive characteristics distinguishing between rural and urban is "surely excessive" (he finds forty in the typological literature) and that "the lack of consensus is remarkable." Further, he finds numerous cases of *gesellschaft* in rural areas and *gemeinschaft* in urban areas. Dewey does admit that some urban/rural characteristics do seem to fit the typological approach, but he concludes that "it is of minor importance for sociology." His point seems to be that sociologists now know about all there is to know from this approach and that it is now time to study "society in the large."[6] Mark Gottdiener and Ray Hutchison (2006, 188) make similar criticisms of the typological approach and then argue that its minimal explanatory value is related to the changes brought by urbanization and industrialization. Thus, they maintain that the paradigm and the city/rural distinctions are obsolete in accounting for patterns of social interaction in postindustrial America.

Has the typological "vein" been mined to exhaustion? Dewey and others (e.g., Miller 1992; Fischer 1995) maintain that it has lost meaning in terms of a cultural distinction based on how "urban" a particular *place* is. Gottdiener and Hutchison (2006) and others (e.g., Tittle and Stafford 1992; Castells 2000; Wellman 2001) maintain that it is also exhausted when referring to the modernization of *entire societies*. Thus, whether *gemeinschaft/gesellschaft* is seen as a typological approach to a geographic form of community (a specific urban place à la Wirth) or a social interaction form of community (a lifestyle for an entire society à la Tönnies), a strong case has been made for its abandonment.

Perhaps Not.

Yet the typological approach endures, partly because it stirs a nostalgia for a more static, simple, and personal time (Williams 1973; Molotch, Freudenburg, and Paulsen 2000). Partly, it endures because it describes real differences in social behavior (Fischer 1995; Beggs, Haines, and Hurlbert 1996). It endures partly because it still provides important advancements in social theory (Brint 2001). And it endures mostly because, as Horace Miner (1952) noted over fifty years ago, "the continuum stands as an insistence that social science has something to explain here." That statement is relevant today. So is Miner's insight about the "bottom-line" question for evaluating this approach: The real query is whether we have a better initial answer than the folk-urban continuum to the general question of how to account for the similarities and differences observable among societies Do we have a better answer? Is the conflict approach more powerful? What about systems theory? The ecological approach? Perhaps, but before such questions can be answered, these other approaches to community must be considered.

NOTES

[1] In *Man in Reciprocity* (1956, 171) Becker refers to "Germans 'turning back the clock' from the Weimar secularity to Nazi sacredness." While this is an uncommon occurrence, it is a continuing phenomenon (e.g., the revival of sacred authority in the Arab world) related in no small part to the "quest for community" thesis discussed throughout this book.

[2] For some, the distinction between "ideal" and "constructed" types was of considerable importance (Becker 1940; Sjoberg 1965; McKinney 1966) because the constructed type is derived from empirical data and possibly superior to the more abstract ideal types. This distinction is, however, technical and somewhat ambiguous. For most purposes the terms can be treated as interchangeable.

[3] We chose to use the term "post–*gesellschaft*" societies (as opposed to "globalization" or "postmodernization") because it best describes the changes occurring in local communities. "Globalization" is most commonly applied to the economy of international markets. The process of globalization usually describes the changes in the overall society or nation but rarely addresses the impacts on the local community. The basis of globalization is the emergence of a single social system, characterized by a worldwide network of economic, political, and social relationships (Dasgupta 2004). Globalization, often a term from the political economist perspective, is used to describe a capitalist state with a single, world economy. Postmodern society (which is more of a theoretical term in nature) is also inadequate to describe the "post-*gesellschaft*" societies we attempt to describe in this chapter. Postmodernity refers to a social and political epoch that is generally seen as following the modern era in a historical sense (Ritzer 1997).

[4] See chapter 7, The Quest for Community.

[5] It should be remembered that Tönnies also associated capitalism with the highest forms of *gesellschaft*.

[6] This is related to the rise of the "mass society" perspective discussed in chapter 1.

chapter three

The Ecological Approach
Community as a Spatial Phenomenon

[handwritten annotation: ↳ has to do w/ geography ↳ where ppl work becomes part of dis Where they end up living]

The ecological approach to community is more specialized than the typological approach. The typologists are a diverse group including "grand" theorists from Europe and America, field anthropologists, and even popular "futurists," but the ecologists are smaller in number and more specific in their approach of focusing almost exclusively on the spatial patterns of the urban environment (Weinstein and Pillai 2001). Still, the ecological approach is not so narrow that it cannot be subdivided. Four main divisions comprise the ecological approach (Theodorson 1961) and reflect its temporal development: classical, sociocultural, neo-orthodox, and the related technical analyses of social area analysis/factorial ecology/GIS.

The Chicago School: Classical Ecology

Just as we can trace the origins of community typologies to Tönnies, the classical ecological approach can be traced to the sociology department of the University of Chicago and its chairman, Robert Park. At a time when sociology was competing for academic acceptance, Park was able to establish its scientific credentials by borrowing evolutionary principles from biology. And, to a degree, the current legitimacy of sociology as a discipline in the curricula of American universities is a reflection of the ecological approach pioneered by Robert Park.[1]

Community and Society: The Human Ecology of Robert Park

Human ecology is the study of the process of human group adjustment to the environment. For Park, human organization is a dichotomy. One part, community, is an expression of human nature that is revealed in Darwinian competition for supremacy. The other, society, is a collective phenomenon revealed in the consensus and common purpose of social groups. Society is the cultural, consensual part of human existence. Community is its biotic, competitive counterpart, and community was the area of study for the urban ecologists at the University of Chicago.

The distinction between community and society is both crucial and obscure. "Ecology," Park (1952, 251) wrote, "is concerned with communities rather than societies, though it is not easy to distinguish between them." Indeed it is not. In fact, we shall see how this obscure and probably artificial distinction became a major criticism of Park's urban ecology, but first it is necessary to examine the major concepts of the ecological approach to community.

Competition.   Borrowing from Darwin's web of life, Park emphasized the interrelationship between the various parts of the environment. The social organization of the city resulted from the struggle for survival. Competition is the master process that determines the spatial form and ecological functions of the interrelated web. For example, in a city competition arises for the most desirable land. Because commercial interests can use the land most efficiently (i.e., profitably), they will prevail in the competition and dominate the city's spatial and functional development. In Park's (1952, 151–52) terms,

> the struggle of industries and commercial institutions for a strategic location determines in the long run the main outlines of the urban community . . . the principle of dominance . . . tends to determine the general ecological pattern of the city and the functional relation of each of the different areas of the city to all the others.

Once competition has determined the spatial patterning of the city, a "symbiotic" relationship develops based on the interdependence of the various groups. For example, competition is tempered by the need of business for supplies from areas of industrial land use and customers from residential areas; industry needs retail outlets from business and workers from residences, and so on.

Competition exists at the community level, and similarly the symbiotic relationships that develop after the competition are community based. Further, this symbiosis is the basis for normative consensus of society. Thus, competitive community is the basis for consensual society.

Natural areas.   Natural areas are the product of competition. As early as 1926, Harvey Zorbaugh (190) explained that "in this competition for position the population is segregated over the natural areas of the city. Land values, characterizing the various natural areas, tend to sift and sort the population." Park and his fellow ecologists believed that the land in any city possessed certain characteristics that would make it more efficient for one particular function. For example, land in the center of the city might be especially useful for retail business or office development. Land near a port or rail line would hold special advantages for industry. The downtown business district, the slum, the ghetto, the warehouse district, the suburb, the red light district, and the immigrant colony are all natural areas. They are culturally distinct land-use patterns determined not by society-based urban planners, but rather by community-based competition.

Natural areas were the most basic unit of analysis for urban ecologists. And since they were the product of *natural* competitive forces, it should be possible to generalize from the findings of their study. "Natural areas," Park (1952, 198) writes, "not only tell us what the facts are in regard to conditions in any given region, but insofar as they characterize an area that is natural and typical, they establish a working hypothesis in regard to other areas of the same kind." However, the generalization from studies of natural areas never reached the levels Park predicted.

Under Park's direction, his students and colleagues studied Chicago's natural areas. Zorbaugh's *The Gold Coast and Slum* (1929) and Wirth's *The Ghetto* (1928) are two of the finest examples of such studies, but even the best studies of natural areas are largely descriptive. That is, the primary goal is to define the geographic boundaries of the natural area and then describe the lifestyles and land use within it. Hence, the classic Chicago studies of this period—*The Hobo* (Anderson 1923), *The Gang* (Thrasher 1927), *The Ghetto, The Gold Coast and Slum, The Jackroller* (Shaw 1930), and *The Taxi Dance Hall* (Cressey 1932)—are classic *descriptions* of urban life, not classic *explanations* of urban phenomena. It may be that the unit of analysis (the natural area) was so small that rich description of individual detail was easy while general propositions about urban phenomena were difficult. In fact, we shall encounter a similar example of atheoretical description in the descendants of the natural area approach: social area analysis and factorial ecology. In any event, it was not until the focus was directed toward the entire city that the major theoretical contributions of urban ecology were developed.

Urban Growth

When urban ecology borrowed its major principles from biology, a special view of urban growth resulted. Just as a more dominant species succeeds another in nature, the human community will have changes in land-use patterns as areas are "invaded" by dominant competitors that can use the land more efficiently. If the business area of a city grows, it may invade a residential area; and since it can use the land more efficiently (i.e., profitably), it can pay more for the land than a homeowner could. Succession occurs as the land values increase, the residents move out, and the land use is transformed to meet the needs of the dominant competitor. Then a new equilibrium is established, and the successional sequence comes to an end.

The land uses of a city, then, reflect the dominance of various users. Since dominance is established by competition and since the competition is won by those who can use the land most efficiently, the city reflects a natural, evolutionary efficiency. Thus, the scorn with which urban ecologists viewed municipal administrators' attempts to plan the land use of cities is understandable.[2]

Burgess's concentric zones. Perhaps the crowning achievement of the ecological approach was Ernest Burgess's use of dominance, invasion, and succession to account for urban structure and growth. He explained that the city could be conceptualized ideally as five concentric zones (see figure 3-1). The land use in each zone reflects the dominance of the user. For example, Zone 1, the Central Business District (CBD), contains "quite naturally, almost inevitably, the economic, cultural, and political centers" (Burgess 1925, 50) because it is the most desirable, valuable property in the city. Beyond the CBD

> there is normally an area of transition, which is being invaded by business and light manufacture (II). A third area (III) is inhabited by the workers in industries who have escaped from the area of deterioration (II) but who desire to live within easy access of their work. Beyond this zone is the "residential area" (IV) of high-class apartment buildings or of exclusive "restricted" districts of single-family dwellings. Still farther, out beyond the city limits, is the commuters' zone—suburban areas, or satellite cities—within a thirty-to sixty-minute ride of the central business district.

Each zone is inhabited by those who can use it most efficiently. Skyscrapers in the CBD can build above the congestion and noise, workers living in Zone III are close enough to the factories to walk or use public transportation, and suburbanites in Zone V have the private transportation necessary for living so far from the city. Each zone reflects the dominance of the user.

The growth of the city is largely the result of one zone invading the next outer zone. The CBD will invade (expand into) the zone of transition, which

Figure 3-1A   The Burgess Concentric-Zone Model of Urban Structure

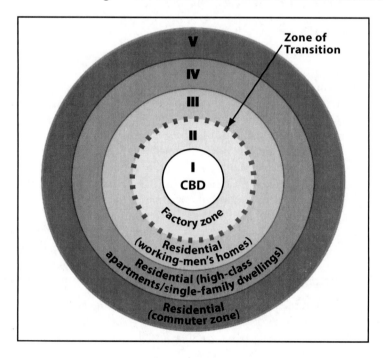

invades the workingmen's zone, and so on until a new and efficient equilibrium is established.

Hoyt's urban sectors.   While Burgess's concentric zone theory is the most widely cited ecological approach to urban structure and growth, there are two subsequent theories of note. One is Homer Hoyt's (1939) sector theory (figure 3-2).

While employing land-use principles similar to those of Burgess, Hoyt maintained that cities grow not by expanding concentric rings, but rather along major transportation lines that radiate from the CBD. Thus, the spatial patterns resemble geometric sectors more than they do concentric circles. Heavy industry and warehouses will be located along waterways, railroad lines, and major highways. Wealthy residents consume the best remaining land, typically high ground along a major transportation artery. Poor residents occupy whatever is left over, the least desirable land. As the CBD expands and industry grows, the wealthy move farther out to avoid the accompanying noise, crime, traffic, and pollution. Some of their former homes are leveled for business growth, and others are subdivided and rented by the poor.

Figure 3-1B   Concentric-Zone Theory Applied to Chicago Urban Areas

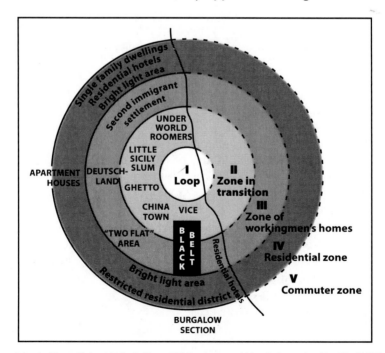

Source: Adapted from Robert E. Park, Ernest W. Burgess, and Morris Janowitz, *The City* (1925, p. 51; repr. Chicago: University of Chicago Press, 1967, p. 47).

Figure 3-2   Hoyt's Sector Theory

1 Central business district
2 Wholesale light manufacturing
3 Low-class residential
4 Medium-class residential
5 High-class residential

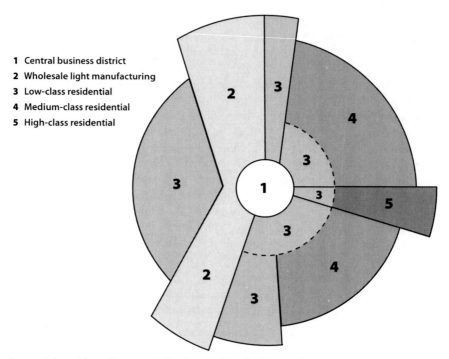

Source: Adapted from Chauncey D. Harris and Edward L. Ullman, "The Nature of Cities," *The Annals of the American Association of Political and Social Science,* 242 (1945): 7–17.

Harris and Ullman's multiple nuclei.   Chauncey Harris and Edward Ullman (1945) developed a multiple nuclei theory of urban structure and growth (figure 3-3). It combined elements of Burgess's and Hoyt's models but was not strictly in the ecological tradition of competition determining efficient land use. Instead, Harris and Ullman were geographers who explained the complex, decentralized structure and growth of a city through four rather commonsensical rules:

1. Certain land uses demand specialized facilities and concentrate where such facilities are available. Industry, for example, requires transportation facilities and will locate along rail lines, a waterway, or major highway.

2. Similar uses of land often benefit from being close to each other. Retailers may locate in the same part of the city so that they can bring a larger number of potential customers to their area.

3. Some dissimilar land uses are typically separated. For example, residential and industrial uses will find it mutually beneficial to remain far apart.

Figure 3-3   The Harris and Ullman Multiple-Nuclei Model of Urban Structure

1 Central business district
2 Wholesale light manufacturing
3 Low-class residential
4 Medium-class residential
5 High-class residential
6 Heavy manufacturing
7 Outlying business district
8 Residential suburb
9 Industrial suburb

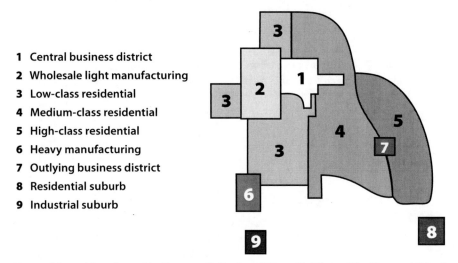

Source: Adapted from figure 5 in Chauncey D. Harris and Edward L. Ullman, "The Nature of Cities," *The Annals of the American Academy of Political Science 242*(1945): 7–17.

4. Finally, the inability to pay for the desired land brings some uses together. Warehousing or grocery wholesaling would benefit from a location in the CBD but require such a large amount of land that the cost is prohibitive. Thus, such uses will cluster together in areas where land is cheaper.

Such rules are similar to what one would learn in an introductory real estate course and are far removed from elegant ecological underpinning developed by Park, Burgess, and others. Still, Harris and Ullman's multiple nuclei theory shares with Hoyt's sector theory and Burgess's concentric zone theory the proposition that urban structure and growth is not random; rather, it is systematic and predictable. Later in this section, we look at the factorial ecologists' attempts to test the validity of that proposition and the reliability of predictions based on these three theories.

For now, however, it is sufficient to note that Harris and Ullman's model more closely approximates the new American cities of the Southwest (e.g., Houston, Dallas, Phoenix, Las Vegas, and especially Los Angeles) that grew after the mass production of the automobile. And, if you extend the Harris and Ullman model far enough, you set the stage for "the Los Angeles school" of postmodern urban ecology. Stemming primarily from the efforts of geographers such as Michael Dear, Allen Scott, and Edward Soja, the Los Angeles school posits a new paradigm for urban structure and growth that replaces the Chicago school, especially the Burgess concentric zone model. While this new approach is sometimes regarded as a form of civic and academic boosterism for Los Angeles (Beauregard 2003), it does provide a useful model of urban development in the 21st century, with gated residential communities, edge cities, and all of the other land uses illustrated in figure 3-4 below.

Figure 3-4   The Youth Stage of a Postmodern Metropolis

Note that land use parcels are functionally unrelated but tend to become physically adjacent as they are successively developed.

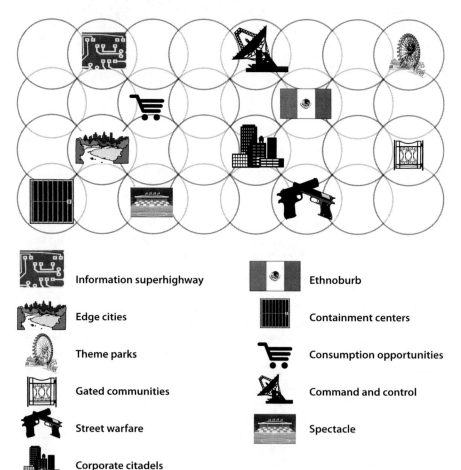

Information superhighway		Ethnoburb	
Edge cities		Containment centers	
Theme parks		Consumption opportunities	
Gated communities		Command and control	
Street warfare		Spectacle	
Corporate citadels			

Source: Adapted from Michael J. Dear, "Imagining Postmodern Urbanism." In Michael J. Dear (ed.), *From Chicago to L.A.: Making Sense of Urban Theory* (Thousand Oaks, CA: Sage, 2002, p. 88).

The Demise of Classical Urban Ecology

The demise of the classical ecological approach was a gradual one, brought about by cumulative criticisms that began with Milla Alihan. She examined Anderson's *The Hobo* and Zorbaugh's *Gold Coast* to conclude that the supposedly crucial distinction between the biotic community and the cultural society levels is, in practice, nonexistent. Alihan noted that Anderson and Zorbaugh did "not discriminate between certain activities carried on within a society as those of 'society' and others which are those of 'community'" (Alihan 1938, 82). Walter Firey (1945, 1947) continued the attack on the ecological position with his study of land use in Boston. He showed how the idea of efficient land use through economic competition could not account for the spatial patterning of Boston. Firey argued that such events as the refusal of Beacon Hill's residents to sell homes in their traditional high-status neighborhood to commercial interests and the retention of the Boston Commons Park in the middle of the CBD could be explained only through reference to personal sentiment and cultural symbolism.

W. S. Robinson's (1950) illustration of the "ecological fallacy" was a different but important criticism of the ecological approach. Robinson (1950) demonstrated that the common practice of using ecological correlations (correlations between aggregates, such as the proportion of blacks in a state and the state's rate of illiteracy) to explain individual behavior (in this case, that some states had illiteracy levels because they had high levels of black population) was statistically invalid. And while it was true that ecologists theoretically focused on aggregates, their descriptions and explanations were often highly individualistic.[3]

Despite numerous limitations, the ecological approach and the Chicago school studies brought forth some positive aspects. The Chicago school connected the spatial patterns with social occurrences. This research took an interactive perspective and included the individuals as they interacted with one another. Finally, the ecological approach attempted to show patterns of development and adjustment to sociospatial location (Gottdiener and Hutchison 2006).

When Robinson's criticism of ecological statistics was combined with Firey's contention that more than economic efficiency was needed to explain land use and Alihan's observation that even the ecologists could not separate the biotic community from the cultural society, the classical ecologists were in serious trouble. In fact, "by 1950 the ecological approach as developed by Park, his colleagues, and students at the University of Chicago was virtually dead" (Berry and Kasarda 1977). Dead perhaps, but not quite buried and forgotten. The ecological perspective remains alive within community and urban sociology. It can still be found in most major texts on urban sociology (e.g., Weinstein and Pillai 2001; Martin 2004; Flanagan 2002; Palen 2008), at least demonstrating historical significance. Moreover, the influence of Robert Park and the classical ecologists lived on in the sociocultural, neo-orthodox, and social area analysis/factorial ecology approaches to community.

Sociocultural Ecology

Firey's study of land use in Boston did more than provide a critique of classical urban ecology. His demonstration of the importance of cultural variables such as sentiment and symbolism on spatial patterns set a new direction for many ecologists. Sociocultural ecologists maintained that urban structure and growth can be understood only if culture and values are made central to ecological theory. Besides Firey, Albert Seeman's (1938) study of how religion influenced the patterns of Salt Lake City and other Utah cities is the most notable early example of this approach. Seeman explained how the Salt Lake Basin had been revealed to Mormon leaders as the place where the Savior and his faithful would gather in the last days. Toward this end, the "City of Zion" was designed to be a utopia where farmers could live within the city and bring their surplus to the centrally located Bishop's storehouse. Salt Lake City developed a distinctive pattern of wide streets running exactly north-south and east-west, large common city blocks at the center for schools and churches, and smaller blocks at the periphery for stables and barns. In a more recent and more secular extension of Seeman's work, August Heckscher and Phyllis Robinson (1977) argued that the spatial patterns of American cities clearly reflect American values of freedom, individualism, growth, and business success. He showed, for example, how the American grid pattern of streets allows people to look down the entire street, even out to the countryside, and envision urban expansion. The regularity of the grid is seen as implying a sense of control over destiny that is absent from the curved streets of medieval Europe.

As the socioculturalists began to emphasize the role of cultural variables, they began to lose the distinctiveness of the ecological approach. The merger with mainstream sociology has become so complete, in fact, that with only a few exceptions such as Heckscher and Robinson (1977), it is difficult today to distinguish the socioculturalists as having a special approach to the urban community. Current analysts tend to: (1) ignore this approach (Berry and Kasarda 1977; Abbott 1997); (2) describe it historically with reference only to Firey and Seeman's research (Gottdiener and Hutchison 2006; Gold 2002; Palen 2008); or (3) merge it with urban ethnographies such as those we consider later in chapter 14.[4]

Perhaps the clearest remaining vestige of sociocultural ecology was in the application of symbolic interactionism to communities. Anselm Strauss's *Images of the American City* (1961) details the transformation of rural America into urban America and, in so doing, shows how our images of what a city is and what it should be have influenced urban development. Gerald Suttles's widely cited and influential *The Social Construction of Communities* (1972) builds on this tradition by presenting a sophisticated collection of articles relating the images of communities to their ecological structure. And Albert Hunter's work (e.g., *Symbolic Communities,* 1974) on symbols and sentiments in Chicago neighborhoods illustrates the blend of cultural symbolism and spatial patterning characteristic of sociocultural ecology. But such works are not common, at least in comparison to the neo-orthodox efforts we examine next.

Regardless of what has actually happened to the sociocultural version of urban ecology, it is now becoming increasingly difficult to identify it as a distinct approach to community.[5] Further, we can conclude that it lost much of its distinctiveness when it lost its primary emphasis on ecological variables. Apparently, it was easier to criticize the classical ecologists than to develop a distinctive blend of cultural and ecological emphases. Thus, we now turn to the version that maintained its primary emphasis on ecological structure and process.

Neo-Orthodox Ecology

The origin of neo-orthodox ecology can be marked by the publication of Amos Hawley's *Human Ecology: A Theory of Community Structure* in 1950. By this time, classic human ecology had died at the hands of its sociocultural critics, but they, in turn, had trouble developing a distinctive ecological approach of their own. Hawley, however, resurrected the ecological approach in a way that insulated it from some of its previous problems.

Amos Hawley (1910–2009):
The Resurrection of Human Ecology

Hawley is often credited with reviving human ecology within the field of sociology (Berry and Kasarda 1977). He did so by moving the focus of the approach away from spatial distributions (which he felt was more a geographical perspective rather than an ecological one) and toward the adaptation of human populations by means of functional differentiation. Technology, culture, and social organizations are his key types of adaptive mechanisms (Hawley 1986). Hawley also dismissed Park's distinction between the biotic and the cultural. He argued that since culture is a mechanism of environmental adaptation, it is within the study of ecology.

Hawley's view of community differed from Park's classic definition. For Hawley, the community is the one unit of analysis where all the key elements of society are present in a relatively small, easily studied place. In the community, an ecological system of interdependence develops between various groups and organizations as the local population adapts to its environment. Thus, the major ecological principle that governs the community is local "interdependence." While Park emphasized the role of conflict and his students chronicled the social disorganization of Chicago, we find in Hawley's approach a community in organized equilibrium, at least until disturbed by outside influences, and even then adjusting back into cooperative balance.

For Hawley, the ecological approach to community is a decidedly macro approach. Hawley was concerned with describing two types of change: the massive increase of suburbanization and the restructuring of the central areas away from manufacturing. The fundamental social organization was created by transportation and communication technologies. The social organizational patterns changed as the means of interaction were changed by technology. There is little room for individual psychology. Hawley (1950, 179) reasoned that since the focus of ecology is on "collective" adaptations, "the irrelevance of the psychological properties of individuals is self-evident."

Hawley's redefinition of human ecology set a course for neo-orthodox ecologists that was followed for another generation of sociologists. One of the most influential neo-orthodox ecologists was Otis Dudley Duncan.

O. D. Duncan (1921–2004): The Ecological Complex

In additional to his many contributions in mathematical sociology, Otis Dudley Duncan (1959) added to the neo-orthodox approach his "ecological complex" of four basic, interrelated, reference variables: population, organization, environment, and technology (or POET). These variables (see figure 3-6 on page ___ in the section on The Process of Suburbanization) include the standard *population* measures (size, heterogeneity), *organization* types (developed as adaptation for survival), *environmental* phenomena (including all variables external to the community), and *technological* developments (skills or tools to aid adaptation). The POET framework allows examination of a wide range of phenomena and ensures that all crucial variables within the ecological perspective are included. In fact, most current ecological research efforts are directed at explicating the interrelationships with the POET complex (Namboodiri 1988; Crenshaw, Christenson, and Oakey 2000; Weinstein and Pillai 2001).

Duncan, perhaps even more than Hawley, has led the way in developing statistical measures of ecological phenomena. His measures of community dominance (Duncan et al. 1960; Duncan and Lieberson 1970), and residential segregation (Duncan and Duncan 1955, 1957) raised the quantitative sophistication of community analysis to levels not equaled until computer-driven analytic techniques emerged in the 1960s.

Social Area Analysis (SAA), Factorial Ecology, and Geographic Information Systems (GIS)

The degree to which social area analysis (SAA), factorial ecology, and geographic information system (GIS) mapping are conceptually distinct from the neo-orthodox approach is questionable, but traditionally they have been categorized separately (Theodorson 1961). It is also questionable whether social area analysis remains a significant methodological tool in light of factorial ecology and the growing emphasis on GIS; regardless, it helped pave the way for the more sophisticated factorial ecology method and eventually, GIS (e.g., Gold 2002). We will briefly review these techniques and assess their relationship to one another and to neo-orthodox urban ecology.

Social Area Analysis

Social area analysis (SAA) was the census-born descendant of classical ecology's natural areas. The natural areas were the indivisible building blocks of the larger city. Each possessed unique environmental characteristics that set it apart from other parts of the city. While the city as a whole might seem an unwieldy, disorganized, unmanageable unit, the classical ecologists believed that urban planning based on the smaller natural areas was more likely to be successful (Zorbaugh 1926; Green 1931).

The natural area's reign as urban ecology's basic unit of spatial analysis was short-lived. In 1940, the US Bureau of Census began publishing data for most large American cities by census tract. Census tracts are similar to natural areas but much smaller, averaging only four thousand residents per tract. A large city would contain several hundred tracts, and for the first time urban ecologists were faced with more statistical data than they could assimilate. SAA was developed in order to group together similar census tracts into larger categories that fulfilled the same functions as the earlier concept of natural areas. Applications of SAA (Shevky and Bell 1955; Bell 1953, 1955, 1959) showed that it allowed the identification and comparison of social areas within different cities so that generalizations could be made about the spatial patterning of urban phenomena. Further, community change could be measured by simply comparing two or more consecutive census dates.

The demise of Social Area Analysis.   SAA was not without its flaws. Critics correctly charged SAA with limited insight (Macionis and Parrillo 2010), arbitrary groupings of variables (Gold 2002), and an inability to provide an analytical model that explains differences from one area to another (Gottdiener and Hutchison 2006). Moreover, computer-driven statistical packages could accomplish the same things with more variables and less time. Thus, the more statistically sophisticated factor analysis technique led to a newer approach to the urban community that complemented and typically replaced SAA. Just as the census tract brought an end to natural areas, we find that with each "new" technique, sociologists have created a new methodology and a more sophisticated, computerized means to analyze the community. These approaches are not new theories, but rather new data (tracts) and new technologies (computers) and new statistical methods (fact-analysis) to continue studying the recurring issues in the community. For community ecology, data collection and technology seem to be driving the approaches and analysis, with theory having only limited relevance. Thus, it is not surprising that new statistical techniques hastened the demise of SAA.

Factorial Ecology

Factorial ecology includes a diverse set of community studies that use factor analysis as their primary research methodology. Like SAA, it is an inherently atheoretical approach in which

[a] data matrix is analyzed containing measurements on *m* variables for each of *n* units of observation (census tracts, wards . . .), with the intent of (1) identifying and summarizing the common patterns of variability of the *m* variables in a smaller number of independent dimensions, *r*, that additively reproduce this common variance; and (2) examining the patterns of scores of each of the *n* observational units on each of the *r* dimensions. The dimensions isolated are an objective outcome of the analysis. *Interpretation of the dimensions (factors) depends on the nature of the variables used in the analysis and the body of concept or theory that is brought to bear.* Theory provides the investigator with a set of expectations regarding the factor structure that can be compared to the actual set of factors produced. (Berry and Kasarda 1977, 123)

Like SAA, factorial ecology seems clearly within the neoclassical ecological paradigm. There is an almost total reliance on aggregate population variables, and the goal is often to plot the spatial patterning of urban phenomena.

Factorial ecology is a complex field and has moved in several directions, many of them cross-cultural, but a brief summary of some of the findings most relevant to the community follows.

1. *Approximately five factors underlie the ecological structure of American communities.* The results of factor analysis depend on the statistical techniques used, the variables employed, and the unit of analysis. Still, such studies of the ecological structures of American communities have been remarkably consistent in their findings. Reviews of factorial ecology in the United States (Rees 1971; Janson 1980; Gottdiener and Hutchison 2006; Gold 2002) conclude generally that American communities vary along five dimensions: (1) socioeconomic status, (2) family status, (3) ethnicity, (4) residential mobility, and (5) population and functional size. In other words, these five factors account for much of the variation or differentiation in American communities. If an analyst wishes to understand why one community or neighborhood is different from another, differences in these five factors should be prime reasons.

2. *Some of these factors are distributed in the community in systematic patterns.* Specifically, the family status dimension is distributed in the Burgess concentric zone pattern; economic status follows sectors radiating from the CBD à la Hoyt; and population growth and racial and ethnic groups tend to cluster around multiple nuclei like those described by Harris and Ullman (Anderson and Egeland 1961; Kleniewski 1997). If city structure and growth were determined entirely by family status, then those families with the fewest children would be near the CBD in order to be near work and the cultural advantages of the central city. Families with more children would locate in outer zones. If economic status were the only factor, all classes would move out from the CBD in sectors. And if race were the only factor, cities would be segregated into racial and ethnic neighborhoods. Of course, all three factors oper-

ate in most cities, producing land-use patterns more complex than any of these models can describe individually (Berry and Rees 1969; Macionis and Parrillo 2010).

3. *Industrialization appears to account for much of the ecological structure of communities.* In much the way the typological approach stressed the role of the industrial revolution in accounting for movement toward social characteristics of *gesellschaft*, cross-cultural factorial ecology stressed the ecological differences between cities in preindustrial and industrial cities (Kasarda and Crenshaw 1991; Sassen 2001; Abu-Lughod 1991, 1999; Soja 2000).

Geographic Information System (GIS) Mapping

As technology advances, geographic information system (GIS) mapping is the most recent technique to examine the spatial patterns of areas, focusing on aggregate, urban data. GIS integrates mapping software and geographic data for managing, analyzing, and displaying all forms of geographically referenced information. GIS allows us to graph, interpret, and visualize data in many ways that reveal relationships, patterns, and trends in geographic community. The "revolutionary" aspect of GIS is the mapping and linking of data (e.g., race, income, age, religion, etc.) to geographic places. GIS can map the data for more than one period in time and combine different types of data (census and survey data) for the same place. It can even incorporate a global positioning system (GPS) to record the location of each household in the sample, allowing for a more sophisticated spatial analysis of the population (Weeks 2002). Figure 3-5 on the following page provides a simple example.

In SAA/factorial ecology/GIS mapping we find a body of research that shares with the neo-orthodox ecologists a focus on aggregate, urban data. Further, the focus on spatial patterning is probably closer to the classical ecologists than the neo-orthodox position (with its emphasis on adaptation). Thus, in neo-orthodox ecology and SAA/factorial ecology/GIS, if not in sociocultural ecology, we find the classic Chicago school of human ecology of Robert Park still influential. It is more empirical and less theoretical now, but the ecological perspective still represents a distinctive approach to the community.

However, there is a challenge to the Chicago school which in some ways harkens back to the multiple nuclei approach.

Suburbanization: An Application of the Ecological Approach

One of the most important changes in the spatial patterns of American cities in the last half of the 20th century is the rapid growth of the urban fringes. Actually, suburban growth was occurring throughout the first half of the 20th century. However, at that time, suburbanization was simply one of

Figure 3-5   GIS Map Representing Distribution of Asian Residents in Northern Chicago

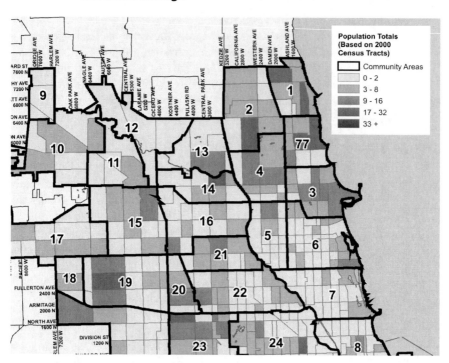

Source: Copyright © 2007, City of Chicago.

several growth patterns affecting the city. Burgess's classic concentric zone model, for example, gave growth in the outlying suburban zone no more attention than growth in the other zones. It was not until the 1950s that the suburbs became virtually the *only* area of substantial metropolitan growth. And, accordingly, since that time, studies of suburbanization have increasingly occupied the efforts of urban ecologists. In fact, recent work in urban ecology argues that suburbanization is not only a dominant center of residential growth (Katz and Lang 2003), but that new views have "changed suburbs from being residential places on the periphery to being the residential, economic, and commercial centers of a new metropolitan form" (Palen 2008, 115, 111). Thus, a substantial body of ecological research has developed in an effort to better understand suburbanization. In the following overview of that research, we further discuss the causes, characteristics, and consequences of suburbanization and simultaneously introduce some examples of modern ecological approaches to an important urban community phenomenon.[6]

Defining Suburbanization

The basic ecological definition of a *suburb* is derived from the US census and includes all areas that are: (1) within either the Metropolitan Statistical Area (MSA) or the more narrowly defined urbanized area, and (2) outside the central city. While the urbanized area is a more precise measure of the degree of suburbanization, the MSA is more widely employed because it can be compared over time. In either case, American suburbs possess a very large, rapidly growing population. In 1950, a mere 24% of Americans lived in suburbs. By the 1960s, the percentage of suburban Americans grew to 33, and then jumped to 40% by 1980. In 2000, most Americans (52%) lived in suburbs.

Suburbanization, in turn, is defined as the general process through which an urban population spreads over an increasingly wider expanse of territory, typically expanding beyond the municipal boundaries of the central city. Within the general process of suburbanization are the more specific processes of *decentralization*—the suburban ring growing faster than the central city— and *deconcentration*—declining population density in the central city. Decentralization has been a continuing process throughout the twentieth century, while deconcentration is a post–World War II phenomenon.

The Process of Suburbanization: The POET Framework

Earlier in this chapter, Duncan's ecological complex was introduced as a framework for much of the current effort in urban ecology. As an example of how the POET variables can be used to explain ecological phenomena, we use the interrelationship among population, organization, environment, and technology to explain the rapid increase in suburbanization (especially deconcentration) in the post–World War II period.

Population underwent a massive demographic transformation with the arrival of the "postwar baby boom." This record number of births between 1945 and 1958 produced an unprecedented demand for family housing. And since little residential development had occurred during World War II and the preceding depression, the United States faced a critical housing shortage.

In other words, the urban *environment* of 1950 predisposed movement toward suburbanization. Central city housing was old and often lacking in the space and modern conveniences desired by the postwar families. Also, the high-density levels in many central cities made new residential developments prohibitively expensive in those locations.

The housing shortage was met through a change in *organization*. While it might have been possible to have constructed new residential areas in the deteriorating central cities, urban renewal programs began to demolish urban housing and replace it with commercial and other nonresidential structures.[7] And while urban renewal was reducing the number of central city housing units, the Federal Housing Authority and Veterans' Administration were subsidizing the costs of new suburban houses (Baldassare 1992). The result was America's first significant deconcentration of urban population.

Changes in *technology* also played a key role in suburbanization. The "baby boom" years witnessed an almost 400% increase in the number of motor vehicles registered in the United States. Without such an increase in individual transportation, the deconcentration of urban population would have been impossible (Palen 2008). Of course, these new automobiles and new suburban homes were expensive, even if the loans were often subsidized. Without the industrial technology that led to the increased productivity and higher per capita income of the 1950s, the suburbanization process could not have been financed.

The result, then, was a fundamental restructuring of an urban environment into a *metropolitan* environment. Old urban housing was either allowed to deteriorate or was demolished, and an exodus to new, mass-produced suburbs began. Figure 3-6 illustrates the ecological relationships necessary to this transformation.

Of course, suburbanization resulted in changes that went far beyond new spatial patterns. There were also accompanying changes in population. Not everyone was equally likely to move to the suburbs.

Figure 3-6   The Ecological Complex and Suburbanization

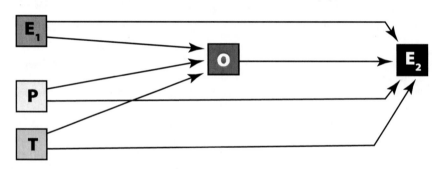

E₁ Urban **environment** (high density, inadequate housing)

P Population (post-war "baby boom")

T Technology (mass production of automobile, high industrial technology)

O Organization (FHA and VA loans)

E₂ Metropolitan **environment** (decentralizing central city, rapid growth in suburbs)

The Characteristics of the Suburban Population

What kind of people moved to the suburbs? Where did they move from? How were they different from their central city counterparts? These have been the driving questions for ecological analysis of suburban populations, and their answers will allow an evaluation of the stereotypic view of suburbs being populated by homogeneous white, middle-class families who have moved from the central city in search of a more family-related lifestyle.

Much of the suburban stereotype is supported from a demographic breakdown of central city and suburban populations. Central cities, on the whole, lost white families of child-bearing age to the suburban ring of the concentric zone. Further, the socioeconomic status of suburban residents is considerably higher than that of central city residents. However, the fact that suburban populations are different from central city populations does not necessarily mean that suburban populations are homogeneous (Frey 2003). They are remarkably heterogeneous and becoming even more so.[8]

In fact, ecologists typically divide the suburbs themselves by type as a partial reflection of their population heterogeneity. Although the categories can be numerous, the most traditional and basic distinction is between *employing* and *residential* suburbs (Palen 2008). There are sophisticated demographic measures that allow precise description of any suburb (Flanagan 2002), but of most general interest is the finding that residential suburbs are the ones that best fit the typical suburban stereotype described above. Employing suburbs (places like Euclid, Ohio, or Pasadena, Texas) are larger, have significant amounts of industry, more racial and social class variation, and less "familism" (Miller 1995). Of course, when ecologists measure familism, they use indicators such as "percent married," "fertility ratio," "percent of population under eighteen years of age," and so on. Whether or not the suburban lifestyle is actually based on family-related values requires more direct measures. Later we introduce the New Urbanism perspective that impacts recent suburban developments, and we will return to the suburban lifestyle in chapter 9 on planned communities and chapter 14 on holistic community research. For now, however, we consider one other dimension of the suburbanization process—the political and economic ramifications.

Suburban/Central City Relationships: Symbiosis or Exploitation?

There are varying views on the effect a large and growing suburban population has on the public services provided by central city governments.

It may be symbiotic.   There are some (although a minority) who maintain that the relationship is mutually beneficial or, in the vocabulary of human ecology, symbiotic. They believe that the central city and the suburb complement each other (Gottdiener and Hutchison 2006). J. C. Weicher (1972), for example, explains that the movement of manufacturing and industry to the suburbs helps to reduce the number of services demanded of the central city government and that sales taxes balance any initial financial advantages the suburbs might appear to enjoy. Mark Baldassare (1992) argues that the political fragmentation that accompanies suburbanization is efficient because it provides a large number of local political entities, each with a unique set of private and public goods. Thus, citizens are free to maximize their own personal preferences through choice of residential location. Gerald Frug (1999) shows how political fragmentation can encourage a sense of community among neighbors with smaller, more accessible towns. Eric Oliver (2001) finds that residents of smaller suburbs are more likely to be engaged in civic activities such as voting, volunteer work, and interaction with neighbors. Robert Dahl (1998) makes a similar argument when he maintains that the fragmentation results in a multiplicity of political areas, so that if groups fail to succeed in one area they are able to try again in others. Further, Dahl maintains that this diffusion of local power provides checks and balances, increases individual freedom, and provides a wider option in policy choices.

It's probably parasitic.   An even more common view is that the central city/suburb relationship is exploitive or, in more ecological jargon, parasitic. The position here is that suburban residents consume many of the central city's services but escape the costs of providing them. Baumgartner (1988) argues that suburbanization allows the affluent middle class to shut out non-middle-class problems and socially withdraw, and hence minimize the social and economic cost to the middle-class taxpayer of solving these problems. Of course, the non-middle-class problems still exist, but the central city residents are the ones most likely to experience these problems and who must pay more for their solution.

Two ecologists, Brian J. L. Berry and John Kasarda (1977), expand on this idea by showing that not only do suburban residents "exploit central cities . . . by not bearing their fair share of the welfare costs," suburbanites also increase the demand for central city services such as libraries, parks, zoos, museums, and other public facilities:

> As metropolitan areas continue to expand, an increasing number of suburban residents make routine use of central-city services and facilities. The additional activity in the central city created by suburban residents has also been reflected in the operating expenditures of central-city governments. Hence, *per capita expenditures for central-city services have been found to be at least as sensitive to the size of the suburban population as the size of the central-city population itself.* (Berry and Kasarda 1977, 225)

The data analyses Berry and Kasarda marshal in support of a case for suburbanites exploiting central-city dwellers are impressive, and most students of metropolitan development would agree that certain elements of the suburban/central city relationship are inherently exploitive. This does not mean, however, that any major restructuring of this relationship is forthcoming. In fact, an extension of Berry and Kasarda's work by Jeffrey Slovak (1985) concludes that the exploitation of the central cities by the suburbs is greater than when Berry and Kasarda's data were gathered.

Regardless, it's not going to change politically.   The most widely advocated solution to this problem is metropolitan consolidation, i.e., combining the politically autonomous suburban units with the central city and forming a metropolitan-wide government. While this is certainly an equitable solution, it is also an impractical one. Too many vested interests support suburban fragmentation. Suburban residents will naturally want to maintain this system, and central city residents (especially black and Hispanic residents, who for the first time are assuming numerous positions of municipal power) feel they might lose their influence in a metropolitan government. There are other barriers to consolidation. Mark Baldassare (1992) explains that what initially appears to be a step toward consolidation—single-purpose metropolitan agencies—is in reality a preference for decentralized services and a strong desire for local rule, thus another force against consolidation. The single-purpose districts, by providing those services most easily consolidated and integrated (water supply, mass transit), reduce the need to completely recombine the city and suburbs for other services. The point is that, except for a handful of American communities (most notably Miami and Nashville, which have consolidated metropolitan governments), the complexity and inequality of multiple governments within a single urban area will continue. And the reasons for the continuation will lie at least as much with cultural values about family, race relations, and politics as with efficient land use.

NOTES

[1] Remember that a key component of Park's definition of community was that residents were "rooted in the soil." Such biological imagery was deliberate.

[2] For example, see Zorbaugh's (1926) analysis of the "futile" attempts of the Chicago Zoning Commission to influence land values and growth patterns. However, more recent analysis of zoning in Chicago by Shlay and Rossi (1981) concludes that urban growth is significantly influenced by zoning regulations.

[3] The problems associated with interpreting ecological correlations continue. Note, for example, Van Poppel and Day's (1996) discussion of the difference between ecological explanations of suicide that are based on communities and explanations based on individual psychological factors. See also Barry Barnes's (2001) and Allen Liska's (1990) concerns about linking micro and macro analysis and John Betancur's (1996) questions about the applicability of using the macro ecological model to explain micro level Latino settlements.

[4] Examples of this third approach (combining the sociocultural works with urban ethnographies) include books by Peter Saunders (1981), William Schwab (1982), Alex Kotlowitz (1991), and Jay MacLeod (2009).

[5] See Firey and Sjoberg (1982) for a different view, one that sees sociocultural ecology as alive and well with vigorous, ongoing research. However, much of the research they cite as examples of the sociocultural approach seem more appropriately placed within the category of the urban ethnographies mentioned above and further discussed in chapter 14 of this text.

[6] The ecological approach is not the only way to study suburbanization, but it has produced more research on the subject than any other approach. The typological approach (chapter 2) can explain much of the motivation for suburban growth, i.e., a desire to recapture the *gemeinschaft*-like lifestyle in the suburb. Similarly, the lifestyles within the suburbs have been studied with a more, holistic, ethnographic approach (chapter 14).

[7] In fact, Domhoff (1978) argues that there was initially a national plan for urban renewal supported by a liberal labor coalition that would have emphasized building new housing in the central city. However, it was defeated in favor of a business-backed plan aimed at increasing

downtown property values. Domhoff explains this decision from a conflict perspective; ecologists would emphasize, rather, the lower property costs in the suburban fringe.

[8] The continuing work of Richard D. Alba and John R. Logan (e.g., Alba and Logan 1993; Logan, Alba, and Leung 1996; Alba, Logan, and Crowder 1997; Alba, Logan, Stults, Marzan, and Zhang 1999; and Alba, Logan, and Stults 2000) clearly illustrates the diversity of American suburbs.

The Community as a Social Network

The third major approach to the community employs social network and systems theory perspectives. Since systems theory, unlike the typological and ecological approaches, is not usually associated with community analysis, it is necessary to provide an overview of general systems theory before making specific reference to community applications.

General Systems Theory

The term *social system* is extremely broad, and general systems theory can take many forms, depending on the predisposition of the systems theorist. Nevertheless, it is possible to sketch an outline of systems theory by referring to some of its basic concepts. It must be remembered, however, that these concepts will have somewhat different meanings for different theorists.

The Social System

The concept of a social system is based on the idea of a structured, socially significant set of relationships between two or more units. Talcott Parsons (1951, 5–6), the foremost system theorist in American sociology, defines the social system as a

> plurality of individual actors interacting with each other in a situation which has at least a physical or environmental aspect, actors who are motivated in terms of a tendency to the "optimization of gratification" and whose relation to their situations, including each other, is defined and mediated in terms of a system of culturally structured and shared symbols.

Thus, a social system could be a family, a football team, a multinational corporation, a university, or even a community. Parsons, however, developed his systems theory with applications to small groups, large organizations, and entire societies; the community was notably absent. Even Charles Loomis, whose community research was discussed in chapter 2, ignored community applications in his book *Social Systems* (1960).[1] One reason for the exclusion of the community was that systems theory developed during the same time period that the idea of America as a mass society was rising to ascendency. But as we examine some of the major dimensions of systems theory, another reason will become evident: The community is a unique social phenomenon with characteristics that are particularly problematic for systems analysis.

Interaction and Systemic Linkage

A second look at Parsons's definition will show that social systems are essentially networks of *interaction*. In systems theory there is interaction both within and among social systems. Individuals may interact within their family system, and in turn the family as a system may interact with a religious system by worshiping at church. Analysis of the types, bases, and structures of systems interactions constitutes most of the applications of systems theory.

The concept of interaction is difficult to apply at the community level. The individuals in a community system do not interact with all the other individuals in the community. There are too many individuals for that much face-to-face interaction. Rather, the idea of "systemic linkage" is typically used to explain community interaction. In the formal language of systems theory, systemic linkage refers to "a process whereby one or more elements of at least two social systems is articulated in such a manner that the two systems in some ways and on some occasions may be viewed as a single unit" (Loomis 1960, 32). In the case of the community, then, we have a system linked both to microsystems such as individuals, families, and institutions and to macrosystems, usually the larger national society.

Boundary Maintenance

Although social systems are interrelated, each system is also distinct. A system can endure only as long as it can encourage cohesiveness and loyalty among its member units. Loomis (1960, 31) defines *boundary maintenance* as "the process whereby the identity of the social system is preserved and the characteristic interaction pattern maintained." Loomis (1960, 32) provides several examples of boundary maintenance:

> They may be primarily physical, as political boundaries, prison walls, zoning restrictions, or prescribed use or nonuse of facilities; or they may be primarily social, as are the life styles of social classes or the preference for endogamy. They may be spontaneously or unconsciously applied, as in the family display of company manners; or they may be planned and rationally applied, as in the travel restrictions imposed extensively by totalitarian states and less extensively by democratic societies. They may be expressed in group contraction as in casting out deviants; or they may be reflected in group expansion, as in the uniting of parallel labor unions, as similar groups find boundary maintenance facilitated by joint effort.

Notice that none of these examples specifically includes the community. Such an exclusion is understandable because the boundaries are difficult to define. Roland Warren (1978, 156) refers to St. Augustine's definition of God when trying to establish the boundaries of community: "an infinite circle whose center is everywhere and whose periphery is nowhere." Communities do have boundaries—sometimes geographic, sometimes psychological, sometimes social—but the imprecise nature of these boundaries makes systems theory difficult to apply. Nevertheless, systems theory can be applied to the community, despite the inherent difficulties. One of the best contributions to date on systems theory is by Roland Warren.

Applications of Systems Theory to the Community

Currently, systems theory has provided three significant contributions to our understanding of the community: (1) macrosystem dominance of society over community, (2) horizontal and vertical patterns linking community and society, and (3) the interactional field, paving the way for network analysis.

Roland L. Warren (1915–2010): Macro-System Dominance and Systemic Linkage

Roland L. Warren made significant and continuous contributions to community theory, most of it within the framework of systems theory (Palen 2008). The basis for Warren's analysis is the macrosystem dominance of community subsystems that results in what Warren calls "the great change."

The great change.   The change, Warren (1978, 52) explains, "includes the increasing orientation of local community units toward extracommunity systems of which they are a part, with a corresponding decline in community cohesion and autonomy." In an extensive and insightful extension of Tönnies's *gemeinschaft* and *gesellschaft,* Warren traces the "great change" through seven developments in society–community relations: (1) the increasing division of labor and the breakdown of mechanical solidarity á la Durkheim; (2) growing differentiation of interests and associations; (3) increasing systemic relationships to the larger society via Durkheim's organic solidarity; (4) more bureaucratization and impersonalization á la Weber; (5) the transfer of functions to profit enterprise and government, functions traditionally allocated to families and local ad hoc groupings; (6) urbanization and subsequent suburbanization; and (7) changing values, such as the gradual acceptance of governmental activity in traditionally private concerns, the shift from moral to causal interpretations of human behavior, and a change in emphasis from the "Protestant Ethic" of work and production to enjoyment and consumption. The cumulative effect of these seven changes is to create a new kind of American community almost totally dependent on the larger mass society.

Macrosystem dominance.   The community becomes a reflection of the larger society, or in Warren's terms, "a node of the macro system." Thus, one finds similar land use, values, and behaviors in all American communities:

> To be sure, there are differences among communities in values, norms, dominant interests, styles, and other cultural aspects. But again, if one is to watch the *public behavior* of people on a busy street corner, or at the supermarket, or in their homes, or at athletic events, one would be hard put to it to know that one is in Pittsburgh rather than St. Louis, in Bridgeport rather than in Rockland, in Atlanta rather than in Denver. Surely, the thought systems, the ideational and behavioral patterns indigenous to the locality are important, but an observer from Mars would be struck by their overwhelming similarity as one moves across the country, indicating once more that they may best be considered local enactments or implementations of thought and behavior systems of the national culture. (Warren 1978, 429)

There are two inferences that can be drawn from the dominance of the macrosystem. One is that a research focus on the community is clearly misplaced. For example, Brian Taylor (1975) argued that community studies analyzing local systems typically miss the prime cause of the social problems they encounter:

> To begin with, so far as problems have been examined at all, the use of a *locality framework* has tended to restrict attention to problems within the settlement-area, and thus either to miss some problems altogether or to ignore their true locations, which in many cases are in social systems which extend beyond the village, parish, slum, suburb or town itself, in the context of the wider society.

The causes of crime, poverty, pollution, and other community problems lie not so much with the characteristics of the local subsystem as with the society's macrosystem. The state of the national economy, for example, will be reflected in local unemployment rates. In terms similar to those used for the mass society, the macrosystem is the prime mover. Causes and cures for social problems will be found at the national, not the local, level. Thus, one implication of macro-system dominance is that community studies are no longer justified.

Warren (1978, 442), however, reached a different conclusion about macrosystem dominance and the role of community studies:

> There must be some broad area of middle ground for investigation between the incurably romantic conception of community as a focal point of virtually all meaningful social activity and the equally remote conception of a territorially undifferentiated mass society in which people's relation to the macrosystem is utterly independent of their geographic location. For in this admittedly difficult theoretical area lie numerous questions not only of theory, ideology, and social policy but also of focal issues around which people are increasingly involved. Many people want locality to be made more, not less, relevant to the adminis-

tration of the police, to the operation of the schools, to the ownership and operation of business enterprise, to the operation of the sanitation department, the health department, the social agencies, the location of highways, transit systems, and on and on through some of the most hotly contested issues of the day. Like Mark Twain's comment about the fallacious report of his own death, the death of the community has been highly exaggerated. Transformed, sí—muerto, no!

The theoretical task, and also the practical one, is to determine with greater depth of analysis those areas—many of the critical issues of our time—where the local organization of social life is an integral component of the social problem.

Yes, but how is this transformed community to be studied? How does one reach the "middle ground" where the role of the community in the macrosystem can be analyzed? Warren's answer—the conceptualization of horizontal and vertical patterns—provides one of the major contributions of systems theory to community.

The horizontal and vertical pattern of systemic linkage. According to Warren (1978, 243), a community's vertical pattern is "the structural and functional relation of its various social units and subsystems to extracommunity systems." The great change greatly strengthened the vertical pattern. The horizontal pattern is "the structural and functional relation of the community's various social units and subsystems to each other." And after the great change, the existence of a significant community system depends upon the strength of its horizontal pattern. In other words, the local units within the community are now so closely linked (vertically) with extracommunity systems that the question of whether the community remains a significant social system depends largely upon the degree of linkage (horizontally) among the various local units (Gilchrist 2004).

Warren's analysis of "locality-relevant functions" can illustrate the distinction between the vertical and horizontal patterns. He specifies five functions (production-distribution-consumption, socialization, social control, social participation, and mutual support), their typical community unit, and their typical horizontal and vertical patterns.

We use production-distribution-consumption as an example. It is an economic function that is at least partially locality-relevant.

Major locality-relevant function	Typical community unit	Typical unit of horizontal pattern	Typical superior unit of vertical pattern
production-distribution-consumption	company	chamber of commerce	national corporation

The company in this example is linked to two systems: the extracommunity national corporation and the community-based chamber of commerce. When production quotas are changed, workers are hired or fired, or wage scales are modified, the vertical pattern is in evidence. These events will have significant effects on the community, but their impetus is extracommunity. Typically, they are results of decisions made by the national corporation or by the local company in consultation with the national corporation. Since the great change, more local companies are controlled by corporations headquartered elsewhere.

This is far removed from the locally owned factories of the X family in Middletown that we examined in chapter 1. In fact, today the X family no longer owns those factories; they are, rather, owned by a conglomerate based in Chicago. Even the local workers will now be affiliated with national unions based outside the community. Note, as an example, how Warner and Low (1947, 108) describe the strengthening of the vertical patterns in their classic holistic study of Yankee City:

> Two fundamental changes have been occurring concomitantly, in recent years, in the social organization of Yankee City shoe factories. The first is the expansion of the hierarchy upward, out of Yankee City, through the expansion of individual enterprises and the establishment by them of central offices in distant large cities. The second is the expansion of the structure outward from Yankee City through the growth of manufacturers' associations and labor unions, also with headquarters outside Yankee City and with units in many other shoemaking communities in New England and elsewhere. Both . . . decrease Yankee City's control over its shoe factories by subjecting the factories, or segments of them, to more and more control exerted from outside Yankee City.

In short, the great change has significantly strengthened the vertical patterns of systemic linkage for locality-based economic functions, but what of the horizontal patterns?

The great change has not strengthened the horizontal patterns to the degree it has the vertical patterns. Still, horizontal patterns continue. In Warren's example, the company's membership in the local chamber of commerce would be a link between it and other units in the community. Thus, chamber-sponsored programs such as a local Better Business Bureau or a merchants-supported promotion of "Founders' Day" would be evidence of horizontal patterns within locality-based economic functions. A complete analysis of the systems related to the community economy, then, would require studying both vertical and horizontal patterns.

Table 4-1 shows all five locality-based functions and Warren's examples of horizontal and vertical patterns. In each case, the great change has strengthened the vertical pattern of systemic linkage. And it would appear that in some cases the vertical pattern has become considerably more important than its horizontal counterpart.

Warren's systems theory approach has emphasized the growing dominance of the macro-system (the *gesellschaft*-like mass society) on the local sub-

Table 4-1   Schematic Analysis of Major Locality-Relevant Functions

Major locality-relevant function	Typical community unit	Typical unit of horizontal pattern	Typical superior unit of vertical pattern
production-distribution-consumption	company	chamber of commerce	national corporation
socialization	public school	board of education	state department of education
social control	municipal government	city council	state government
social participation	church	council of churches	denominational body
mutual support	voluntary health association	community welfare council	national health association

systems, but he has also provided a conceptual tool (the horizontal pattern) for discovering and perhaps strengthening the local subsystem (the *gemeinschaft*-like community). Thus, it is Roland L. Warren who has made some of the most significant demonstrations of the applicability of systems theory to the community. And in some ways, Warren's contributions to systems theory paved the way for network analysis, studying the community as an interactional field.

Community as an Interactional Field

The concept of the community as an interactional field within which various forms of interaction take place emphasizes the social rather than physical elements of community. Harold Kaufman has pioneered this approach. "The interactional field," writes Kaufman (1959, 10), "probably has several dimensions, the limits and interrelations of which need to be determined. The community field is not a Mother Hubbard which contains a number of other fields, but rather is to be seen as only one of several interactional units in a local society." The community, then, is not a geographic place where all local interactions occur. It is a narrower concept that refers only to community-related actions.

Community-related actions.   What constitutes community-related actions? The answer is not clear, but according to Willis Sutton, Jr., and Jiri Kolaja (1960), it depends on the relative amount of "communityness" they possess. Communityness depends on the degree to which: (1) an activity is locality related; (2) the actors are identified with a locality; and (3) local people participate in an activity. For example, a local bond election or fluoridation decision would rank high on communityness, but an increase of postal rates at the local US Postal Service office would rank much lower. With this perspective of community, then, the focus is exclusively on those interactive fields "through which actions expressing a broad range of local activities are coordinated" (Wilkinson 1972, 44).

The interactive field approach has proven to be particularly effective in applying a more social-psychological, individualistic view of the community. In contrast to the aggregates of the ecological approach, individual values, motivations, and actions are important to the field theorists. Note, as an example, Norton Long's (1958, 254) reference to individuals in his analysis of community game playing:

> Individuals may play in a number of games, but, for the most part, their major preoccupation is with one, and their sense of major achievement is through success in one. Transfer from one game to another is, of course, possible, and the simultaneous playing of roles in two or more games is an important manner of linking separate games.
>
> Sharing a common territorial field and collaborating for different and particular ends in the achievement of overall social functions, the players in one game make use of the players in another and are, in turn, made use of by them. Thus the banker makes use of the news reporter, the politician, the contractor, the ecclesiastic, the labor leader, the civic leader—all to further his success in the banking game—but, reciprocally, he is used to further the others' success in the newspaper, political, contracting, ecclesiastical, labor, and civic games. Each is a piece in the chess game of the other, sometimes a willing piece, but, to the extent that the games are different, with a different end in view.

People are accustomed to playing games—for employment, for entertainment, for obtaining successes, and in general, for daily living (Flanagan 2002). The interconnection of game theory and narrative theory brings both place and time into the picture (Abell 2000). When the community is viewed as an interactional field, there is an emphasis on *people* as individual actors that provides an important counterbalance to the aggregate, territorial analysis of the urban ecologists.

The nonterritorial community.   This focus on the individual (and corresponding dismissal of territorial space) has produced an emerging nonterritorial view of the community. An early proponent of the nonterritorial community, Israel Rubin, was among the first analysts to eschew the concept of place and view the community as those interactive links that bind the individual to the larger society. These links are typically found in religious groups, occupational roles, and ethnic identifications, and thus the locality is relatively unimportant:

> The territorial view of community is probably responsible for most of the fuzzy theorization that we have discussed above. For example, the romantic theme that modern man has "lost" his community is fed by the common observation that the neighborhoods, towns, and cities have ceased to serve as significant foci of identification for the mobile man of industrial society. However, from our vantage point we see no reason for

saddling the concept with the territorial element. Individuals may mean-
ingfully relate to their respective societies through nonterritorial as well
as through territorial substructures. (Rubin 1969, 115)

Thirty years after Rubin's observations, network analysts like Barry Wellman (Wellman and Gulia 1999b, 169) want to "educate traditional, place-ori-
ented, community sociologists that community can stretch well beyond the
neighborhood." If the interactions of community members transcend the arbi-
trarily defined ecological boundaries, then the claim here is that it is necessary
to reevaluate the territorial basis for community (Karp, Stone, and Yoels 1991).
The social networks need not be confined to the local neighborhood (Wellman
and Wortley 1990). Network analysis (discussed in the next section) has uncovered the non-neighborhood basis of personal ties and networks that are not territorially concentrated, but rather dispersed among nonterritorial forms of
community social organizations (Fuchs 2007; Gottdiener and Hutchison 2006).

Network analysis. The interactional field's emphasis on individual
interactions and the resulting conception of a nonterritorial community provide the basis for much of the current work in network analysis.[2] With the
advances in survey research and the development of powerful computer technology for the statistical analysis of social networks, the quantity and quality
of social interactions can be empirically assessed.[3] Network analysis is an
interactive systems "perspective that focuses on structured relationships
between individuals and collectives" (Wellman and Leighton 1979). Social
network analysis maps social relationships across group boundaries (Fuchs
2007).[4] By precisely measuring and mapping the interactions among individuals, it is possible to test hypotheses, such as a hypothesis about nonterritorial
communities. If the most common and significant personal interactions
occur among people within the same geographic area, then Rubin is wrong.
If however, most of the interactions occur with people who do not live in the
same area, then a nonterritorial community does exist. However, the results
have not allowed such a definitive acceptance or rejection of territorial vs.
nonterritorial community.

Network analysis of residents in several urban neighborhoods has documented the existence of both territorial and nonterritorial communities (Laumann 1973; Wellman and Leighton 1979; Fischer 1982; Freeman 2004).
Barry Wellman (1979) was among the first to demonstrate this application of
network analysis by tracing the networks of social interaction reported in his
surveys in East York (a working-class neighborhood in Toronto). Wellman
concluded that while significant social interaction occurs within the neighborhood, more of it is outside East York. According to Wellman's network
analysis, the nonterritorial community (i.e., liberated) appears stronger than
the territorial community (i.e., saved).

Claude Fischer (1982) methodologically extended Wellman's network
analysis by surveying a larger and broader sample that included residents
with substantial variation in social class, family status, and residence (urban

San Francisco, suburbs, small towns, and rural North California). Fischer examined the effect of location on the structure of interpersonal networks and found social class to be extremely important in defining the nature of networks and social interactions. The residents in the upper class have the means and inclination to move beyond their neighborhoods and establish broad, metropolitan social networks. Fischer also finds significant rural/urban differences in networks and social interaction beyond those associated with social class and family status. Urban residents, for example, are much less likely to have relatives in their social networks than their rural and small-town counterparts. Subsequent research supports the proposition that the rural/urban distinction is real and has yet to disappear. The urban network is more dispersed, loosely knit, and open (Flanagan 2002; Gottdiener and Hutchison 2006). The personal networks in rural settings contain more intense ties based on kinship and territorial neighborhoods that tend to be small, dense, and homogenous (Beggs et al. 1996).

In sum, network analysis suggests that territorial communities are typically built around local kinship structures and/or workplace propinquity. Nonterritorial communities extend out to distant parents, friends, co-workers, and so on. Thus, personal interactions can either link a person to the local territorial community or to the larger nonterritorial society.

So, while the influence of society's macrosystems (à la Roland Warren) is an important part of the systems theory approach to community, systems theory remains out of favor in sociology. More recently, network analysis has been recognized as an important addition to the systemic linkage between the individual and society, and it is likely that social networks will continue to replace social systems as an approach to community.

NOTES

[1] To a large degree, the functional systems theory of Parsons and Loomis is ignored in modern sociology (Hassard 1995, Bausch 2001). It does, however, provide the foundation for the work of Roland Warren and other more recent and relevant approaches discussed later in this chapter.

[2] The ecological view (discussed in chapter 3) can be broadened when it accounts for social networks. Examining networks in ecological terms enriches network analysis with concepts like competition, density, and dependency. Network analysis explores the internal structure, yet it can be strengthened with the inclusion of POET characteristics (see Perrow 2000).

[3] The theoretical roots of network analysis and systemic linkages can be traced back to Georg Simmel's "Social Circles" (1908/trans. 1955) (see Abu-Lughod 1991). The theory of social networks has evolved into an operational tool and sophisticated methodology applied to social research. As the theoretical constructs of networks have been empirically tested, the advanced computer techniques often replace the theory.

[4] Recently, developments in statistical techniques and models have been adapted for use to empirically test social networks. The statistical analysis of networks has blossomed as seen with statistical causality (Doreian 2001), path analysis and symmetric structures (Doreian 1986), linear models (Doreian 1981), cluster analysis (Abu-Lughod 1991), canonical analysis (Wasserman and Faust 1989), correlation and association models (Faust and Wasserman 1993), logit models (Skvoretz and Faust 1999), and GIS mapping.

The Conflict Approach
Marx Finally Comes to the City

Systems theory, with its basis in inherently conservative structural functional-ism, is often seen as the theoretical antithesis of conflict theory, with its basis in Marxist analysis. Yet, in one important characteristic they are similar: both are major social science paradigms with relatively limited relevance to the community.[1] Classic Marxists, much like system theorists, typically focus on nation-states, not the communities within them. Hence, just as with the pre-ceding section on systems theory, we must first outline the major dimensions of the theory before turning to the local applications.

Considerable confusion can develop in discussing Marxism, since the term can refer to a political ideology, an economic system, an epistemological philoso-phy, or any combination of the three. And when these broad terms are often used interchangeably with neo-Marxism and the conflict approach, the lack of defini-tional precision expands geometrically. For our purposes, however, *Marxist analy-sis* will refer to the classic statements of Marx and Engels. *Neo-Marxism* refers to positions developed by largely European social scientists in the 1960s and 1970s—positions built on Marx's principles of economically based class conflict. In the 1980s, this approach began to be called the *new urban sociology* (by the time it was no longer "new"). More recently, the *urban political economy approach* began to extend the ideas of the neo-Marxists in the twenty-first century, focusing on political and economic forces that shape the city. Finally, the *conflict approach is* the most inclusive term, referring to both Marxist and neo-Marxist approaches, as well as the non-Marxist analysis of conflict provided by American sociologists in the 1950s and 1960s. We examine the variations in this section, beginning with what is arguably the most influential theory ever developed by social scientists.

Classic Statements: Marx and Engels

The nineteenth-century analysis of Karl Marx and Friedrich Engels set in motion debates and controversies in both academic and political spheres that continue unabated over a hundred years later. Although Marx's writings are typically (and correctly) given more consideration than those of his friend and collaborator, Engels, in terms of the community their writings are more equal. Engels, in fact, provided more examples of local analysis than Marx. Thus, we will examine Marx's writings for the theoretical underpinnings of this approach and then turn to Engels's works for the few existing local applications of classical Marxist analysis.

Karl Marx (1818–1883)

The German philosopher, economist, and sociologist Karl Marx[2] explained the movement toward *gesellschaft* in terms of a change in the "means of production," in this case, a change from agricultural production based on the land to industrial production based on the factory. Further, this change in the means of production brought about a change in the ruling class—the owners of the means of production. Thus, while the structure of medieval Europe supported the class interests of the landed aristocracy, the emerging structure of industrial Europe would support the capitalist class, the new owners of the means of production. The industrial-based capitalists, the *bourgeoisie*, were the new ruling class. Since the bourgeoisie owned the means of production, the working class (the *proletariat*) was completely dependent upon them for jobs. Thus, the proletariat could be exploited through low wages and poor working conditions.

Marx, however, believed there were inherent, dialectical contradictions within industrial capitalism that would inevitably lead to its demise. Specifically, the desire for greater profits would lead to even greater exploitation, alienation, and degradation of the working class. At this point, a "class consciousness" would develop among the proletariat as they realized that their class interests were in opposition to those of the bourgeoisie. The proletariat would revolt and overthrow the bourgeoisie, which in turn would lead to a classless workers' utopia:

> If the proletariat during its contact with the bourgeoisie is compelled by the force of circumstances to organize itself into a class; if by means of a revolution it makes itself into the ruling class and, as such, sweeps away by force the old conditions of production, then it will, along with these conditions, have swept away the conditions for the existence of class antagonisms and of classes generally, and will thereby have abolished its own supremacy as a class.
>
> In place of the old bourgeois society, with its classes and class antagonisms, we shall have an association in which the free development of each is the condition for the free development of all. (Marx and Engels 1848, "Manifesto of the Communist Party," quoted from Feuer 1959)

Marx's analysis was almost exclusively on the macro level. The industrial city was merely a place where the evils of capitalism were particularly visible (Ritzer and Goodman 2004). Engels also viewed the city as the site of capitalistic excesses, but unlike Marx he devoted much of his writings to a description and analysis of urban capitalism.

Friedrich Engels (1820–1895)

Engels, in his first major work, *The Condition of the Working Class in England* [1845], describes the *gesellschaft*-like conditions of the city in terms that echo Simmel's "The Metropolis and Mental Life." Engels' analysis, however, is much more critical. While Simmel finds increased freedom in the impersonal city, Engels finds only unnatural alienation:

> The very turmoil of the streets has something repulsive, something against which human nature rebels. The hundreds of thousands of all classes and all ranks crowding past each other, are they not all human beings with the same qualities and powers, and with the same interest in being happy? And have they not, in the end, to seek happiness in the same way, by the same means? And still they crowd by one another as though they had nothing in common, nothing to do with one another, and their only agreement is the tacit one, that each keep to his own side of the pavement, so as not to delay the opposing streams of the crowd, while it occurs to no man to honour another with so much as a glance. The brutal indifference, the unfeeling isolation of each in his private interest becomes the more repellent and offensive, the more these individuals are crowded together, within a limited space. And, however much one may be aware that this isolation of the individual, this narrow self-seeking is the fundamental principle of our society everywhere, it is nowhere so shamelessly barefaced, so self-conscious as just here in the crowding of the great city. The dissolution of mankind into monads, of which each one has a separate principle, the world of atoms, is here carried out to its utmost extremes. (Engels 1958, 30–31)

While capitalism creates the urban ills, it is unable to cure them. Neo-Marxists (e.g., Tabb 1999; 2004; Tabb and Sawers 1984) still refer to Engels's critique of what today would be called urban renewal, and the neo-Marxist solution to the problems of urban slums is still the same as Engels's:

> The breeding places of disease, the infamous holes and cellars in which the capitalist mode of production confines our workers night after night, are not abolished; they are merely shifted elsewhere! The same economic necessity that produced them in the first place produces them in the next place also! As long as the capitalist mode of production continues to exist it is folly to hope for an isolated settlement of the housing question or of any other social question affecting the lot of the workers. The solution lies in the abolition of the capitalist mode of production. (Engels 1969, 75)

Still, the city represented more to Marx and Engels than simply an extreme example of capitalist exploitation. The city was to play a crucial role in bringing about the overthrow of the bourgeoisie. Marx and Engels, in the *Communist Manifesto* (1848), argued that the bourgeoisie had actually rendered a service to the proletariat by creating cities that have "rescued a considerable part of the population from the idiocy of rural life." Engels expanded on this idea in *The Condition of the Working Class* [1845]:

> The great cities are the birthplaces of labour movements; in them the workers first began to reflect upon their own condition and to struggle against it; in them the opposition between proletariat and bourgeoisie first made itself manifest. . . . Without the great cities and their forcing influence upon the popular intelligence, the working class would be far less advanced than it is. (Engels 1969, 152)

In classical Marxism, then, there was an ambivalent view of the city. On the one hand, the city manifested the most extreme evils of capitalism; on the other hand, it provided the necessary conditions for the proletarian class consciousness that would lead to capitalism's destruction. In either case, however, it remained only a reflection of the larger, capitalistic society. The city is not the major focus of classic Marxist analysis.

Non-Marxist Conflict Approaches

Conflict has not always been a popular subject for American sociologists. We saw how neo-orthodox ecologists replaced competition with equilibrium. Similarly, systems theory, with its structural–functional underpinnings, tends to view conflict as an unnatural and negative phenomenon. Some of this reluctance to include conflict was due to the conservatism of the 1950s and the linking of conflict with Marx and Marxism. Even when an elaborate theory such as Lewis Coser's *The Functions of Social Conflict* (1956) was built on conflict, it was based on Simmel rather than Marx. When examining the analysis of community conflict by American sociologists, then, it is not surprising that two major studies treat conflict as a somewhat negative phenomenon and make no reference to the works of Marx.

James S. Coleman (1926–1995): *Community Conflict*

James Coleman's most enduring contribution to community sociology is his analysis of local controversy. Coleman's monograph, *Community Conflict* (1957), gathers together reports of numerous local controversies and seeks out their commonalities to develop a general theory of community conflict. According to Coleman, conflict typically stems from three local sources: (1) *economic issues* such as bond elections or zoning, (2) *political disputes* such as elections or revising town charters, and (3) *value conflicts* reflected in controversies such as school integration. In some communities, disputes from these sources may rekindle dormant but deep-seated hostilities between local groups. In such cases, the disputes are likely to produce controversy.

Although the sources of community conflict may differ, "once the controversies have begun, they resemble each other remarkably" (Coleman 1957, 9). The dynamics that transform an initial specific issue into a widespread community conflict do not vary by issue. Rather, as figure 5-1 illustrates, there is a general sequence of events that produces a dispute independent of the issue that leads to the initial disagreement.

The first step is when specific issues give way to general ones. For example, an attack on certain books in the school library might lead to a more general assault on educational policy (curricula, teaching methods). This is most likely to occur when the aforementioned latent hostilities exist in the community. At this point there is a shift from dispassionate *disagreement* to emotional *antagonism.* The hostility is characterized by personal slander and rumor.

Figure 5-1   Coleman's Model of Community Conflict

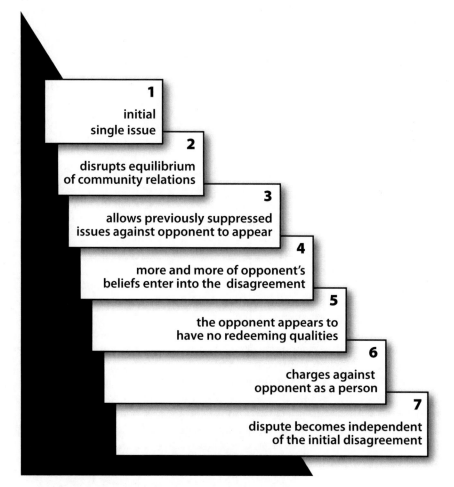

1

initial
single issue

2

disrupts equilibrium
of community relations

3

allows previously suppressed
issues against opponent to appear

4

more and more of opponent's
beliefs enter into the disagreement

5

the opponent appears to
have no redeeming qualities

6

charges against
opponent as a person

7

dispute becomes independent
of the initial disagreement

Source: Adapted from James S. Coleman (1957), *Community Conflict* (New York: The Free Press).

As this antagonism develops, associations *within* the quarreling groups flourish while associations *between* the groups wither. New leaders, not governed by traditional norms of debate and compromise, emerge

> who have not been community leaders in the past, men who face none of the constraints of maintaining a previous community position, and feel none of the cross-pressures felt by members of community organizations. (Coleman 1957, quoted from Warren and Lyon 1983, 325)

At this point the controversy is likely to develop into a major conflict. Various organizations and individuals begin to choose sides, and those who advocate community conflict win out over those who would maintain order.

In spite of his generally negative views of community conflict, Coleman[3] does not offer much in the way of conflict control and resolution. He does emphasize that since the events leading to community conflict are mutually reinforcing, it is best to break the cycle early in the process. If traditional community leaders take an early and united stand against the dissident groups, the conflict can be diverted into normal, nonthreatening channels.

William A. Gamson: The Causes of "Rancorous" Conflict

Most of Coleman's analysis was directed toward the dynamics of community conflict, with little concern paid to *which* communities are the most likely to experience conflict. William Gamson, however, made the likelihood of "rancorous" community conflict the focus of his research.

Gamson (1966) studied fifty-four issues in eighteen New England communities to learn why some communities would experience "rancorous conflicts" characterized by actions that are "'dirty,' 'underhanded,' 'vicious' and so forth," while other communities experienced more "conventional conflicts" where "established means of political expression are used." Using elite interviews and available data sources, Gamson labeled each community as characterized by either rancorous or conventional conflict.

Gamson discovered a strong relationship between rancorous conflict and political instability, finding that "only one of the conventional towns is undergoing political change while two-thirds of the rancorous towns are undergoing such change" (1966, 78). Further, he found that "the average degree of acquaintance among opponents is substantially lower in rancorous than in conventional towns" (Gamson 1966, 79). Thus, he concludes that: (1) shifts in political control produce a structural strain that is conducive to rancorous conflict, and (2) a lack of community integration (i.e., few opponents being acquainted with one another) can also lead to more rancorous conflicts.

In what was a rather remarkable observation for the times, Gamson (1966) noted that rancorous towns were not all bad. In fact, the conventional towns were often boring:

> Because of the negative connotations of a term like "rancorous conflict," some final observations about the towns studied here are worth making. Many of the conventional communities are rather dull and stagnant,

while some of the rancorous ones are among the most vital. Some of the conventional towns not only have an absence of rancorous conflict but a general absence of change; the rancorous towns have the strains that accompany change but some of them also have the advantages of stimulation and growth. The absence of rancorous conflict is no necessary sign of an ideal community. (81)

In later research, Gamson (1992) examines group consciousness, identity, and solidarity in the community. He notes that external attacks on a community can have contradictory effects, sometimes increasing the solidarity within the community.

Every attack is a test, forcing participants to consider whether the group deserves their loyalty and is worth the risks involved. The willingness of people to maintain or even increase their commitment by linking themselves to the collective entity under attack is a powerful stimulus for others to do the same. (Gamson 1991, 45)

While Gamson reports politically positive contributions for community conflict, it is still a long and radical stretch to the ideas of European neo-Marxists, who were beginning to turn their attention to the urban community in the 1960s.

Neo-Marxist Conflict Approaches

Traditionally, neo-Marxists followed in the footsteps of their founder and focused almost exclusively on the nation-state. In the late 1960s, however, several Marxist perspectives on urban phenomena suddenly appeared. Why? Two American neo-Marxists, William Tabb[4] and Larry Sawers (1984, 4–5), offer this explanation:

One may ask why suddenly in the 1960s and 1970s have so many Marxists begun studying cities and so many urbanologists turned to Marx. Indeed, why did not Marxists pay attention to urban problems before the 1960s? Marx's followers prior to the last decade or so have tended to focus on the core relations of capitalism. While cities were often considered to be the site of class struggle, the space itself hardly seemed important or worthy of special study. . . . This changed in the 1960s. The middle-class exodus from the cities and consequent loss of the tax base, the civil-rights movement, and the urban conflagrations all drew attention to the cities. Struggles over urban space intensified as community groups fought for their homes against highways and urban renewal. Many came to see these struggles over "turf" as forms of class struggle. . . . As the antiwar movement drew to its successful conclusion in the early 1970s, many radicals redirected their attention away from imperialism and to urban problems. By the mid-1970s, the left-right punch of inflation and unemployment had brought several cities to the point of fiscal disaster and pushed many others close to the brink. Marxists, therefore, could no longer ignore the urban crisis, and Marxist urbanology blossomed.

Still, the initial neo-Marxist approaches to community were almost exclusively a European phenomenon. Marxist analysis has always had a larger following in Europe than in the United States, and even today variations in Marxist theory are typically European in origin. So, it is with a Spanish sociologist that we begin our examination of neo-Marxist conflict approaches.

Manuel Castells

Castells' conflict approach to the community is most fully developed in his book *The Urban Question* (originally published in 1972 and translated into English in 1977). Like many Marxists, he begins the book by characterizing all non-Marxist approaches as "ideological." By ideological he means that they are not scientific but rather are falsely "giving the reassuring impression of an integrated society, united in facing up to common problems" (Castells 1977, 85). Hence, the typological approach and urban ecology are rejected along with community power studies and urban planning as ideological justifications of the status quo. However, Castells goes even further and dismisses other neo-Marxian approaches as ideological as well.[5] It is Castells' position, apparently, that his is the only truly scientific approach to the city.

Castells views the city as the place where a dialectical contradiction between production and consumption appears—a conflict between the need to produce at the highest possible level of profit and the need to reproduce labor power through local consumption. Individual capitalists will find little reason to invest in the consumption commodities necessary to replenish the workforce. Thus, the quality of life of the workers deteriorates. It falls, then, to the state to maintain the capitalist system by constructing low-cost housing units, subsidizing food costs, maintaining social facilities, and so on. This is why, Castells argues, consumption had become increasingly political. The state, by creating a capitalist welfare system, protects the capitalists from their own excesses:

> The state apparatus not only exercises class domination but also strives, as far as possible, to regulate the crises of the system, in order to preserve it.
>
> It is in this sense that it may, sometimes, become reformist. Although reforms are always imposed by the class struggle and, therefore, from outside the state apparatus, they are no less real for that: their aim is to preserve and extend the existing context; thus consolidating the long-term interests of the dominant classes, even if it involves infringing their privileges to some extent in a particular conjuncture. (Castells 1977, 208)

While state support of local consumption supports the system by replenishing the workforce and reducing class conflict, it nonetheless generates a new set of contradictions. Since the state pays the increasing costs of replenishing labor power while the private capitalists reap the profits created by labor power, the state goes deeper into debt:

> In fact, the fiscal crisis of the inner cities was a particularly acute expression of the overall fiscal crisis of the state, that is, of the increasing bud-

getary gap created in public finance in advanced capitalist countries because of the historical process of socialization of costs and privatization of profits. The crisis is even more acute for the local governments of larger inner cities because they express the contradictory expansion of the "service sector." On the one hand, corporate capital needs to build directional centers which require concentration of service workers and public facilities downtown. On the other hand, if social order is to be maintained, the state has to absorb the surplus population and to provide welfare and public services to the larger unemployed and underemployed population concentrated in the inner cities. (Castells 1977, 415)

The fiscal crisis of New York City in 1974–75 and its threatened bankruptcy are symptoms of these problems (Castells 1977, 415–20).[6] One would further suppose that the growing national debt and reduction of local services during the great recession of 2010 is another example of this contradiction, though Marxist critiques of this most recent economic crisis are rare and focused on global rather than local conditions (e.g., Wolff 2010).

As the level of state debt increases, there must eventually be a reduction of labor-replenishing commodities. This reduction in the workers' quality of life may lead to "urban social movements" against the capitalist state, but such a development is problematic since there must also be a "socialist organization" (for Castells, this would be a communist party) to organize and politicize the unrest. Without the party, "urban contradictions are expressed in a 'wild' way," with youth gangs and urban unrest (Castells 1977, 271–72).

Castells' next book, *The City and the Grassroots* (1983), analyzed "urban social movements" in the form of neighborhood organizations building a common "community." His book is an apparent recognition that urban violence declined rather than increased, as he had predicted. Moreso than *The Urban Question,* this book focuses on social movements and political contests. *The City and the Grassroots* sets forth the way cities are shaped by urban social movements. The urban social movement and collective political activity is the basis for urban change. These urban conflicts affect the urban spatial form, and Castells believes in the necessity for grassroots action if the good city is ever to be built. This lengthy book presents several case studies of urban social movements, emphasizing the specific historical contexts. The series of case studies includes the tenants' movements in high-rise *grands ensembles* in suburban Paris in the 1960s and 1970s; the gay and Hispanic communities in the Mission District of San Francisco; the squatter community in Latin America; and the citizen movement in Madrid in the 1970s. Castells's discussions of historical change seems clearly within the Marxist tradition; however, Castells tries to separate himself and rejects the Marxist view of social transformation.

More recently, Castells is concerned with the growth of *The Informational City* (1991) and the development of the network society in *Communication Power* (2009). The introduction of new technology designed to create and spread information has a great impact on the way people organize an urban world (similar to the POET model that incorporates the technology in the assessment of community, yet with a conflict twist). According to Castells, the flow of computerized information has allowed the transformation of our cities and created problems in the process (Ritzer and Goodman 2004). *The Informational City* is set in the context of economic restructuring in the United States, exploring a specific set of interactions between restructuring, technology, and space. His hypothesis is that "the interaction between modes of production and modes of development is at the source of the generation of new social and spatial forms and processes" (*ibid.*, 7). Thus, Castells highlights the conflict between social relations rooted in place versus social relations that are increasingly reliant on recent technological innovations.

Castells continues with his focus on the network society and offers a modern perspective of our new technological and computerized world in his trilogy (2000a, b, c; 2010) with the overarching title *The Information Age: Economy, Society, and Culture*. Castells's core argument is that the technological revolution and the restructuring of world capitalism have revolutionized the organization of production on a global scale with implications for our work and private lives. And in the only consideration of community issues, he describes the search for identity as it has shifted from civil society to a more communal experience such as religious fundamentalism, nationalism, and ethnicity. *The Information Age* represents Castells's movement away from questions of urban community and onto the stage of grand global theory. At this new level, despite an opaque writing style that sometimes makes the exact meaning and implications of his work unclear, Castells's work continues to garner broad critical acclaim.

David Harvey: *Social Justice and the City*

English geographer David Harvey has approached the city in a manner that parallels Castells in a somewhat more humanistic way. Harvey's major work, *Social Justice and the City* (revised 2009; original in 1973), contains two major approaches to the city: Part I, which is a liberal approach, and Part 2, which is a conflict approach. Like Castells, his distinction between them is based on a Marxian concept of ideology:

> I leave it to the reader to judge whether Part I or Part 2 contains the more productive analyses. Before making this judgment there are two points I would like to present. First, I recognize that the analysis of Part 2 is a beginning point which opens up new lines of thought. The analysis is rather unfamiliar (of necessity) but its freshness to me may have made it appear at times rather rough and at other times unnecessarily complicated. I beg a certain amount of indulgence on this score. Second, Marx gives a specific meaning to ideology—he regards it as an *unaware* expression of the underlying ideas and beliefs which attach to a particular social situation, in contrast to the *aware* and critical exposition of ideas in their social context, which is frequently called ideology in the West. The essays in Part 2 are ideological in the Western sense, whereas the essays in Part I are ideological in the Marxist sense. (Harvey 1973, 18)

Although the reader is invited to choose between liberalism and Marxism, Harvey clearly prefers the neo-Marxist perspective developed in Part 2. He argues that liberal approaches are probably insufficient and that a new conflict approach based on Marxism should be considered. As a geographer, Harvey's major concern is with how social processes are expressed in spatial forms. His thesis in Part 2 is that the spatial patterning of capitalist cities reflects the exploitative injustices inherent in capitalism. These spatial patterns are dynamic because the dialectical contradictions of capitalism require constant adjustments to maintain the system.

Harvey illustrates how capitalism changes urban spatial patterns in an attempt to save itself from its own excesses. In order to maximize profits, individual capitalists produce more than can be consumed, leading to glutted markets, falling prices, and rising unemployment. This problem can be temporarily solved by switching investment from "primary circuits" (production) to "secondary circuits" (warehouses, offices). By reinvesting in their capital, capitalists are able to temporarily reduce production, and (at the same time, of course) they are remaking the urban environment through expansion and construction. Eventually, however, production is increased to even higher levels. The recurring problems of market glut are now exacerbated by the demolition of structurally sound buildings for new, but now largely vacant, blocks of offices. Thus, the physical patterns of urban structure and growth reflect the exploitation, development, and contradictions of capitalism.

Harvey's analysis is better suited to pointing out the injustices and inefficiencies of capitalist cities than to projecting the changes necessary to create a more just city. He ends *Social Justice and the City* with the following observations:

> An urbanism founded upon exploitation is a legacy of history. A genuinely humanizing urbanism has yet to be brought into being. It remains for revolutionary theory to chart the path from an urbanism based in exploitation to an urbanism appropriate for the human species. And it remains for revolutionary practice to accomplish such a transformation. (Harvey 1988, 314)

The exploitive nature and process of capitalism is further discussed in Harvey's case study of Baltimore in *The Urbanization of Capital* (1985b), the case study of Paris in *Consciousness and the Urban Experience* (1985a) and *Paris, Capital of Modernity* (2003b). He discusses the historical view of capitalism in *The Urban Experience* (1989) and *A Brief History of Neoliberalism* (2007). Harvey demonstrates that urban development is not a single growth process but rather a boom, recession, or uneven growth that is basic to the cycles of urbanism within a capitalist system.

Harvey continues to build on the Marxist and neo-Marxist perspective in his book, *Spaces of Hope* (2000) and *Spaces of Capital* (2001), showing how territories are continually reorganized, redefined, and changed by a world dominated by capitalism. Finally, in true Marxist tradition, Harvey describes the future utopian space and offers hope for the oppressive spatial patterns of today.

Since Harvey's publication of *Social Justice and the City* (1988), *Spaces of Hope* (2000), and *Spaces of Capital* (2001), neo-Marxist analysis of local phenomena has continued to expand considerably (Soja 1996, 2000, 2003; Tabb 1999, 2004). However, the neo-Marxist approach remains much as it was in the 1970s: (1) pointing out the contradictions and exploitation inherent in urban capitalism, and (2) accounting for the survival of capitalism in spite of these contradictions and exploitations. The "revolutionary practice" still awaits the development of "revolutionary theory."[7] The natural progression from neo-Marxism leads us to the political economy approach.

Urban Political Economy and the New Urban Politics

Closely associated with Neo-Marxism are the terms *urban political economy* and *new urban politics*. These two somewhat interchangeable terms are not substantially different from neo-Marxist and new urban sociology; they are generally the preferred terms for applying the conflict approach to the city in the first decade of the twenty-first century. The political economy paradigm assesses the changing nature of the economy and its impacts on the community (Tabb 1999; Kleniewski and Thomas 2010). The viewpoint draws from the works of Karl Marx, Manuel Castells, and David Harvey, arguing that urban changes are best understood in the framework of economic *and* political forces, thus the new urban politics label. Broadly, urban political economy assumes that Marx's emphasis on those who control the means of production remains relevant. Cities reflect the desires of those with the greatest resources to maintain and increase their control. As the economy changes from a basis on local manufacturing to one of global information, urban structures and setting change accordingly. While this may not seem all that different from what was called neo-Marxist or new urban sociology, it is a bit more general and does appear to be the preferred term as of this writing.

The political economy paradigm examines local phenomena such as the growth of suburbs, the closing of industrial facilities in the urban center, the relocation of companies to the suburban areas, and the decline in industrial jobs. While Marxists and neo-Marxists focus on the conflict between competing groups, political economists focus on the changing economic structure of the city. The characteristics of political economy are described by Nancy Kleniewski and Alexander Thomas (2010, 37–39):

1. Cities are part of the political, economic, and social arrangements of their times rather than products of natural processes.

2. Competition and conflicts over the distribution of resources help shape urban patterns and urban social life.

3. Government is an important institution influencing urban patterns.

4. Economic restructuring, or a pattern of widespread shifts in the economy, is one of the most important factors affecting local communities.

Beyond the key focus on the role of economic development in shaping cities, the political economy approach also examines conflicts between races, classes, industries, and economic institutions as influencing the characteristics of the city. Neo-Marxists are sometimes critical of the political economy approach, suggesting that its potential to promote radical change in urban environments is limited (Harvey 2006, 2007). The urban political economy paradigm is also criticized for a macro approach that overemphasizes uniformity of the cities and ignores local political and economic variations (Kleniewski and Thomas 2010). As with the other Marxist and conflict approaches, the community is typically acted upon by global forces rather than being an actor. Still, promising exceptions that focus on local institutions and local places do exist, with John Logan and Harvey Molotch's widely-cited *Urban Fortunes* (1987) as perhaps the most important. Logan and Molotch borrow heavily from Marx and Harvey in their concept of a "growth machine" that includes local elites influencing local land use. This idea is explored more fully in chapter 12 (Community Politics), and it may be this area that shows the most promise for conflict approaches to community.

NOTES

[1] However, most urban and community scholars include a discussion of the conflict approach and neo-Marxism in their texts (see Palen 2008; Macionis and Parrillo 2010; Gottdiener and Hutchison 2006; Kleniewski and Thomas 2010; Abu-Lughod 1991).

[2] The most complete statement of Marx's ideas is in his classic treatise *Capital* (1867). For an outline of his views, see the *Communist Manifesto* (1848).

[3] In the latter part of his career, James Coleman changed his approach and focused on rational choice theory (see Coleman 1988; 1990a; 1990b; 1993). Coleman founded the journal, *Rationality and Society*, in 1989 to highlight work from the rational choice perspective. His widely influential book, *Foundations of Social Theory* (1990a), also reflects this perspective. James Coleman died in 1995.

[4] More recently, William K. Tabb (Tabb and Sawers 1984; Tabb1999, 2004) identifies himself with the urban political economy approach instead of Neo-Marxism, although he claims to have been heavily influenced by the ideas of Karl Marx. Tabb examines the role of the economy and political structure in *The Economic Governance in the Age of Globalization* (2004).

[5] Especially interesting is Castells' (1977, chapter 6) rejection of the Marxist-humanist analysis of Henri Lefebvre (1976), who develops a more individualistic interpretation of Marx similar to the works of David Harvey that are discussed in the following section. Castells is more structural than Lefebvre, and this apparently accounts for the rejection.

[6] See Friedland, Piven, and Alford (1984) and Block (1981) for somewhat similar analyses of the urban fiscal crisis. See Friedland, Palmer, and Stenbeck (1990) and Friedland and Robertson (1990) for the fiscal impact of the urban industrial system. See Morin and Hanley (2004), Abu-Lughod (1999), and Sassen (2001; 2006) for the economic restructuring and fiscal state of urban areas. See Palen 2008 for an overview of fiscal health, Hendrick (2004) for assessing local fiscal health, and Ruhil (2003) for fiscal effects on local reformism.

[7] For example, while David Harvey's *The Enigma of Capital* (2010) provides an explanation of the financial disaster in the American economy in September 2008, a feasible alternative to capitalism remains elusive.

chapter six

The Multiple Approaches to Community

We have now examined four approaches to community. There could have been more. Roland Warren (1978) distinguished between six approaches and later expanded it to eight (Warren 1983). Dennis Poplin (1979) employed six. Heather Haveman (2000) also described six paradigms. Jessie Bernard (1973) listed two general and seven more specific approaches to (or paradigms of) community. Steven Brint (2001) identified two lines of development of the community approaches following either Tönnies's or Durkheim's ideas, with four major subtypes related to behavioral and organizational outcomes of community. There is no complete and exhaustive list, but if there were a "magic" number that encompassed the totality of community approaches, it would probably be substantially less than the total number of community definitions. Remember that Hillery (1955) found almost a hundred separate definitions of community, and even more have been added since then (Sutton and Munson 1976). Still, there is a causal relationship here. Since the community can be defined in such a large number of ways, it can be approached in different ways as well.

Multiple Definitions Yield Multiple Approaches: Examples with Area, Common Ties, and Social Interaction

We can illustrate the degree to which the multiple community definitions produce multiple community approaches by referring to Hillery's three most common types of definitions: those including (1) area, (2) common ties, and (3) social interaction.

Defining the community in terms of people in a specific geographic area implies focusing on the physical environment of the community, emphasizing the relationship between the population and the physical environment and the resultant spatial patterns. Thus, it is not surprising that those who employ an ecological approach to community are likely to define the community as a specific territorial entity. The classic human ecologists of the Chicago school, neo-orthodox ecologists such as Hawley and Duncan, sociocultural ecologists like Firey, and modern applicants of factorial ecology and GIS all define community in terms of specific and important geographic boundaries. In short, conceiving of the community as a geographic area is more likely to lead to an ecological community study.

A similar relationship exists between defining the community in terms of common social ties and the typological approach. Common social ties are a basic component of *gemeinschaft* (Tönnies), mechanical solidarity (Durkheim), the folk society (Redfield), and diffuse relationships (Parsons). Conversely, the absence of such ties would be characteristic of *gesellschaft*, organic solidarity, urbanism, and specific relationships. If a community is defined as people who identify and interact with one another, then the amount of identification and interaction and the reasons for the growth or decline in identification and interaction become important. The typological approach supplies a particularly relevant perspective for such concerns.

As a final example, a definition of community that emphasizes social interaction fits well with systems theory, especially the interactional field and network analysis variations. For example, an interactional field approach to community focuses primarily on community-related social interactions. Without these types of locally relevant interactions, there is no community. And network approaches, of course, are based on measuring the level and type of interaction that occurs in the community.

Certain community definitions, then, are especially well-suited for particular community approaches. And this is one reason there are multiple approaches to community. There is another, equally important reason for the multiplicity of approaches, however, and it has nothing to do with the special definitional characteristics of community. Rather, it involves the special nature of paradigms in sociology.

Sociology as a Multiparadigmatic Science

Ever since Thomas Kuhn's *The Structure of Scientific Revolutions* (1962), the idea of sciences being built around paradigms has become common and widely accepted. Although the exact meaning of *paradigm* is debatable, we can take it to mean something very much like a combination of "definition" and "approach," as they were used in the preceding section. A paradigm is "a fundamental image of the subject matter within a science. It serves to define what should be studied, what questions should be asked, how they should be asked, and what rules should be followed in interpreting the answers obtained" (Ritzer and Goodman 2004, A-10). For example, when a certain definition focuses attention on certain elements of community and predisposes the selection of a complementary approach to community, which in turn guides the choice of community research techniques, then that is a community paradigm.

It was Kuhn's thesis that science progresses not in an inexorable, cumulative march toward greater understanding but rather through abrupt scientific revolutions in which the current paradigm is found to be insufficient and replaced by a new one. Because Kuhn's examples always dealt with natural sciences possessing single paradigms, he inferred that the social sciences, with their lack of a single viewpoint, had yet to reach even an initial paradigmatic stage. Thus, as long as the social sciences cannot agree on a single paradigm, they will be unable to develop the "normal" science that followed the appearance of paradigms in the natural sciences.

Yet, more and more it is becoming recognized that the social sciences in general and sociology in particular do not fit Kuhn's model of scientific development. There is no hegemonic paradigm in any social science, though neoclassical comes close in economics. Rather, within each social science there are multiple paradigms, and no single paradigm appears capable of establishing hegemony over the discipline.

The three major paradigms in sociology are typically labeled: (1) structural functionalism, (2) conflict sociology, and (3) symbolic interactionism. These three labels are not universally accepted and are not always viewed as the only major paradigms.[1] What is becoming universally accepted, however, is the position that sociology is and will remain a multiparadigmatic discipline (Abell 2000). A phenomenologist, Alfred Schutz, was one of the first to recognize this phenomenon:

> What is happening at the present time in sociology is that different schools are each choosing . . . levels of interpretation as a starting point. Each school then develops a methodology suitable to that level and initiates a whole new line of research. The level of structure of meaning which was the starting point soon gets defined as the exclusive, or at least the essential, subject matter of sociology. (quoted in Ritzer 1975, 32)

Since the 1960s, the perception of sociology as a multiparadigmatic science has become common (Friedrichs 1970; Effrat 1972; Greisman 1986; Rosenberg 1989; Falk and Zhao 1990a, 1990b; Guba and Lincoln 1994; Ritzer and Goodman 2004).

If sociology continues as a multiparadigmatic science, then no single paradigm will win out and become the dominant and unquestioned sociological perspective. Accordingly, then, the conflict between proponents of competing paradigms will not be resolved through one paradigm achieving hegemony. And if there is no promise of conflict resolution, the desirability of political infighting among the supporters of various paradigms is questionable.

George Ritzer and Douglas Goodman (2004, A-17) assess the problems stemming from interparadigmatic conflict:

> The result is a wide open theoretical world, one that is so unrestricted and contested that it borders on, if it has not already descended into, chaos . . .

perhaps the most important point to be made about such a theoretical universe is that it was inherently constraining of the individual theorist who was under pressure to choose a theory, work within it, and defend it from external attack and, in turn, attack competing perspectives.

Ritzer continues his analysis of interparadigmatic conflict by describing the tendencies of paradigmatic proponents to exaggerate the explanatory power of their perspectives and to downgrade the contributions made by rival paradigms. He concludes that a willingness to "bridge" paradigms and use multiple approaches to a social phenomenon is sorely needed. We can draw similar conclusions for community sociology.

Reflections in Community Sociology

There are multiple approaches to the study of community, and most reflect basic paradigmatic splits within sociology itself. Further, the competition between paradigms in sociology is reflected in similar competitions by community sociologists. In the preceding chapters, we have witnessed conflict between classical, sociocultural, and then neo-orthodox ecologists, between conflict and structural-functional systems theorists, and in subsequent chapters there will be conflicts between supporters of a mass society view of community and those who argue for the community's continued relevance (chapter 7), and between elitist and pluralist approaches to community power (chapter 12).

Fortunately, these often bitter and usually dysfunctional conflicts between paradigms are mostly a thing of the past in community sociology, as they are in sociology more broadly. However, if community sociology is now a "mature" subdiscipline in which diversity has replaced controversy, then new questions emerge: How is a community to be studied? Which approach is to be used? Roland Warren (1983), in an address to the Community Section of the American Sociological Association, suggests that since no single community paradigm can establish dominance:

> . . . let us have a multiplicity of paradigms. Those which endure, despite their shortcomings, will find supporters and utilizers only because they can do some things—though not all things—better than can their alternatives. Let us have a kit of good tools; but why use a screwdriver when we need a saw, or why use a hammer when we need a foot rule?

Most students of community would probably agree with Warren, but his conclusion leads to another set of questions: Which approach is to be used when? When do we need a hammer rather than a saw? Are community researchers to take turns, choosing one approach and then another until all are exhausted? Or are they to somehow combine all approaches into one all-encompassing package of community theory and research?

Choosing the Best Approach

There are no easy answers to these questions, but it is possible to develop some general guidelines for applying different community paradigms to different community phenomena. For example, each of the four basic approaches outlined in the preceding chapters tends to be better suited for some research areas than for others.

The Typological Approach

The large body of theory and research that has built up around Tönnies's original *gemeinschaft/gesellschaft* distinctions has proven applicable in several areas. It has the ability to account for change, especially in relation to the individual lifestyle changes that occur as a society is transformed into a modern *gesellschaft*-like state. Possibly no other approach can so effectively combine a macro theory of social change with micro descriptions of individual behavior.

The typological approach is also a powerful tool for quality of life studies. Descriptions of the blasé urban way of life and the resultant "quest for community" continue to strike a responsive chord in urban America. It would be impossible to fully understand the American animus toward cities, our movement to and now beyond the suburbs, the continuing appeal of rural communes, and our nostalgic yearnings for a simpler, more *gemeinschaft*-like time (even if it never really existed) without an appreciation of the typological literature. Research on the degree of primary group relations, neighboring, and neighborhood identification (chapter 7) demonstrates the continuing relevance of this approach. Philosophical questions about the quality, and ultimately even the meaning, of life appear here as well. The trade-offs of communalism for urbanism, of integration for independence, are fateful ones; it is the stuff of which penetrating sociological, psychological, and philosophical insights are made.

Finally, considerable discussion has developed around applying the typological approach to studying and even guiding third-world modernization efforts. Remember that the chapter on typologies was introduced with a quotation from Robert Nisbet arguing that while the approach may have developed to account for social change in an industrializing Europe, it is applicable to other situations as well. Steven Brint (2001, 5–8) concurs in his discussion of the typology approach to community.

> One point is clear, however: This change in orientation cannot be attributed to the disappearance of all forms of communal relations in the modern world. Communities and communal relations continue to exist in neighborhoods and small towns; in bowling and soccer leagues; . . . among the regulars at local taverns; in the interchanges of core members of usenet groups; among the active members of churches, synagogues, and mosques. . . . The current tendency to focus on short-term interaction rituals linked to social network structures risks distorting (and effacing) the reality of those *gemeinschaft*-like structures that continue to exist.

> If an emphasis on community-like social relations has been one of the great contributions of sociology to a world imbued with the spirit of *gesellschaft*, this contribution became possible only by separating out variable aspects of social relations from the larger concept in which they were embedded. In this sense, the fate of the community concept indicates a maturation of social science—a movement from commonsense, but imprecisely defined, aggregates to more precise analytical concepts.

Thus, the typological approach, although it is the oldest approach to community, would still seem to have much to offer.

The Ecological Approach

Although the theoretical base of the ecological approach may not have the sophistication or acceptance that it had when human ecology reigned at the University of Chicago, its *methods* are more sophisticated and widely accepted than ever. With the increasing amount of statistical data about urban phenomena, the mathematical techniques developed by urban analysts to explain city placement, population growth, density, and land-use patterns borrow heavily from the aggregate urban data approach pioneered in human ecology.

City placement.   The question of why a city is where it is rather than someplace else has long intrigued urban ecologists. And with the traditional focus on environmental influences upon spatial patterns, a number of theories have been proposed to account for the location of cities. Three of the best-known are: (1) *break-in-transportation theory* (Cooley 1894; Cottrell 1951; Ruben 1961),[2] positing that cities are most likely to develop at points where one form of transportation stops and another form begins; (2) *specialized function theory* (Ogburn 1937; Ullman 1941), positing that some cities develop where and how they do because they are near a natural resource (e.g., mining or resort towns); and especially (3) *central place theory* (Christaller 1933, Lösch 1954), positing that since a certain amount of land is required to support a city, the size and location of a city is determined by the size of its trade area, its "hinterland." The result is a centrally placed city surrounded by a hexagonally shaped trade area that borders the adjacent city's hinterland.[3] An example of city placement can be seen in the world dominance of global cities like New York, London, Tokyo (Sassen 1991, 2001), Chicago, and Los Angeles (Abu-Lughod 1999). However, more recent technologies have given rise to less emphasis on physical place and more emphasis on virtual place within various global networks (Castells 1996; Neal 2011).

Population growth.   Estimating population growth has become a major subfield within itself (indeed an industry within itself, since the demand for population projections is strong from both government and business). And whether the growth projections are based on standard census data,[4] administrative records (e.g., building permits, utility hook-ups, tax records), sample surveys, computer simulations (Foot 1981), social area analysis (Goldsmith, Jackson, and Shambaugh 1982), or some combination of these techniques, ecological units of analysis and ecological methods of combining aggregate data are predominant.

Density. Ever since Wirth's "Urbanism as a Way of Life," urban ecologists have been interested in population density. Generally, ecologists have focused on two density-related phenomena: (1) the density–distance relationship, and (2) the various pathologies associated with high levels of density.

The basic density–distance model simply states that as distance from the center of the city increases, population density experiences an exponential decrease (Clark 1951). Figure 6-1 illustrates this relationship for two hypothetical cities. The comparisons of variation in density over time and between cities have allowed the development of elaborate models of density–distance patterns and projections for urban growth patterns in both industrial and nonindustrial societies (Hawley 1971).

This preoccupation with such precise measures of population density is typically justified by the assumption that density affects human behavior. Since Wirth's classic work, widely publicized research with rats ("the behav-

Figure 6-1   Urban Density and Distance

The density–distance curve for City A shows substantial density near the Central Business District and then a rapid reduction as one moves toward the fringes. Such a pattern is typical of cities in the Northeast that developed prior to the mass production of the automobile. The curve for City B shows a less dense center with a more gradual decline in density toward the fringe. This is a typical Southwest pattern.

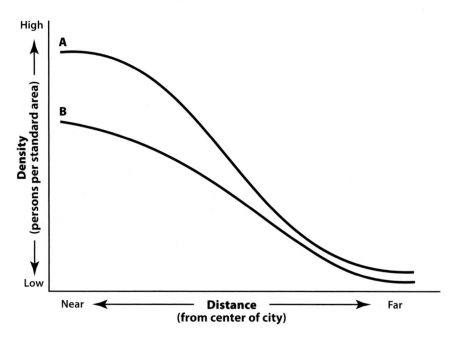

ioral sink" in Calhoun 1961, 1962) and into various social pathologies in Honolulu and Hong Kong (Schmitt 1963, 1966; Forrest, La Grange and Ngai-Ming 2002), and Chicago (Galle, Grove, and McPherson 1972) have supported a number of variations on the idea that density produces deviance. *Social overload* (Altman 1975; Saegert 1978) posits that high levels of density lead to interference with and confusion in normal social processes. *Territoriality* (Ardrey 1966) claims that density creates stress since human beings, like other animals, have a territorial instinct. *Stimulus overload* (Milgram 1970; Mitchell 1971; Baum and Paulus 1991; Evans, Rhee, Forbes, Allen and Lepore 2000) argues that crowded conditions are overly stimulating and thereby create anxiety and withdrawal. *Personal space* (Hall 1966; Sommer 1969) posits that, for cultural reasons, individuals need "space bubbles" surrounding them and that high density violates this personal space. Finally, *spatial constraint* (Saegert 1978) posits that high density resulting from crowding people into a small space can limit traditional behavior patterns to the extent that psychological stress results.

Most ecological research on these density → pathology theories simply concludes that there are no negative consequences of high residential density (Fischer, Baldassare, and Ofshe 1975; Whyte 1989; Lepore and Evans 1991; Rousseau and Standing 1995), or rather that the pathologies are due to some other factors (Bonnes, Bonaiuto, and Paola 1991; Lepore, Evans, and Palsane 1991; Oliver 2003). However, some studies by urban ecologists (Gove, Hughes, and Galle 1979) suggest that the relationship between density and pathology may be a real one. In either case, the effects of density will probably continue to be a researched and debated topic in urban ecology (Regoeczi 2002).[5]

Land use.   Finally, perhaps the most basic application of the ecological approach involves land use. The classic models of Burgess, Hoyt, and Harris and Ullman still have relevance to urban planning schemes. Later refinements such as William Alonso's "Theory of Rents" (Alonso 1965), moving (Rossi 1955; Wolpert 1965), and suburbanization (Greer 1962; Farley 1976; Baldassare 1992; Frey 2003) are all squarely within the ecological focus on spatial patterning. This research, along with the references above to research in population growth, city location, and population density, points out areas in which the ecological approach is particularly relevant.

Systems Theory

In chapter 4 we argued that although systems theory has achieved wide acceptance in the social sciences, its specific applications to community phenomena remain limited. Still, it can be demonstrated that when systems theory has been applied to the community, it has been directed toward some of the most important issues in community sociology: community power, interpersonal relationships, and community development.

Community power.   Power can be conceptualized as either an individual or a structural phenomenon. Most of the community power research reported in chapter 12 focuses on individuals, and the few times it has been treated as a structural phenomenon, it has been typically approached from an ecological perspective. However, there is a relatively new structural approach to community power that is based on a variation of systems theory: *network analysis.* The network analysis approach shares with systems theory a common focus on boundary maintenance and systemic linkage and is becoming something like a mathematical, computer driven update of Long's "Ecology of Games" approach (discussed in chapter 4).

Building on the earlier and simpler network analyses of communities by Floyd Hunter (1953) and Herman Turk (1970), this method combines individual and organizational linkages to provide multidimensional maps of local exchange networks. Thus, this technique has been used quite productively to analyze community politics by measuring the intersystem linkages of money, information, and political support (Knoke 1994).

Interpersonal relationships. Another systems-related variation of network analysis also has been used to address the question of how much *gemeinschaft* remains in our increasingly *gesellschaft*-like society. Again focusing on linkages in social systems, Barry Wellman and Barry Leighton (1979, 364) have used this technique to study "how large-scale divisions of labor in social systems affect the organization and content of interpersonal ties." Their research into interpersonal linkages leads them to conclude that the locality-based *gemeinschaft*-like community persists in our *gesellschaft*-like society, "but only as specialized components of the overall primary networks. The variety of ties in which an urbanite can be involved—with distant parents, intimate friends, less intimate friends, co-workers and so on—and the variety of networks in which these are organized can provide flexible structural bases for dealing with routine and emergency matters" (Wellman and Leighton 1979, 388). In short, they argue that the territorial community retains a part, but only a part, of our interpersonal ties. We now are able to have close, *gemeinschaft*-like relationships that are not territorially based.

Network analysis, then, has direct application to one of the most fundamental questions in community sociology: the *gemeinschaft/gesellschaft* issue. Systems theory also has provided the basis for improving the local quality of life by providing a guide for community development.

Community development. Just as Wellman and Leighton were concerned with the degree to which interpersonal ties are locality based, a systems theory approach to community development shares a similar focus. The concern here is with locality-based community fields, which are social fields in which actions relating to a broad range of local interests are coordinated. And from a systems theory perspective, any actions that strengthen the structure of the community field are also actions of community development. For example, Kenneth Wilkinson (1972; 1989) has developed a field approach to community development that stresses the need to increase the generalization potentials of local interactional relationships. Thus, actions such as establishing an organization to coordinate community action projects or even simply introducing a leader in one local interest field to a leader in a different field would constitute community development because both are attempts to strengthen the structure of the community field by increasing the scope or generalization of local interaction.

In a similar vein, Roland Warren (1978, 325) defines community development as "a deliberate and sustained attempt to strengthen the horizontal pattern of a community." Warren's horizontal pattern is very much like Wilkinson's community field, and actions that strengthen the structure of Wilkinson's community field should strengthen Warren's horizontal pattern as well. Warren, however, gives major emphasis to actions strengthening those local organizations that provide "major locality relevant functions"— organizations such as the chamber of commerce, school boards, the city council, a local council of churches, or a United Way chapter.

With either Wilkinson or Warren, however, the principle is the same: systems theory allows the definition of what a community is and does—and what actions are most likely to strengthen it. Hence, systems theory has substantial relevance to community development.[6]

Conflict

The application of a conflict approach to local phenomena became common only in the 1970s. It is not surprising, then, that one of the most popular local subjects for conflict analysis was the severe fiscal crisis that beset many American cities in that decade.

Urban fiscal crises.   Castells's (1977) analysis of these economic problems was reviewed in chapter 5, but there have been many others (Friedland, Piven, and Alford 1984; Tabb and Sawers 1984, 2004; Friedland, Palmer, and Stenbeck 1990; Friedland and Robertson 1990), and unfortunately, the fiscal problems facing American cities seem never ending (Muro and Hoene 2009). Although there are variations in these conflict approaches, they share a common focus on extracommunity causes of local difficulties. From the conflict perspective, contradictions within the national or international capitalist system led to a local fiscal crisis. World systems theory maintains that since the city's economic problems stem from the capitalistic structure of larger regional systems, the city can do little to help itself.

Urban environment.   A similar body of analysis emerges from a conflict approach to urban renewal and New Urbanism. Castells (1977, 1996, 1997, 1998, 2000a, b, c) and Harvey (1985b, 1988, 1989, 2000) have analyzed America's urban renewal and New Urbanist (Lehrer and Milgrom 1996) programs from a conflict perspective. And although their separate analyses contain important differences, they all conclude that urban renewal and New Urbanism were counterproductive responses to *national* economic problems. In other words, just as with the fiscal crisis, the cause lies in the structure of society; the effect (suburban sprawl) occurs in the community. In fact, the neo-Marxist versions of the conflict approach typically view the national economic structure as the fundamental cause of local phenomena (Ritzer and Goodman 2004).

Is it always the national economic structure that matters?   If the neo-Marxists are correct in assigning the basis for local events to the national economic structure, then the local environment doesn't matter very much. This means, then, that a neo-Marxist application to community phenomena typically focuses on national analysis rather than local change, since short of a fundamental restructuring of society (a proletarian revolt leading to a socialist society), little can be done to assist the community.

The lack of local applications for neo-Marxists' structural approaches has been noted before,[7] and as long as the cause of the local phenomena is invariably the national economic structure, this problem will remain. This can account for David Harvey's comment (see chapter 5): "It remains for revolutionary theory to chart the path from an urbanism based on exploitation to an urbanism appropriate for the human species." And it accounts for the potential significance of a more locally oriented book like *The City and the Grassroots* (1983) by as influential a neo-Marxist as Manuel Castells.

This is not to say, however, that a neo-Marxist focus on extracommunity structure is necessarily irrelevant to producing social change. It is possible that such analysis can sufficiently raise the consciousness of the exploited and eventually lead to a restructured, noncapitalist society. William Tabb and Larry Sawers (1978, 19), for example, believe that the neo-Marxist analysis presented in their book *Marxism and Metropolis*

> shows the key to solution of the crisis of capitalism and its cities, is gaining steadily in influence both in the United States and throughout the world. The ideas in this book are being used as a guide for many who go on to work for fundamental social change. The popular forces for change are building even as the crisis of capitalism deepens. We do not await this "inevitable" occurrence. We put our scholarship at the service of the class forces which will bring about this transition.

The transformation, of course, is a transformation of the national economic structure because from the neo-Marxist perspective, it alone is the major cause of local phenomena (Tabb 2004). Still, there are *non*-Marxist conflict approaches that do not grant such preeminence to the national economic structure. Coleman's (1957) and Gamson's (1966) analyses of community conflict were considered in chapter 5, but for the present purposes, it is sufficient to simply remember that both men argued that local characteristics influenced local conflict. Thus, both have community applications that do not require a restructuring of society.

A similar case can be made for Harvey Molotch's (1976) analysis of "The City as a Growth Machine," which we consider in chapter 12. However, it is important to note here that although he argues that national capitalism fuels the local drive for community growth, Molotch believes that local antigrowth forces can wrest control from the community's capitalists and thereby improve the local quality of life. In other words, Molotch employs a conflict approach that views state capitalism as an important but not overpowering variable.

Finally, an example can be drawn from the community development literature that we review in chapter 8. Saul Alinsky (1971), a major figure in the field, developed an explicitly conflict-laden methodology for community organization and change. We will look at his methods later, but for our present purposes it is sufficient to note that for Alinsky the community is the locus for significant social change.

Choosing the Approaches that Work Best

It should be clear by now that the community is probably best viewed from several perspectives and that each approach has merit and relevant local applications. Each paradigm offers a different and important vantage point. The most accurate description and most complete understanding of the community comes from employing multiple approaches, but this conclusion is easier to draw than implement. The community researcher usually has a special affinity for a particular approach, and the local research topic is usually better suited to one approach than another. So, we tend to use an approach that corresponds to both our own perspective on the community and the particular topic of research within the community.

Broad research questions on large-scale social change, industrialization–modernization, and the quality of local life in a mass society lend themselves to the typological approach. Conversely and more specifically, more technical questions about city placement, population growth, density, and land use are particularly well suited to the ecological approach. Systems theory has direct applications for community development because of its ability to locate the local community systems within the larger network of national systems. And when dealing with the interpersonal relationships within a community, systems-based network analysis is particularly effective. Finally, the conflict approach has proven popular for the analysis of local economic problems such as the urban fiscal crises.

In a sense, then, community researchers use whatever works best. If a lot of demographic data are available and the research question is a technical one, an ecological approach is almost assured. On the other hand, a broader, more critical concern with the unequal access to local goods and services is tailor-made for a conflict approach. Such pragmatism may seem to be unethical or at least disloyal to the one "true" paradigm; but remember, sociology has no dominant paradigm, and there is none on the horizon. Hence, attempts to stretch a perspective into areas for which it isn't applicable are unnecessary. Or, in Warren's (1983) terms, "let us have a kit of good tools" and use a tool that is appropriate for the job.

NOTES

[1] A fourth approach with potential to reach "paradigm" status includes the newly developed postmodernism and globalization theories (Clark 2000; Ritzer and Goodman 2004).

[2] Cooley 1894 is Charles Horton Cooley, later known for his concept of the *looking glass self*.

[3] This theory applies especially well in flat terrain such as in Kansas or Nebraska but must be modified considerably for environments dominated by mountains or lakes.

[4] The Census Bureau regularly makes projections for over thirty thousand different places.

[5] Much of the debate centers around: (1) what measure of density is most appropriate, (2) which pathologies should be considered, and (3) what variables should be used as controls.

[6] Systems theory also relates to community development via the analysis of local service delivery systems. See Garkovich and Stam (1980, 163–70) for an overview of this input/output approach to community development.

[7] Roland Warren (1971), for example, argues that although community poverty can be explained in terms of a national economic structure that produces poverty, this explanation has no accompanying means for combating local poverty. See Katharine Coit's (1978) explanation of why the low level of American class consciousness has inhibited local participation in neo-Marxist community-action groups.

COMMUNITY AND THE QUALITY OF LIFE

Community sociology, in both its theory and application, has been especially concerned with the nature and quality of our lifestyles. The typological theorists focused squarely on how *gemeinschaft* life differs from *gesellschaft* life, often pointing to problems associated with moving from one type to another and sometimes concluding that the quality of life may decline in our increasingly *gesellschaft*-like society. The ecologists focused initially on the low quality of life during the period of rapid urbanization and social disorganization in Chicago by associating various pathologies with demographic variables such as density. Systems theory has direct applications for improving the quality of local life through community development, and the conflict approach typically focuses on how capitalism reduces the quality of urban life.

While concerns with the quality of life were indirectly reflected throughout the chapters in Section I, they are the primary focus of the chapters in Section II. In chapter 7, the theory and research that relate the community with the quality of life are reviewed, as well as attempts to reestablish *gemeinschaft* qualities of cyberspace.

The community theories or paradigms that make up Section I also influence the attempts to improve the quality of local life described in chapters 8 and 9. Chapter 8 shows that how one goes about community development depends on the paradigmatic assumptions one makes concerning what a community is, what its problems are, and how those problems are best addressed. Chapter 9, on planned communities, is based on three of the approaches predominant in Section I: the typological, ecological, and conflict approaches. A careful comparison of these first two sections shows that community theory and applications are so closely intertwined that even the most abstract theory can influence local applications, and even the most pragmatic community developer or planner will be indirectly influenced by some theoretical views of community.

chapter seven

The Quest for Community

Critiques of modern societies often include the loss of community due to increasingly weak connections with local places and changing modes of social interactions. The idea that Western societies lose community as they modernize has been an ongoing theme in sociology since Tönnies' *Gemeinschaft und Gesellschaft*. We saw in previous chapters how Tönnies, Simmel, Wirth, and to a lesser degree, Durkheim, Marx, and Weber all concluded that, on balance, the quantity and quality of community is reduced when a society becomes more urban, more industrial, more *gesellschaft*-like. Simmel's (1936) famous observation that "one nowhere feels as lonely and lost as in the metropolitan crowd" illustrates a common theme of alienation and lost community in classic social theory. More recently, analysts (e.g., Bellah et al. 1996 and Putnam 2000) traced this theme in the United States., concluding that community is indeed diminished. Often, then, assessments of modern and even postmodern societies include the "eclipse of," "decline in," or "loss of" community. While the nature of community decline remains debatable, there is nonetheless a wide acceptance of this decline and numerous searches for the lost community.

Losing Community

While the attempts that have been made to measure the decline of *gemeinschaft*-like relations in the United States and other Western societies are relatively recent, nonetheless, a long-term acceptance of this decline exists along with numerous prescriptions for appropriate remedies to restore the lost community. In this chapter, we look first at the research tracing the decline in *gemeinschaft*-like relations, and then we will examine attempts to guide our quest toward reestablishing them.

The Loss of the Territorial Community

Although few terms can match "community" in definitional imprecision, most sociologists could accept a working definition of community that included a specific geographic area, an identification by the residents with that area, and social interaction among the residents. The lost community thesis often argues that what was lost was a village, a small town, or an urban neighborhood, a place where one was born, was raised, and died—a local place with inherently intimate, holistic relationships. Tönnies stresses the importance of place in his original description of the *gemeinschaft*-like community:

> A common relation to the soil tends to associate people who may be kinsfolk or believe themselves to be such. Neighborhood, the fact that they live together, is the basis of their union . . . this type is the rural village community. (Tönnies [1887] 1957, 257)

In order to assess the necessity of an identification with place for community, it is important to note that when sociologists speak of the "loss" of community there are at least two distinct meanings: psychological and territorial (Bernard 1973; Driskell and Lyon 2002). The psychological meaning focuses on the social interaction dimension of the community and analyzes the alienation that can come from the loss of community.[1] The territorial meaning focuses more on the specific area and the diminishing identification with place.[2] Both meanings share the same primary source for the loss of community—the urban, *gesellschaft* society—and both describe similar problems: excessive individualism, alienation, and a resultant lower quality of life.

Although the two types of community that are "lost" can be conceptually distinct and are treated as separate phenomena in most literature, they are, nonetheless, closely related. Robert Nisbet, in the preface to the more recent printings of his famous treatise on individual alienation in the mass society, *The Quest for Community* (originally published in 1953), relates the decline in identification with the place and property of the territorial community to the more psychological alienation from close, personal interaction.

> Similarly, I think alienation from place and property turns out to be, at bottom, estrangement from those personal ties, which give lasting identity to each. Native heath is hardly distinguishable from the human relationships within which landscape and animals and things become cherished and deeply implanted in one's soul. (Nisbet 1976, xii)

Some research indicates that the territorial community still matters (Guest, Lee, and Staeheli 1982; Ahlbrandt 1984; Chaskin 1997; Driskell and Lyon 2002), but most studies document a decline in the importance of place (Fischer 1982; Oldenburg 1999; Wellman 1979), and the decline in the relevance of and identification with the territorial community is related to the decline in *gemeinschaft*-like interpersonal relations; both reinforce one another, and both are seen as symptoms of a modern society.

The idea that territorial community does not affect psychological community is a relatively new idea. The original concept of community was an ideal type that emphasized local place as a basis for the common ties, and social interaction that is intimate, holistic, and all-encompassing. Tönnies contrasted the types of relationships typically appearing in extended families or rural villages (*gemeinschaft*) with those found in modern, capitalist states (*gesellschaft*). *Gemeinschaft*-like relationships are based on sentiment, tradition, and common bonds. The basis for these relationships is in either the family or the "soil" (i.e., living and working in a local place). *Gemeinschaft* is characterized by a strong identification with the community, emotionalism, traditionalism, and holistic conceptions of other members of the community (i.e., viewing another as a total person rather than only as a segment of one's status—as significant in one's own right rather than as a means to an end). Since *gemeinschaft* is an ideal type, there is no place where one can find total *gemeinschaft* or, for that matter, complete *gesellschaft*. Rather, they are hypothetical, extreme constructs, existing solely for the purpose of comparison with the real world. This "gold standard" community where residents identify with the local place, where common ties bind them together, and where all interactions are completely holistic, has never existed. Instead, human organizations and relationships fall somewhere in between *gemeinschaft* and *gesellschaft*. However, analysts such as Tönnies, Simmel, and Wirth clearly believed that an identification with place was essential for true *gemeinschaft* relations.

So, does place still matter? Not as much as it did before the Industrial Revolution, certainly; but residents (especially long-term residents) still identify, to a degree, with their territorial communities (Goudy 1990), and the place one lives directly impacts lifestyles and economic opportunities. For example, the size of a community once mattered a lot, with large places offering more opportunities than small ones, but more recently the degree to which a community is networked within the larger global network is increasingly important (Neal 2010). Still, the basic question about the continuing importance of place for *gemeinschaft*-like relationships remains, and it is a question we consider again at the end of this chapter.

The Loss of Psychological Community

Although distinguished sociologists from Tönnies to Parsons to Bellah have described various social pathologies associated with the move from *gemeinschaft* to *gesellschaft*, the preponderance of research shows that psychologically significant neighboring (Kasarda and Janowitz 1974; Hunter 1974; Ahlbrandt 1984; Wellman and Wortley 1990) continues to exist. Other research (MacDonald and Throop 1971; Seeman, Bishop, and Grigsby 1971; Fischer 1973) has failed to find the higher levels of isolation thought to be associated with more urban (and therefore more *gesellschaft*-like) populations. The observation that isolating, alienating individualism is replacing community typically receives more popular acceptance than empirical support. A few prominent examples will illustrate this phenomenon in more detail.

***Bellah's* Habits of the Heart.**   Robert Bellah describes the excesses of individualism that can lead to isolation and alienation in his best-selling work, *Habits of the Heart* (1985), and to a lesser degree in *The Good Society* (1992). According to Bellah, many of the ills of today's society result from too great an emphasis on individualism and too weak a commitment to the community. As individualism, selfishness, and greed in America have grown, our civic commitment and our sense of responsibility to society have declined. Bellah believes that it is our moral duty to deny our obsession for material accumulation and consumerism and restore the traditions of civic concern and responsibility now eroded by excess individualism. Bellah offers a solution to these various ills; participation in the community can reduce alienation and "enable people to belong and contribute to the larger society" (Bellah et al. 1996, xxxiii). Bellah's call for the renewal of civic membership is often based on Christian ideologies, biblical accounts, and the beloved community of yesteryear.

Finally, while Bellah (1996) acknowledges that increased individualism is not proven, it is certainly probable. As we shall see in the Putnam example that follows, the idea that we have too much individualism and a lack of consensus over proof continues.

***Putnam's* Bowling Alone.**   A decade later, Robert Putnam (1995, 70) sides with Bellah and ominously notes that we are "bowling alone" in that "more Americans are bowling today than ever before, but bowling in organized leagues has plummeted in the last decade or so." Putnam claims that a decline in the traditions of civic engagement are weakening our society and sense of community, and unlike Bellah he backs up his claim with empirical data. Putnam documents the noticeable lack of Americans' involvement in voluntary associations and the reduced patterns of political participation. The trend is disengagement from membership in fraternal organizations, religious affiliations, labor unions, and voluntary associations (e.g., women's societies, school-service groups, Boy Scouts, and the Red Cross). Putnam acknowledges countertrends but dismisses them. For example, the American Association of Retired Persons (AARP) has grown tremendously in the last decade; but Putnam claims this is not "real" civic involvement because these mass memberships create a situation wherein members are unaware of the others' existence (i.e., there is no psychological community). Thus, Putnam (1995, 75) concludes that due to (1) women's participation in the labor force; (2) social mobility; (3) current demographic trends in marriage and family size; and (4) privatizing leisure time with recent technological advances such as television, Americans are less trusting and the social capital traditionally associated with community is eroding.

***Robert Wuthnow's* Loose Connections.**   Robert Wuthnow (1998) provides a more nuanced version of Putnam's thesis in his book, *Loose Connections.* Wuthnow states that community-mindedness is eroding and civic involvement is indeed declining in clubs like the Rotary, Lions, Jaycees, and Kiwanis and "loose connections" now tend to suit Americans. We are still connected to some extent, but in different, usually weaker ways. Organizational membership is not necessarily decreasing, but rather shifting from traditional voluntary organizations to new types of groups. However, these new support groups and specialized hobby groups demonstrate that they have become a rather poor substitute for traditional communities[3] and their loose connections.

> The social contract binding members together asserts only the weakest of obligations. Come if you have time. Talk if you feel like it. Respect everyone's opinion. Never criticize. Leave quietly if you become dissatisfied. . . . We can imagine that these small groups really substitute for families, neighborhoods, and broader community attachments that may demand lifelong commitments, when, in fact, they do not. (Wuthnow 1998, 3–6)

Wuthnow's more complex explanation based on qualitative gradation in membership may come closer than Putnam to describing the current changes in community. However, it is the more sweeping claims of Putnam that have generated the most interest and debate. In any case, while there are compelling theories associating various psychological problems with modern mass society, the analysts who promote these theories have produced much more popular support for their positions than for empirical research support. It may well be that the effects of the mass society and individualism have been overestimated, and the same may be said for the loss of community. It is a qualitative decline rather than a total loss, and therefore most quests for community proceed accordingly.

Finding Community

In this section we search for and find the community through various avenues. We look at attempts to find territorial community in the neighborhood and in the New Urbanist architecture. We also explore the aspects of the psychological community as it is found through voluntary associations and in cyberspace. A relatively new and especially appropriate method with which to search for territorial and psychological community is network analysis (see chapter 4). We use this network approach to define the broad parameters of the quest.

Network Analysis and the Community Question

Additional evidence for *gemeinschaft*-like relationships has now emerged from a more objective type of community research. With the advances in survey research and the development of powerful, computer-supported tools for the statistical analysis of social networks, the quantity and quality of social interactions can be empirically assessed.

Barry Wellman (1979) was among the first to demonstrate the applications of network analysis by positing three possibilities to the community question. The possible answers include: (1) community *lost*, in which communal ties have disintegrated with the rise of industrial bureaucratic nations; (2) community *saved*, in which the territorial neighborhood remains an important means of support; and (3) community *liberated*, in which the social interactions have expanded well beyond the neighborhood and are no longer tied to the community. Based on the networks of social interaction reported in his surveys in East York (a working-class neighborhood in Toronto), Wellman concluded that community is definitely not lost, partially saved, and clearly liberated. While some significant social interaction occurs within the neighborhood, much of it is outside East York. According to Wellman and Leighton (1979), psychological (i.e., liberated) community appears stronger than the territorial (i.e., saved) community.

Claude Fischer (1982) extended Wellman's analysis by surveying a larger and broader sample that included residents with substantial variation in social class, family status, and residence (urban San Francisco, suburbs, small towns, and rural North California). Fischer found social class to be extremely important in defining the nature of social interactions, with what Wellman called the "community liberated" arrangement being especially common among higher-class respondents who more often move beyond their neighborhoods and establish broad, metropolitan social networks. Current research on networks in community relations suggests that although spatial location matters, its effects are not large (Gottdiener and Hutchison 2006). Fischer finds that significant rural/urban differences in social interaction exist beyond those associated with social class and family status. Studies also show that in most cases territorial locality still matters for interactions in rural communities (Goudy 1990; Beggs, Haines, and Hurlbert 1996), and it is to the territorial community that we now turn.

The Territorial Neighborhood

Wellman's (1979) "community saved" argument maintains that neighborhoods have survived despite urbanization, industrialization, and technological advances. Residents still have a sense of local ties for social support and sociability. The local neighborhood serves various functions for its residents, providing primary relationships, social support, organizations, local pride, and numerous facilities and services near their place of residence (Ahlbrandt 1984;). According to Wellman the thesis of the saved community includes heavy involvement of residents in a single neighborhood, strong network ties, extensive networks that are densely knit, solidarity of activities and sentiments, and the mobilization of assistance.

Wellman found some support for the saved community. More research shows that communities still exist in which residents identify with an area known as the neighborhood, and personal interactions may still be examined within the boundaries of the neighborhood (Chaskin 1997). Although individuals may define the boundaries of the neighborhood differently, residents who define the neighborhood in terms of network interactions and personal relationships tend to identify with the geographic unit compared with those considering the neighborhood in terms of the institutions and facilities.

In fact, saved ideologies often stress the importance of preserving existing neighborhoods against the destructive, alienating impact of urban institutions.[4] Neighborhood improvement associations typically seek to protect the quality of life in the local environment through place-based associations. Membership and participation in these neighborhood associations strive for social solidarity among the residents and attachment to the community (Oropesa 1992).

Previous research finds that neighborhood sentiment is often dependent on the social integration of the residents and in turn, the social integration has a significant impact on the attachment to the neighborhood (Austin and Baba 1990). Many factors, such as statuses and personal network characteristics, will influence the level of involvement in and attachment to the neighborhood (Campbell and Lee 1992); but it is usually argued that whenever social integration can be enhanced, it is beneficial to the resident as well as the neighborhood. In sum, neighborhoods remain the spatial focus of meaningful social interaction, important political organization, and significant psychological attachment.

Finding Psychological Community

Much of the literature provides evidence for communities without propinquity (Webber 1963), communities of limited liability (Suttles 1968), or liberated communities (Wellman 1979) that transcend the geographic boundaries of the neighborhood. The idea is that we have experienced an eclipse of territorial community (Stein 1960) and that community interactions now occur outside the neighborhood.

Voluntary Associations

It can be argued that community had not really been lost since common ties and social interaction can exist without the local place. They can exist in a more generic, nonresidential shared space, such as a school, workplace, church, or social club. The common tie could be to a company or a religion; the social interactions could be of an intimate and holistic nature. Therefore, some analysts believe that voluntary associations, the workplace, or other meeting places can meet the same psychological needs that we assumed small towns and neighborhoods once met (Webber 1963; Rubin 1969; Zablocki 1979; Fischer 1982; Oldenburg 1989).

Urban planner Melvin Webber was among the first analysts to suggest that the concern for the lost local community is unnecessary and that attempts to revive the territorial community are misplaced. In a remarkably prescient article subtitled "Community without Propinquity," he argued that the concerns of analysts such as Nisbet over the standardization and centralization of the mass society are unfounded because "rather than a 'mass culture' in a 'mass society' the long-term prospect is for a maze of subcultures within an amazingly diverse society" (Webber 1963, 29). However, the basis for this subcultural variation is not the territorial community. Rather, "Americans are becoming more closely tied to various interest communities than to place communities" (*ibid.*).

Webber's views are echoed by Wellman's influential concept of the liberated community where residents' involvement and membership is partial, recognizing numerous associations and relationships both within and outside of the neighborhood. The sense of community is based on informal interpersonal ties often derived from friends and family who live outside the residential community (Wellman and Wortley 1990). These nonterritorial community ties are further strengthened with community involvement in voluntary associations. In general, networks in voluntary organizations provide emotional support, small services, financial aid, and companionship that were once supplied through the local, territorial community. Warner (1999) explains how social capital is accumulated by community residents through membership in voluntary associations, and he shows how government aids community development through support to community-based voluntary associations. The community, then, when it becomes an interactional field of social networks to voluntary organizations, ceases to necessarily be a place. It is, rather, a space, a setting in which individuals link themselves to the larger mass society.

However, the idea that voluntary organizations can replace the territorial community as the primary basis for the psychological feelings of community is questionable (Driskell, Lyon, and Embry 2008). A minimum level of community rises naturally from propinquity. While professional associations, labor unions, religious groups, and other voluntary organizations can provide a measure of *gemeinschaft,* the territorial community seems certain to remain a primary basis for the psychological community. For example, Benjamin Zablocki (1978, 108) maintains that a psychological community requires an "infrastructure" of interpersonal interactions to maintain itself. He observes that while a voluntary organization

> must nourish this infrastructure out of a surplus of its members' vested resources, if any such surplus remains after the manifest goals of the organization are met," in the territorial community, "proximity itself provides for the greater part of the maintenance of this infrastructure without the deliberate intention of the individuals involved. (*ibid.*)

In other words, when people live near one another, a level of interaction and common identification is forced upon them. Voluntary organizations can supplement the territorial community, but it is difficult to foresee a time when *gemeinschaft is* no longer associated with the territorial community.

Although the extreme position of Webber and Rubin—that the psychological feelings of community are possible (and even common) without a relevant territorial community—is in direct contrast with community development strategies intended to strengthen the local community, both voluntary organization and community development strategies represent "quests" for community. The method through which the "lost" community is "found" varies, but the common concern with the local or individual quality of life remains. In the next two chapters we examine more closely the attempts to improve the quality of community life through community development and urban planning.

The idea that community can exist without territory commands considerable support, but much of the more recent focus on psychological community goes not only beyond the territorial community but beyond voluntary organizations as well. The search for community continues in the virtual environment of nonspatial cyberspace.

Cyberspace

The most recent extension of the idea that community can exist without local place is the concept of a virtual community existing in cyberspace. Now the argument is pushed further: Not only is local place not necessary,[5] neither is shared space of voluntary associations. This means that face-to-face contact is not necessary for the common ties and social interaction associated with community.

This section addresses the qualities of virtual communities in cyberspace and assesses the degree to which they contain *gemeinschaft*-type elements of identification with place, common ties, and social interaction necessary for community. We will discover that communities in cyberspace are spatially liberated from geographic and social boundaries, are socially ramified in their connections, have only limited liability for their members, and are psychologically detached from close interpersonal ties. In other words, we will discover that they are very unlike *gemeinschaft* communities.

Spatial liberation.   Certainly the most visible and possibly the most crucial difference in cyberspace is the absence of place from the physical community. Almost by definition, the virtual community in cyberspace has been liberated from confines and constraints of place (Wellman 2001). It may be that relations in virtual communities are sufficient to offset the declining importance of local place (Katz, Rice, and Aspden 2001; Wellman 2001). Whether or not this is the case depends, of course, on the level of common ties and quality of social interaction in virtual communities.

The Internet certainly provides the opportunity for associations based on all manner of shared interests. However, two distinctive characteristics emerge from the literature on the types of ties that develop among Internet users; neither lends itself to a *gemeinschaft*-like community.

Social ramification.   In comparison to the communities of local place and shared space, cyberspace communities tend to be more numerous and more heterogeneous in social characteristics such as race, religion, or income (Hiltz and Turoff 1993). Thus, we may follow Fischer (1975) and conclude that the virtual community is ramified in its ties and social interactions. The Internet allows participants to increase both the number of community ties and the diversity of the people whom they encounter. The ready accessibility of e-mail and Internet chat rooms make it easy to send messages to large numbers of people and remain in contact with multiple social environments

(Wellman and Hampton 1999). While we are likely to resemble our family, neighbors, fellow worshipers, and co-workers in racial and social background, a chat room of Star Trekkers, for example, may be of any racial category, educational level, religion, political party, or income level. Of course, the participant may also join social network groups like Facebook, but these sites do not necessarily contain qualities of *gemeinschaft*. In fact, studies of Facebook friends show them to be more diverse than face-to-face friends, and lower in social capital (Seder and Oishi 2009; Byler 2009).

Limited liability.   The virtual community holds only limited liability for its members. The ties binding virtual community relationships are typically weak, reflecting a marketplace approach to community much like that described in Wuthnow's (1998) discussion of "loose connections." Virtual communities are self-selecting, contingent, and often transient with short attention spans. Virtual members, however, can shut others out with one click of the mouse (Dear 2000). It is not easy to leave one's family, move from a familiar neighborhood, change or renounce one's religion, or find a new workplace, but one can obtain a new e-mail address, chat room, website, or Usenet with just the click of the mouse. Due to the lack of face-to-face contact and the weak ties, virtual communities in cyberspace have only limited liability for their members.

Psychological detachment.   The quality of social interaction necessary to create and sustain community requires a significant level of trust and intimacy. Many features of the virtual community do not promote interpersonal knowledge, trust, or commitment. Virtual communities may lack identity recognition in voice and tone, physical responses or gestures, and incremental signals from others, resulting in deception or manipulation (Donath 1999). Although there is little empirical data, the commonly expressed view is that the virtual community lacks an element of trust due to its limited information on and lack of social cues about the other community members (Donath 1999; Etzioni and Etzioni 2001). Robert Putnam comments that while the Internet is a tool of communication, he is unsure whether computer-mediated communication can foster social capital and genuine community.

> Anonymity and fluidity in the virtual world encourage "easy in, easy out," "drive-by" relationships. That very casualness is the appeal of computer-mediated communication for some denizens of cyberspace, but it discourages the creation of social capital. If entry and exit are too easy, commitment, trustworthiness, and reciprocity will not develop. (Putnam 2000, 177)

Given the relatively low level of commitment to digital communities, we should not be surprised to encounter studies of sites such as Facebook that find they have little or no affect on social capital (Valenzuela, Park, and Kee 2008; Byler 2009). Thus, while the possibility for virtual communities with close psychological ties exists in theory, in practice members of virtual communities are likely to maintain psychological ties quite similar to those that existed before joining the web-based community.

   The lack of true community in cyberspace.   In evaluating virtual communities, we find them unlikely to contain many aspects of the ideal gemeinschaft-type relationships. Without exception, the non-gemeinschaft characteristics of the virtual community in cyberspace reflect the absence of a spatial reference. The fact that virtual communities are spatially liberated increases the likelihood that they also possess characteristics antithetical to *gemeinschaft*. Relationships in communities without a spatial reference are more likely to be socially ramified, resulting in community members who are psychologically detached and feel only limited liability to the community.

   The decline in the relevance of and identification with the local place is related to the decline in *gemeinschaft*-type relationships. While the shared space of voluntary associations may provide a suitable environment for community, it seems plausible at this point to conclude that most virtual communities do not contain the necessary qualities of true community. However, such a conclusion does not address the related but conceptually distinct questions concerning the effects of the Internet on community.

Net Effects of the Internet on Community

   While virtual communities, lacking a spatial component, have a difficult time providing the common ties and social relationships associated with *gemeinschaft*, it does not necessarily follow that this is a problem. Most social entities do not create *gemeinschaft*; even the traditional local place community often falls short (Fischer 1995; Bellah et al. 1996; Wuthnow 1998; Putnam 2000). Holding virtual communities to the "gold standard" of *gemeinschaft* may be unrealistic. Perhaps a more reasonable metric would be the impact of virtual communities on *gemeinschaft*-like relationships. Are communications via the Internet likely to hinder or help the development of the common ties and social interaction associated with *gemeinschaft*?

   A significant body of research concerning Internet use and its effects on community is emerging. Many of the initial studies indicated a negative effect on community. While these reports were often limited methodologically, the common view of detrimental effects on community persisted.

Negative Effects

   Observations that an isolating, alienating individualism induced by the Internet is replacing community typically generate more popular acceptance than empirical support. Initial reports indicated that long-term and intense Internet users would indeed replace community activities with solitary cyberspace activities. Many authors are concerned that Internet use may result in spending more time alone, communicating with strangers, or forming relationships with weak ties, thus displacing the higher-quality face-to-face relationships of family and friends (Putnam 2000; Thompson and Nadler 2002). Although lacking empirical support, Norman Nie (1999) suggests that people who spend even a few hours on the Internet each week suffer higher levels of depression and loneliness than less frequent users. According to Nie (1999), isolation is reinforced, not reduced, in cyberspace. Internet use provides a refuge for social isolates who avoid real-world relationships. Robert Kraut and associates (1998) conducted a small, nonrandom study known as the "HomeNet" study and concluded that Internet use is associated with subsequent reductions in social involvement and increases in loneliness and depression.

Positive Effects

While debate continues, most survey data indicate that the Internet may be a catalyst for creating and maintaining friendships. Users report the Internet has had a modestly positive impact on both increasing contact with others and communicating more with family (Katz and Rice 2002), and a few (less than 10% of users) report Internet use leading to new face-to-face friendships (Katz and Rice 2009).

Due to its innovative research design, probably the strongest evidence for positive effects comes from Wellman and Hampton's (1999) two-year study of approximately sixty families living in a newly built, wired (equipped with Internet technologies) suburb of Toronto—"Netville." The residents' ties tended to extend not only to those in close proximity, but throughout the Netville community (Wellman 2001), and wired residents reported increased contacts with neighbors, family, and friends (Hampton and Wellman 2001).

Emerging Consensus

While it is hardly uncommon to find contradictory positions in the social sciences, the emerging consensus seems to be that the Internet has a limited but positive effect on users' face-to-face interactions. In fact, some recent research reexamines and backs away from the claims of social isolation, loneliness, and depression (Nie 2001; Kraut, Kiesler, Boneva, Cummings, Helgeson, and Crawford, 2002). In an updated study, Nie (2001) tries to reconcile some of the negative findings by arguing that the key to the isolating effects is often the *amount of time* spent on the Internet rather than the effect of the Internet itself. His survey results indicate that excessive time spent on the Internet takes away from time once spent interacting and socializing with family and friends (Nie and Erbring 2000). When spending excessive amounts of time in cyberspace, users may actually reduce their personal interactions and face-to-face contacts (Nie 2001). Further, Nie (2001) found that individuals who already exhibit a high degree of social ties and community participation continue to be social and maintain a high degree of social interactions.

Given this emerging consensus, rather than having the effect of replacing virtual communities with local place communities, the Internet may actually enhance community in the local place or shared space of voluntary associations. Wellman and Gulia (1999b, 179) provide accounts of community ties that combine both online and offline relationships and appear rooted in a shared space and local place: "Despite all the talk about virtual community transcending time and space *sui generis*, much contact is between people who see each other in person and live locally." Their research indicates that communication, via telephone or the Internet, takes place with people who live nearby, and the communication "filled in the gaps between in-person meetings and made arrangements for future get-togethers." It appears that cyberspace provides an excellent arena to initially establish and subsequently maintain the network of social ties necessary for community. As Internet use expands and telecommunications technology evolves, what is true now may be quite different in the near future.

Thus, the Internet is better conceived not as a substitute for community but rather as a new, enhanced means of communication with effects on community similar to those of the telephone (Pool 1983; Fischer 1992; 1997). For example, an e-mail relationship may enhance community just as a telephone conversation could, by leading to more holistic, more personal, face-to-face interactions. Both media are capable of initiating the first limited contact that can lead to developing closer levels of community (e.g., when asking for a date), and they can provide important substitutes when face-to-face encounters are impossible (e.g., when families are physically separated). Most of the interaction that occurs on the Internet consists of relatively narrow communication of specific information. Although communication is necessary for community, communication alone cannot create community.

Thus, as we search for community, the Internet may: (1) *reduce community,* with hours devoted to impersonal searches of websites for information leading to social isolation and the absence of community, by any definition of community; (2) *create a weak community replacement* by including significant amounts of e-mail correspondence and chat room conversations, leading not to a *gemeinschaft*-like community but rather to a virtual community of specialized ties with a weak set of secondary relationships; or (3) *reinforce community* by providing the initial or supplemental connections that lead to the *gemeinschaft*-like community. All three connections to community currently exist in cyberspace; and if the telephone is a reasonable analogy, our growing use of the Internet will continue to simultaneously reduce, replace, and reinforce community.[6]

The quest for community continues in cyberspace. However, after the first few years of this search, the proposition that nonspatial virtual communities can replace the local-place and shared-space community as the primary basis for the psychological feelings of community remains questionable. For now, at least, Internet relationships can complement the community found in the local place and in voluntary associations, but they are poor replacements for the *gemeinschaft*-type relationships found in the place called *The Community.* Communities still exist most readily, most naturally, and most often when people identify with place—the neighborhood, the school, the church, or the workplace—and when personal, face-to-face interactions are still important within the boundaries of a geographic area.

NOTES

[1] See, for example, the widely cited works of Vidich and Bensman (1958), Stein (1960), Castells (1977), Nisbet (1976), Bellah et al. (1996), and Putnam (2000).

[2] Though not as numerous or influential as studies of the loss of psychological community, the loss of identification with place has inspired the works of Gans (1962), Greer (1962), Kasarda and Janowitz (1974), Hunter (1975), Ahlbrandt (1984), and Wellman and Wortley (1990).

[3] See Skocpol and Fiorina (1999) for a strong critique of voluntary associations' inadequacies in addressing larger community issues. More generally, in *Civic Engagement in American Democracy* (1999) Theda Skocpol and Morris Fiorina contend that community development efforts and civic engagement are enhanced by and prosper with an active government and inclusive democratic politics, producing a *gemeinschaft*-like community.

[4] Chapter 9 discusses the recent development of New Urbanism in planned communities. Residents seek to reinvent community in their neighborhoods through the defined territorial space. The goal is creating spaces that encourage people to socialize and watch out for each other.

[5] Ironically, references to space and spatial metaphors abound in the electronic environment. Internet users often refer to navigating through cyberspace, traveling the information highway, and visiting different virtual communities around the Net (Hiltz and Turoff 1993; Howard 1997). Further, high-technology facilities that could be located anywhere in the new global economy tend to be spatially congregated in such high-tech centers as Silicon Valley (Webster 2001).

[6] See Boase and Wellman (2004) for a thoughtful extension of this argument that places Internet use in a more general pattern of movement from "spatially proximate and densely knit communities" to "spatially dispersed and sparsely knit communities."

Community Development

In the preceding chapter community development was linked to quests for the economic, political, and psychological relevance of the community that are thought to be lost in a *gesellschaft*-like society. In this chapter we can be more specific and explore various community development strategies for such quests. The exploration will be limited to American community development efforts because in less industrialized societies the concept can have a very different meaning (i.e., the hastening of *gesellschaft*). Even in other industrial and postindustrial societies, there is less of the local political autonomy that distinguishes US community development. Hence, even though community development is an area of international concern, the primary focus here is on community development efforts in the United States.

An Overview of Community Development

Community development became both an academic discipline and an applied profession in the latter half of the twentieth century. Beginning with the "community dynamics" program of William Biddle at Earlham College, Indiana, in 1947, the field grew to include community development courses at over eighty universities and colleges, some with specialized graduate programs in community development. Professionally, the Community Development Society was established in 1970 and in the first ten years had grown to over a thousand members (Christenson, Fendley, and Robinson 1989).While the Community Development Society focuses primarily on rural community development, members are employed by universities as teachers, researchers, and extension agents; by governments as technical advisors, planners, and managers; by private industry as counselors and consultants; and by neighborhoods as advocates or organizers (see http://www.comm-dev.org). The academic training of the community development agent varies, from sociology to psychology to social work to urban planning to physical education to home economics to agricultural economics.

In terms of public policy, community development can trace its roots back to the late nineteenth century in US housing settlements and services for low-income neighborhoods. By the 1960s, an emergence of social policies focused on community improvement through community development corporations (CDCs). CDCs were an outgrowth of the civil rights movement (Peterman 2000) and the federal government's War on Poverty in the 1960s (Vidal 1997; Vidal and Keating 2004), providing community-based strategies for problems typically associated with individual pathologies (Chaskin, Joseph, and Chipenda-Dansokho 1998). CDCs were a business-oriented response to these problems, revitalizing deteriorated neighborhoods through housing renovation and economic development (Lowe 2006; Palen 2008; Peterman 2000). As federal support for CDCs declined in the 1980s, "a growing number of foundation-funded, neighborhood-based initiatives are renewing their effort to develop a viable alternative to fragmented community-change strategies" (Chaskin et al. 1998, 19). Today, both public and private community development efforts are addressing the needs of individuals and neighborhoods through a variety of coordinated strategies to improve the community environment.

Defining Community Development

Community development is yet another of those important, widely used but variously and differently defined concepts. Surprisingly little of the ambiguity surrounds the first term—*community*—which is usually defined as it is in the initial chapter of this text. After reviewing the major uses of the term in conjunction with development, James Christenson, Kim Fendley, and Jerry Robinson, Jr. (1989, 9) concluded that "a community is defined and best described by the following elements: (1) people, (2) within a geographically bounded area, (3) involved in social interaction, and (4) with one or more psychological ties with each other and with the place [where] they live."

Development, however, requires more elaboration. The term *development* has been used broadly and frequently in all types of situations throughout the world. "It is not a uniformly defined methodology; different themes dominate its application in different places (McNeely 1999, 742)." Generally, it is a dynamic, value-laden concept that implies positive change. Perhaps the most common use is economic, where the focus is on technological transformations that increase economic productivity. Nationally, a common measure is the Gross Domestic Product (GDP). The value-laden implication here is that transformations resulting in a higher GDP are desirable. As a similar example, political development would entail changes that result in a more representative government. Democratic politics, in this example, is the favored way of distributing and justifying governmental authority. In other words, development is regarded as a desirable change that improves the quality of life among residents (Green and Haines 2008). The ambiguity, of course, comes in distinguishing desirable from undesirable change. We will consider that problem shortly, but for now it is sufficient to simply combine "community" and "development" and come up with a working definition of the concept. *Community development typically includes voluntary cooperation and self-help efforts by neighborhood residents and professionals to improve the physical, social, and economic conditions of the community.*

Community development efforts will often focus on the enhancement of community through the development of leadership, self-help initiatives, and local institutions (Berner and Phillips 2005; Green and Haines 2008). It is assumed that these efforts are not necessary for affluent communities, since community development is "asset building that improves the quality of life among residents of low- to moderate-income communities" (Ferguson and Dickens 1999, 5). The various assets include the physical buildings and land, individual skills and knowledge, all formal and informal relationships, financial capital, and political capital. Thus, this approach aims at improving and building up each asset within the community (usually a low-income, urban neighborhood).

Community development activities are diverse and can include anything from community organizing and planning, advocacy and empowerment, the creation of neighborhood associations or community development corporations, and neighborhood revitalization (Lowe 2006; Peterman 2000) to social services integration, and the economic, physical, or social development of an area (Robinson and Green 2010). More recent community development attempts integrate tourism as a strategy for development (see Beeton 2006; Phillips and Pittman 2009). Sara Stoutland (1999) identifies ten types of community development activities including (1) housing development, (2) building commercial property; (3) business/economic improvement; (4) planning, advocacy, and organizing; (5) education and youth development; (6) security and public safety; (7) workforce development; (8) emergency assistance; (9) religious services; and (10) public health. One way to organize the multiple community development activities is to focus on their basic goal. Is the goal a completed task or an ongoing process?

Task versus Process

Two basic dimensions of community development exist in the literature: task and process. While they are not incompatible, they differ considerably in emphasis. Task conceptions focus more on a tangible goal (e.g., a new hospital, a school, or a water treatment plant), while process conceptions emphasize the more abstract goals of strengthening community ties and local autonomy. Again, borrowing from Christenson, Fendley, and Robinson (1989, 14), we can define the task orientation to community development as: "(1) a group of people (2) in a community (3) reaching a decision (4) to initiate a social action process (i.e., planned intervention) (5) to change (6) their economic, social, cultural, or environmental situation." More succinctly, Roland Warren (1978, 325) refers to the process aspect of community development "as a deliberate and sustained attempt to strengthen the horizontal pattern of a community."

As an example of the difference between these two approaches, consider a large corporation locating a branch plant in a community in response to a request from the local chamber of commerce. From a task perspective community development clearly occurred, since the goal of securing a new factory was successfully reached. From a process perspective, however, the verdict is not so clear. If the chamber's activities were episodic rather than continuous, and if the new factory's presence increases the dependence of the vertical patterns while weakening local ties and identification, then community development did not occur. The difference is one of emphasis and value. Is the local quality of life enhanced by the new factory? From the task perspective the answer clearly is affirmative, but from the process perspective it is possibly negative.

The best of all possible worlds occurs when a specific task is accomplished and the horizontal ties are simultaneously strengthened, but when pursuit of the task is likely to weaken local ties, the approaches are in conflict. We employ both definitions in this chapter and try to reconcile their differences when they occur.

Approaches to Community Development

In a review of the publication of the *Journal of the Community Development Society* (from 1970 to 1988), James Christenson (1989) identified three broad approaches to community development: (1) self-help, (2) technical assistance, and (3) conflict.[1] As we have come to expect, one's definition of community development has a lot to do with how one goes about it. We will see that the task definition is particularly well suited for the technical assistance approach, while the conflict and self-help approaches are usually best viewed from a process perspective.

Self-Help

The self-help approach is based on democratic principles of self-determination. The priority assumption is that people can become meaningful participants: "the more so if participation goes beyond 'listening to beneficiaries' towards their active role in decision-making . . . self-help, finally, can be seen as participation squared" (Berner and Phillips 2005, 18). The community development agent is primarily a *facilitator*. The local residents take primary responsibility for: (1) deciding what the community needs, (2) how this goal is to be accomplished, and (3) doing so. The goal of the community development agent is to enhance the horizontal pattern of decision making and implementation. The self-help approach often finds a level of community anomie and a lack of relationships within the community. The ultimate goal is integration of *gemeinschaft*, thus building the community's ability to make informed decisions and promote feelings of accomplishments and *gemeinschaft*.

The self-help approach is designed to promote and build community through "the development of increased neighborhood capacity for planning, advocacy, service delivery, and the implementation of a broad range of development strategies" (Chaskin and Abunimah 1999, 57). This involves some degree of voluntarism from friends, neighbors, and other members of the community (Peterman 2000; Robinson and Green 2010). Creating such involvement can bolster community spirit and trust and encourage local solutions. While the local residents take the primary role as the change agents, the practitioner or community organizer is an enabler, catalyst, and coordinator (Eichler 2007; Rothman 1996; Swanepoel and De Beer 2006). The specific task is almost irrelevant. It can be directed toward any goal selected by the community. The most important part of this approach is the *process* of bringing local residents together (Eichler 2007).

Application.   The process of strengthening horizontal patterns within the community is both difficult and complex. One of the first obstacles to overcome is the potential for fatalistic apathy among local residents (Littrell and Hobbs 1989; Littrell and Littrell 2006). Fostering "inclusive participation" when the citizens and their contributions "are valued and appreciated, overcoming institutionalized exclusion (and the complementary acquiescence of the powerless) is no simple task" (Mathie and Cunningham 2003, 483). The idea that ordinary people in the community can affect the local quality of life is often hard to sell to justifiably skeptical local residents. Such apathy, of course, is supposedly a symptom of our *gesellschaft*-like mass society. Thus, an initial task of the community organizer is instilling the *gemeinschaft*-like conditions of mutual assistance and collective action (Diers 2004).

From the self-help perspective, the community development agent's role in this process of building *gemeinschaft* is a limited one—very much like what group theorists have referred to as the "maintenance functions" of a group (Thibaut and Kelley 1959; Ritzer and Goodman 2004). Robert F. Bales and his associate at Harvard (Parsons and Bales 1955) found in their research that groups typically require two types of leaders: a *task* leader who proposes actions and assigns roles, and an *expressive* leader who notices how people feel and works to soothe the tensions that develop within the group. The local change agent role can be seen as that of an expressive leader. The task leader, on the other hand, should be someone indigenous to the community since only local residents are qualified to set the group's goals (O'Brien, Raedeke, and Hassinger 1998).

Task/process relationship.   Although the process of strengthening horizontal patterns is given precedence over the task of achieving a specific goal, the task remains an important component of the self-help approach. In fact, it can often gain too much importance—that is, the task can become the primary reason for being, and when it is accomplished the local organization that was formed to achieve the task fades away.

This emphasis on task to the exclusion of process is a problem that is especially common to community development. Bureaucracies, à la Weber, in contrast, often give more emphasis to preserving the organization than to accomplishing a specific task. A "goal displacement" occurs in which most of the bureaucracy's energies are directed toward maintaining the organization itself rather than accomplishing the original goals of the organization (Ritzer and Goodman 2004). Roland Warren (1978, 331) maintains that exactly the opposite situation occurs for community development organizations. Although the community development organization begins with the goal of strengthening the horizontal pattern,

> the organizational goal becomes displaced as the task accomplishment usurps it. This reverse goal displacement should not be surprising when we recall that community development, like community action episodes through which it takes place, involves an activation of the horizontal pattern of the community in ways in which it is not customarily activated. (If it were, the "community development" would not be necessary.) Thus, the community, as a social system, has not been made to pay the price of bureaucratic goal displacement largely because it has not received the values that bureaucratic organization affords. When it attempts to achieve these values through a rational, administered approach to creating or restoring a strong horizontal pattern in a deliberately "administered" fashion, this goal is easily displaced by the more immediate task goal of the action episode involved—be that a new school bond issue, a community center, the attraction of a new industry, an urban renewal program, or whatever.

Kenneth Wilkinson (1989, 342) also maintains that the process of strengthening horizontal ties often is more important than the task.

> A process is never fully "developed"; it consists simply of behavior in process. The development is in the doing—in the working together toward a shared goal. To require success in goal achievement—even in achievement of the goal of being able to continue working together—before accepting an activity as community development would violate the process approach and would ignore the many other factors in social change.

Still, the achievement of specific tasks does not have to be as detrimental to strengthening horizontal ties as Warren or Wilkinson imply. It can be beneficial, perhaps even necessary to the maintenance of the horizontal patterns. While failing to achieve a goal can cause participation to wane, achieving a goal can generate increased participation and enthusiasm (Edwards and Jones 1976). Lucius Botes and Dingie van Rensburg (2000, 51) warn against stressing the importance of only the process or only the task.

> Some people and organizations tend to emphasize process and fail to deliver product (task), whilst other are so product-driven that they neglect community processes. Both are dangerous: process without product leaves communities feeling that nothing is really happening other than a lot of talking, and that time, money and social energy is lost. Product without process runs the risk of doing something communities do not want or need, or cannot sustain.

Robert Chaskin and Ali Abunimah (1999) provide a cautionary tale about the Community Action Program (CAP), which originally stressed the coordination of activity and maximum participation of the residents. The CAP experienced opposition from municipal government and local formal agencies who felt left out and threatened. The program was restructured, with citizens becoming marginalized while the mayor and local government agencies gained control. As the local residents were removed from the process, the CAP became ineffective. The horizontal pattern of integration necessary for continuance was dissolved. Community development, Chaskin and Abunimah argue, is impossible without special local tasks and horizontal ties.

With the self-help approach to community development, then, there is a constant tension between process and task. The successful completion of a task aids in building support for the community development process, but too much emphasis on the task can divert energies from maintaining horizontal patterns. A tightrope must be walked, and a tilt too far in either direction can be fatal to community development efforts.

Evaluation.   When does the self-help approach work best? Under what conditions should one expect difficulties? What kinds of difficulties? How can they be overcome? The research necessary to answer these questions is still being done, but it is possible to make some broad suppositions about the efficacy of the self-help approach.

First, the self-help approach probably works best in a homogeneous community (Berner and Phillips 2005; Botes and van Rensburg 2000; Robinson and Green 2010). To the degree the community encompasses different groups (family status, race, social class) with different needs and values, a democratic approach to community development may become hopelessly deadlocked (Warren 1978).

Second, predominantly middle-class communities may be best suited for a self-help approach since it assumes that local residents have the power, predilection, and resources to help themselves (Berner and Phillips 2005). For often powerless and sometimes justifiably apathetic lower-class residents, this may be a naive assumption. And upper-class residents, since their interest is more likely to be on extralocal events (Wellman and Leighton 1979), may be more difficult to organize around local issues.

Third, communities with a pluralistic power structure should have a tradition of open and democratic decision making conducive to the self-help approach (Fabiani and Buss 2008). Communities with a covert elite decision-making structure may have little experience with, and little existent structure for, the type of politics associated with the self-help approach. However, the poor are not always equipped with the necessary skills to navigate the infrastructure of elite decision-making processes (Berner and Phillips 2005; Eichler 2007). Further, the ruling elite may (quite accurately) perceive this type of community development as a threat to their power (Botes and van Rensburg 2000).

Finally, this approach will probably be easiest to implement in relatively isolated, autonomous communities (Littrell and Hobbs 1989). Since the self-help process emphasizes local residents' assumption of responsibility for their environment, communities with strong vertical (and weak horizontal) patterns will be less receptive to the self-help approach. Of course, this comes close to saying that the self-help approach works best where it is not needed. A more accurate assessment, however, would be that those communities with weak horizontal patterns will present difficulties for community development from a self-help perspective, but they will also be the communities most in need of community development; hence, they will also be the communities that will benefit most from a self-help approach (Green and Haines 2008; Robinson and Green 2010).

Although each of these four propositions is open to further research and revision, collectively they imply that the self-help approach will be more effective in some situations than in others. And in keeping with the eclectic approach of this text, it is reasonable to assume that other approaches might do better under other conditions. Thus, we now turn to the other two basic approaches: technical assistance and conflict.

Technical Assistance

In many ways, the technical assistance approach is the opposite of the self-help approach. Whereas self-help emphasizes the horizontal process, technical assistance emphasizes the vertically imposed task. While self-help is based on reestablishing *gemeinschaft,* technical assistance is often the product of increasing *gesellschaft.*

The technical assistance approach is based on the presumed need for expert planners who, through their technical skills (e.g., in grant writing, non-profit management, cost-benefit accounting, law, counseling, urban design), can guide and evaluate the community development process. Community development, from this perspective, typically includes tasks such as economic development (e.g., attracting new industry), improving social service delivery systems (e.g., Meals on Wheels), and coordinating existing services (e.g., regional planning).

The most common form of technical assistance can be found in community development corporations (CDCs)—expert-based organizations that can manage the highly technical aspects of development (e.g., housing construction, management, and job and business development). CDCs, while not for profit, typically operate in cooperation with for-profit agencies—banks, real estate, insurance, contractors. The CDC approach, funded by government grants and philanthropic organizations, is based on functionalist models of common interest and cooperation among agencies. CDCs typically focus on refurbishing housing or bringing in new businesses, structures that can be built or rebuilt and are little threat to the status quo (Swanepoel and De Beer 2006).Of course, a fundamental, structural rebuilding of poor communities would involve a dramatic redistribution of wealth across the entire society and is, therefore, unlikely (Stoecker 1997; 2001), but CDCs have emerged as a major player in providing technical assistance for multiple ameliorative projects (Shanklin and Rayns, Jr. 1998).

This is a common form of community development, but as Frank Fear, Larry Gamm and Frederick Fisher (1989, 79) point out in their review of the technical assistance approach, the lack of attention to psychological community can be a problem: "Frequently in community development we naively assume—sometimes with disastrous consequences—that sufficient levels of community-ness exist, in the psychological and sociological sense, so that all practitioners need to do is focus attention on the substantive problem(s) at hand."

Application.   What has accounted for the popularity of the technical assistance approach? Who decides when expert technicians are needed? Who decides who qualifies as an expert? Who designs the project or program that needs the technical assistance? In most cases, the answer to all these questions is an extralocal (typically federal) government. In short, the process of technical assistance is almost exclusively a vertically patterned phenomenon. The task will impact the community, but the impetus for the task originates outside the community.

Today, most community development programs (for education, law enforcement, the elderly, job training, transportation) are funded by categorical state or federal grants. The government funds these programs for specific community applications and often determines the basic qualifications of the experts (usually from state agencies, universities, or private consulting firms) who provide the technical assistance and evaluation. In other words, the technical assistant must meet the requirements of the state or federal government, and then the technical assistant helps insure that the state or federal guidelines are being followed by the community that receives the funds (Phillips and Pittman 2009).

Task/process relationship.   In most cases of technical assistance, the specific task takes total precedence over the process of strengthening horizontal ties. In fact, because of its base in the vertical patterns of the community, the task may cause the horizontal patterns to atrophy. Technical assistance often leads local residents to look to the state or federal government or to outside experts rather than to one another for solutions to community problems.

There are rare but important exceptions to this relationship. In some cases, providing technical assistance can actually strengthen horizontal patterns. Leadership training programs have this potential (Phillips and Pittman 2009). In this case, federal-, state-, or foundation-supported programs employ consultants to teach local residents the analytic and management skills necessary for community development. For example, in the International City Management Association's provision of technical expertise to member cities, a local city manager can receive expert advice on similar problems that other cities have encountered (Fear, Gamm, and Fisher 1989). Still, such programs are more the exception than the rule. And the general rule is that the task takes precedence over the process (Robinson and Green 2010).

Evaluation.   There is little doubt that when community problems require only facts and funds for their solution, when both the problem and the solution can be clearly defined, and when the concern is largely and simply with delivering goods or services efficiently, the technical assistance approach is preferable (Phillips and Pittman 2009; Rothman 1996). However, most local problems don't fit these criteria. Problems like crime or poverty, with their complex causes and controversial solutions, would seem to fall outside the province of this approach, but this has not proved to be the case. We often like to conceptualize the solutions to our complex problems as technical manipulations rather than structural change. Thus, technical assistance is by far the most common approach to community development. Even if it seldom solves the local problem it is meant to address, the very fact that we try the technical assistance approach so often means that it probably has more lasting local impact than the self-help and conflict approaches combined (Christenson 1989).

Still, the evaluation of this approach by community development professionals is always colored by the neglect of horizontal ties. Christenson (1989, 35) argues, for example, that local change agents who rely on the technical assistance approach "end up working *for* people rather than *with* them. While planners and technical assistance workers may argue against this characterization, it is fairly well documented that this orientation has largely ignored public input or participation."

In a similar vein, Fear, Gamm, and Fisher (1989, 83) believe that "the more we attempt to impose technical assistance from the outside, the more we come to realize it does not work either as often or as well as those involved had hoped it would." The "paternalistic roles" of many "development experts" impede development and community participation (Botes and van Rensburg 2000, 42). John Kretzmann and John McKnight (1993, 4) point out that if the needs-based approach (i.e., technical assistance) is the only aid to communities, the consequences can be "devastating." This reinforces the idea that only outside experts can provide real help and further weakens neighbor-to-neighbor links (i.e., horizontal ties). We return, then, to a conclusion much like that reached for the self-help perspective: The most effective community development programs are those that manage to successfully complete tasks *and* maintain horizontal ties.

Conflict

The conflict approach to community development is in many ways the opposite of the self-help and technical assistance approaches. While the latter two approaches are ostensibly value-free (with self-help assuming that values must originate from the local residents and technical assistance assuming that the technical advice provided is unrelated to the more philosophical concerns of values), the conflict-oriented change agent believes there is injustice in the current structure of the community and that conflict is necessary to restructure the community along more egalitarian lines. The conflict approach emphasizes communities (usually poor and underprivileged communities) organizing themselves and using confrontational strategies, involving protest and even disruption, to demand the removal of discriminating practices in order to create equal opportunities (Alinsky 1946; Bobo, Kendall, and Max 2001; Ledwith and Campling 2005; Robinson and Green 2010). The conflict approach is especially well suited for attacking the structural barriers that prevent poor communities from improving. The necessity of conflict is key here, since this approach is the converse of the conflict resolution efforts sometimes associated with community development. In fact, this approach is more often found under the category of community organizing (see Stoecker 2001) rather than community development.

Application.   The conflict approach to community development is identified closely with the community organization efforts of Saul Alinsky (1946, 1971). This is a very popular approach to analyze, but outside of Alinsky it has not proved to be a very popular approach to implement. For example, in his review of articles in the *Journal of the Community Development Society* Christenson (1989, 37) notes that

> Although the conflict theme is interesting to discuss, when it comes down to using the approach it seems that most authors who write for the *Journal* do not become involved in or do not become participant observers of the conflict approach. Instead, they write about Saul Alinsky.

More recently and most famously, Hillary Rodham Clinton's writings on Alinsky were "sealed" during her years in the White House. She could be seen as one who wrote on Alinsky's style rather than implementing his tactics; to a lesser degree, the same could be said for Barack Obama (Stoecker 2009). The reasons it is not widely implemented will become apparent as the steps involved in this approach are presented. The conflict approach requires the change agent to make difficult and subjective choices and often alienates the change agent from powerful groups within the community.

There are, of course, other important applications of the conflict approach besides those of Saul Alinsky (e.g., the civil rights and women's movements), but at the community level his techniques are the most widely used and analyzed.[2] So, drawing largely from Alinsky, how does one do conflict-oriented community development?

The first step is for the outside professional community organizer to *receive a formal invitation* from local leaders. Alinsky typically required invitations from several segments of the community (e.g., white liberals, blacks, churches, unions) so that local acceptance and broad-based interest developed. If the formal invitations are not initially offered, the organizer must create the type of conflict situation that will generate the invitations.

The second step involves *field research* to identify salient elements of community structure: community norms, power structure, divisions, and potential leaders. Alinsky refers to this as the listening, observing, and learning period.

The third step requires the *mobilization of community-wide sentiment for change.* Usually the strategy is to create adversaries that unite the community.

During his work in Rochester, Alinsky (1971, 137) called a press conference and identified the major employer as an adversary by saying, "Maybe I am innocent and uninformed of what has been happening here, but as far as I know the only thing Eastman Kodak has done on the race issue in America has been to introduce color film."

Step four is the difficult processes of *reinforcing existing community organizations and creating a new organization that represents several local groups.* Block groups are established and linkages are formed with existing groups such as churches and unions. Then a new community-wide organization is created:

> The purpose of the organization should be interpreted as proposing to deal with those major issues which no single agency is—or can be—big enough or strong enough to cope with. Then each agency will continue to carry out its own program, but all are being banded together to achieve sufficient strength to cope with issues that are so vast and deep that no one or two community agencies would ever consider tackling them. (Alinsky 1946, 87)

The final step is *winning a confrontation and delivering improved services.* In order to convince local residents that there is power through organization and that their membership is worth the investment of time and energy, a confrontation must be won early in the community development process. Thus, the initial confrontations should be chosen carefully to insure that they are: (1) highly visible, (2) salient, (3) nondivisive, and (4) winnable (Alinsky 1971, 114–59).

> The steps come together as scenes in a morality play of community development: It's the kind of thing we see in play writing; the first act introduces the characters and the plot, in the second act the plot and characters are developed as the play strives to hold the audience's attention. In the final act good and evil have their dramatic confrontation and resolution. (Alinsky 1971, 115–16)

But when a play ends, the audience leaves and the actors move on to other roles in other plays. Unfortunately, this has usually been the case with Alinsky's organizations as well. After the tasks of creating a community-wide organization and winning the initial confrontations are completed, the process of maintaining the horizontal patterns of local identification and action usually has been unsuccessful (Reitzes and Reitzes 1982, 1992; Rothman 1996). The two Alinsky-inspired organizations with the longest tenure are the largely faith-based umbrella organization, the Industrial Areas Foundation (IAF), and the more well-known Association of Community Organizations for Reform Now, better known as ACORN. In 2010, all 30 of ACORN's state chapters closed after hidden camera footage from conservative activists appeared to show ACORN staff providing advice on employing child prostitutes and avoiding taxes. So, with the demise of ACORN only the smaller, less radical IAF remains as a national example of Alinsky's model.

Task/process relationship.   Theoretically, the successful completion of the task should ensure the continuation of the process:

> Once the stated objective has been achieved the clientele need an evaluation to determine what other changes they could realistically attempt in order to better their life situation. At this stage, the conflict agent will help the indigenous leaders assess their situation, assess what they have achieved, and assess where they might go from here. The agent's intentions of leaving the community should be reaffirmed. It is probably best if the agent phases out of the community picture as quietly as possible, leaving the administration and the recognition to the indigenous leaders. The experiences derived from the exercise of planning change through conflict should provide local community organizations with the confidence and ability to carry on in the future. (Robinson 1989, 108)

The above description has not proved to be the case, however. Alinsky's repeated attempts to build a national coalition of community organizations were failures (Reitzes and Reitzes 1992); and even within the same city those organizations that remained in existence would not aid one another, leaving the community segmented (Rothman 1996). Hence, the process of maintaining horizontal patterns has proved to be a major difficulty for the conflict approach.

Evaluation.   As shown above, the process of maintaining the community development organization is a major problem since the conflict approach lends itself to episodic rather than continuous development. Although it is, perhaps, too psychologically and physically demanding to maintain continuous community conflict, the individual tasks that can be accomplished by this approach should not be discounted. The conflict approach can accomplish substantial change in a relatively short period of time (Bobo et al. 2001; Christenson 1989; Shaw 2001).

In fact, the inability to maintain the community development process is hardly unique to the conflict approach. It is also a common shortcoming of the self-help and technical assistance approaches. In other words, the inability to maintain horizontal patterns cannot account for the relatively few applications of the conflict approach. Rather, there are two other difficulties that account for its lack of popularity among community change agents. First, is the nature of the opposition in the conflict—typically the rich and powerful. Even if the change agent is willing to side against the establishment,[3] the resultant backlash from these vested interest groups may outweigh the fruits of the initial victory.

Second, beyond the difficulties associated with going against the establishment, there is an ethical problem with this approach. When does one intervene into community affairs? On whose side? Donal Reitzes and Dietrich Reitzes (1992, 18) suggest that "the external task of the community organizer is to serve as the defender of economic and political interests and as the advocate for new programs, policies, and plans which will foster local community development." The professional change agent should always ask: Is this for the common good of the community? In theory, an affirmative answer to this question would appear to resolve the ethical dilemma, but in practice it is more problematic. Suppose a group home for sex offenders wanted to move from their current lower-class neighborhood to a working-class neighborhood. The group home residents need organization to win the conflict, and the working-class neighborhood could be mobilized to resist them. Both groups are relatively powerless; both wish to determine their own destinies; and the common good is, in this case, open to interpretation. Some community organizers might feel uncomfortable using the conflict approach in such a situation, and such situations are common.[4]

Comparing Approaches

Although each of the three major approaches aims at improving the local quality of life, each makes very different assumptions about community problems and solutions. Table 8-1 contrasts these approaches along several common dimensions of community development. Note that each appears better suited for some situations than for others. Depending on the values of the change agent, the nature of the local problem, and the characteristics of the community, one approach to community development will be preferred over another. Thus, the skilled practitioner needs sufficient insight into self and community to know which approach is most likely to succeed, and then sufficient flexibility is needed to implement that approach:

> Our field studies have produced voluminous evidence that [various] roles are needed, but not always at the same time and place. The challenging problem, on which we have made a bare beginning, is to define more clearly the specific conditions under which one or another or still other types of practice are appropriate. The skill we shall need in the practitioner of the future is the skill of making a situational diagnosis and analysis that will lead him to a proper choice of the methods most appropriate to the task at hand. (Gurin 1966, 30)

While Gurin has been proved correct in his call for the ability to choose between various approaches, in the years since his article it also has become increasingly clear that these approaches are not mutually exclusive.

Mixing and phasing approaches.   In an insightful article comparing the three basic approaches, Jack Rothman (1996, 95) calls for the "mixing and phasing" of self-help, technical assistance, and conflict "on those frequent occasions when more than one value is being pursued at a given time." Most critics of the technical assistance approach, for example, believe it should be mixed with some of the local self-determination that occurs in the self-help approach.

Rothman notes, however, that not all blends are possible, with the conflict approach being particularly difficult to combine with others. In these cases, the approaches may be phased. A community might be best helped by one approach initially and then, at a later stage, by another. Conflict, for example, may be necessary for securing the power and organization sufficient

Table 8.1 Comparisons of the Three Major Approaches to Community Development

Approach	Values of change agent	Typical occupation of change agent	Perception of clients	Relationship to power structure	Ideal community characteristics	Task/process relationship
Self-help	Democratic	Social worker, VISTA volunteer.	Unorganized citizens needing assistance in strengthening horizontal ties.	Attempts to broaden decision-making may be seen as threat to power structure.	Homogeneous, middle class.	Process takes precedence over task.
Technical assistance	Neutral	Sociologist, agricultural extension agent.	Untrained consumers needing more efficient services.	Works for power structure.	"Eclipsed" community dependent on extra-local assistance.	Task is everything, process is irrelevant.
Conflict	Egalitarian	Community organizer, labor organizer, civil rights worker.	Exploited victims who must band together to forcefully change community structure.	Works against vested interest of the powerful; definite threat to power structure.	Numerous working-class or lower-class neighborhoods.	Task and process both important; task has proven more attainable than process.

the successful introduction of a self-help approach.[5] In this case, the change agent must be able to determine when conditions are ripe for a transition from one type of community development to another. Not only is the mixing and phasing of approaches often the best strategy for effective community development, it also is becoming the most common practice for local change agents. Sue Kenny (2002, 296) agrees with Rothman that "mixing and matching of the discourses can assist in the rehabilitation of 'the social' in new and innovative ways that ensure that community-building, trust, mutuality, and collaboration are legitimate concerns for all public policy and business development."

Current Status of Community Development

Community development is becoming decidedly eclectic; just as multiple approaches to community development are being employed, the field itself is opening up to a broader range of professionals with a wider variety of skills. The new global economy has left local government with fewer resources for community development (Pilisuk, McAllister, and Rothman 1996; Warner 1999). Grassroots efforts and CDCs have expanded, filling the gap where government involvement in community development has receded (Fabiani and Buss 2008; Vidal and Keating 2004).

Still, it would not be correct to say that just because the field is becoming more eclectic, all the approaches to community development are flourishing equally well. The conflict approach especially has lost favor in more conservative times. As neighbor-based agitators lose their appeal, Alinsky-type community organizers become less numerous (Callahan, Mayer, Palmer, and Ferlazzo 1999). However, CDCs are flourishing in the United States with over two thousand active CDCs in the field. The increases in the number, scale, and activity of CDCs are supported by increasing resources from foundations. While many CDCs focus on low-income housing, it is much more common for them to have a broad mission of community development (Green and Haines 2008; Lowe 2006; Vidal 1997).

Additionally, as federal and foundation money for community development has become increasingly scarce, there has been an accompanying increase in the demand for accountability. This typically implies a method of program evaluation that produces measurable community outputs. Such evaluations will naturally favor task-dominated approaches to community development, since it is relatively easy to measure how successful one is in building a new school or renovating a housing project. But how does one measure the strength of horizontal ties, and how, then, can process-oriented programs to strengthen these ties be evaluated and justified? The fiscal crunch and tight bureaucratic budgets have required communities to become more responsible for their own fate, but they have also made it more difficult to fund the process-oriented types of community development programs (Kenny 2002).

This may be the major task confronting community development today: The horizontal patterns of the community must be better conceptualized and measured so that techniques for strengthening them can be evaluated. The measurement of these horizontal patterns is considered in the third section of this text, but before proceeding to that final section, one more subject that goes considerably beyond community development requires attention: "planned" or "new" communities.

NOTES

[1] Green and Haines (2008) continue with these three types of approaches. Most researchers agree that three different approaches exist; however, there is little consensus on the labels for each approach. According to Jack Rothman (1996), three approaches to community development are identified as: (1) locality development, (2) social planning policy, and (3) social action. Other typologies of approaches to community development can be found in Eichler (2007), Robinson and Green (2010), Stoutland (1999), and Warren (1978).

[2] For alternative conflict approaches, see Cloward and Elman (1966), Glasgow (1972), Bailey and Brake (1975), O'Brien (1975), and Shaw (2001). Also see the activist framework in Kenny (2002), the social action approach in Rothman (1996), and the applied urban symbolic interaction approach in Reitzes and Reitzes (1992).

[3] Since the change agent is usually an "outside agitator" in this approach, there is less to fear from local elites.

[4] This discussion of the conflict approach has focused exclusively on techniques geared toward *promoting* conflict. In that regard it reflects the usual use of conflict for community development. However, the goals of community development also can be met through conflict *prevention* and *mediation*. See Robinson (1989) for a comparison of these three types of conflict approaches, and for an attempt to escape ethical dilemmas by choosing mediation over promotion or prevention.

[5] The labor and civil rights movements have moved through similar modes of action.

Planned Communities

Most communities just happen. That is, they are much more the product of various unanticipated, uncontrolled, local, and extralocal forces than they are the product of deliberate, planned local development. Some important exceptions do exist, however. A few communities are, at least in part, the result of rational planning. Rather than an improvement of an existing neighborhood as in chapter 8, planned communities are new towns or neighborhoods that are consciously created to improve the quality of life. In this chapter, we: (1) examine the theoretical basis for planned communities, (2) look back at some of the pioneering attempts at planning and building new communities, (3) evaluate the progress of more recently developed planned communities, and (4) try to determine what can be learned from attempts to plan communities.

The Origins of Planned Communities: *Gemeinschaft/Gesellschaft*, Conflict Sociology, and Ebenezer Howard

The planned communities examined in this chapter emerged from the convergence of three classic community themes: (1) the desire to restore lost *gemeinschaft*, (2) a somewhat muted conflict view of the industrial community, and (3) the belief that a community's ecological structure influences its social structure. Thus, one of the major theoretical underpinnings for community planning is Tönnies's original idea concerning *gesellschaft* replacing *gemeinschaft*. The goal of many early planners was to construct a new form of industrial city including features common to rural, preindustrial environments; in this way, the negative effects of *gesellschaft* might be tempered by the positive elements of a *gemeinschaft*-like environment. Note, as a primary example, the position of the most influential planner of new towns since the Industrial Revolution, Ebenezer Howard,[1] in his classic *Garden Cities of To-Morrow* (originally published in 1898):

> The two magnets must be made one. As man and woman by their varied
> gifts and faculties supplement each other, so should town and country.

The town is the symbol of society—of mutual help and friendly cooperation, of fatherhood, motherhood, brotherhood, sisterhood, of wide relations. . . . The country is the symbol of God's love and care. . . . All that
we are and all that we have come from it. Our bodies are formed of it; to
it they return. We are fed by it, clothed by it, and by it we are warmed and
sheltered. . . . It is the source of all health, all wealth, all knowledge. . . .
Town and country must be married, and out of this joyous union will
spring a new hope, a new life, a new civilization. (1965, 48)

While Ebenezer Howard shared a nostalgia for rural *gemeinschaft* with
Tönnies, Howard's critical view of life in industrial cities was similar to the
conflict approach of Karl Marx and Friedrich Engels. Again from *Garden Cities of To-Morrow*, Howard cites observers who believe that "cities tend more
and more to become the graves of the physique of our race, can we wonder at
it when we see the houses so foul, so squalid, so ill-drained, so vitiated by
neglect and dirt?" (1965, 43). Later in the book, he views London as "an eye-
sore and a blot a danger to health and an outrage on decency" (*ibid.*, 156).
Such descriptions of London could just as easily have been made by Engels.[2]

Not only did Howard reflect Marx and Engels in his critical view of
industrial cities, he also was somewhat of a socialist, advocating community
ownership of all the land in his new cities. And though not a revolutionary,
he was a social activist who played a major role in securing support for his
ideas. So, while Howard (1965, 114) claims that "no reader will confuse the
experiment here advocated with any experiment in absolute Communism,"
his plans are certainly experiments in partial communism, and his influential
garden cities movement includes the Marxist tradition of economic criticism
almost as much as Tönnies's tradition of lost *gemeinschaft*.

Howard believed that new, planned communities could free England
from the urban ills that so distressed Marx and Engels. For Howard, much
like Louis Wirth in America, the physical urban environment creates urban
lifestyles; and, going beyond Wirth, Howard believed that modifying the
urban environment would modify the social environment. In the introduction
to his chapter on administering his garden cities, Howard (1965, 89) quotes
from Albert Shaw's *Municipal Government in Great Britain:*

The present evils of city life are temporary and remediable. The abolition
of the slums and the destruction of their virus are as feasible as the drain-
age of a swamp and the total dissipation of its miasmas. The conditions
and circumstances that surround the lives of the masses of the people in
modern cities can be so adjusted to their needs as to result in the highest
development of the race, in body, in mind and in moral character. The so-
called problems of the modern city are but the various phases of the one
main question: How can the environment be most perfectly adapted to
the welfare of urban populations? And science can meet and answer
every one of these problems.

Howard's plans for a new urban environment are based on the environmental determinism reflected in this quotation.

In the next section we discuss how Howard's ideas were put into practice, but now it is sufficient simply to note that his ideas for new towns flowed from the same theoretical streams that produced the classic works of Tönnies, Marx, and Wirth. And to the degree that we will uncover examples of Howard's influence on later attempts to plan new communities, we can see these classic traditions being the ideological basis for modern planned communities as well.

Early Attempts at Planning Communities

Since this book focuses on North American communities, attempts to plan communities in Europe (Herman 1971; Michelson 1977b), South America (Epstein 1974), and Asia (Payne 1977) are not detailed here. Because of the strong influence of Ebenezer Howard's ideas on community planning in North America, however, we must examine his "New Towns" movement.

New Towns in England

As we found in the preceding section, Ebenezer Howard's new towns were a reaction to the growing *gesellschaft*-like atmosphere of industrializing England. In response to the abject poverty, high disease rate, pervasive crime, and near uninhabitability of many dwellings in London, Howard began to plan new towns incorporating elements of rural, natural *gemeinschaft* within the city itself.

A new town with "green belts."   To maintain a rural atmosphere within an urban environment, Howard planned for gardens, parks, and especially for "green belts" of forest land as integral parts of each new city. A major proponent of Howard's new towns, Frederick Osborn (1969, 28) describes the towns as

> a balanced mixture of all social groups and levels of income. Areas are worked out for the zones; public buildings and places of entertainment are placed centrally, shops intermediately, factories on the edge with the railway and sidings. Houses are of different sizes, but all have gardens and all are within easy range of factories, shops, schools, cultural centers, and the open country. Of special interest is the central park and the inner Green Belt or Ring Park, 420 feet wide, containing the main schools with large playgrounds and such buildings as churches.

Not only did Howard conceive of inner green belts that separated various parts of the city, but each city also was to have an encircling outer green belt of forests or open land that was owned by the town and could never be developed. The purpose of the outer belt was to limit the growth of the city. These green belts have become the most enduring aspect of Howard's plans. Today, virtually every planned city in Europe and North America includes such belts.[3]

Letchworth and Welwyn.   Howard's plans were realized in 1902 when, with the financial aid of the Garden City Association, his first city was built at Letchworth, about thirty miles north of London (Osborn 1969). It was not planned to be merely a suburb of London, but rather a self-contained, self-sufficient city of thirty thousand residents living in a blissful, largely *gemeinschaft*-like environment. Unfortunately, it never reached the state Howard and his supporters had envisioned. Financial problems, a lack of industry, and lower-than-desired population growth hindered the new town. In spite of these problems, however, a second city was begun in 1920, Welwyn Garden City; and while it encountered similar problems, Welwyn was more successful (Palen 2008). Although Letchworth and Welwyn were the pioneering attempts, the real impetus for implementing Howard's ideas came with destruction of much of London during World War II. The New Towns Act of 1946 provided government sponsorship of self-sufficient new towns beyond a green belt that was to encircle London and thereby curtail its future growth. The "new towns" part of the Act proved easier to implement than a green

---

Figure 9-1   Howard's Plans for a Garden City
The "Grand Avenue" in these plans is an inner green belt while the "Large Farms" comprise the outer green belts. From Howard (1898, 1965, 52–53).

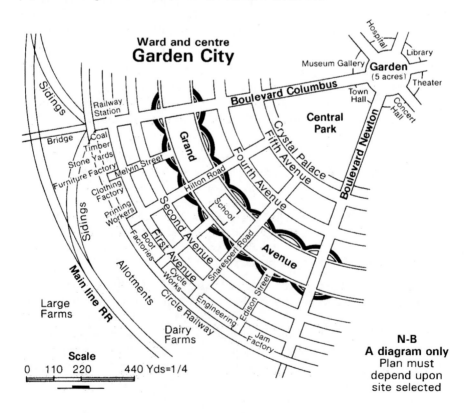

belt around London (just as Howard had predicted), and over thirty new towns were built.

The Mark I and Mark II towns.   The first of these new towns, called Mark I towns, were similar to Howard's plans for Letchworth and Welwyn. The Mark I town of Stevenage, for example, separated housing from industry and pedestrian traffic from autos and trucks, focused social life on the neighborhood, and emphasized single-family housing units. Later communities, Mark II towns, departed considerably from Howard's ideas; they extended population limits to eighty thousand and beyond, dramatically increasing residential density, allowing more private ownership, emphasizing central shopping and recreation facilities rather than the neighborhood, and giving less emphasis to agriculture and green belts.

Although the Mark I and II towns did not follow all of Howard's plans for the ideal industrial community, they represent a large-scale experiment in community planning that can be evaluated even if it is not a true test of Howard's ideas. How successful are these new towns? That is, do they meet either Howard's original goal of restoring the satisfaction of *gemeinschaft* or the government's desire to relieve urban congestion and provide new housing? The general answer, on both counts, is no. Although residents of the new towns appear satisfied with their communities, their attitudes and lifestyles do not differ significantly from those of other Britons (Michelson 1977a). As for relieving London's congestion and providing new housing, the population limits on the new towns limited their impact on London's housing needs. Only 5% of Britain's housing constructed since World War II has been built in the new towns (Palen 2008). Yet, new towns based (however loosely) on Howard's plans were built, they survived, some even flourish, and, most important, they continue to influence community planning, as we shall see in the next section.

Planned Communities in the United States

The idea of new towns came to America almost exclusively as a creation of private enterprise.[4] The lack of government support, planning, and control for new American towns is a unique social phenomenon, almost without precedent anywhere else in the world. As such, it shows how local communities reflect the values of the larger society. Capitalism is more developed in the United States than in other nations; and in the US more than in other nations, new towns were built to produce a profit. In fact, over one hundred new towns have been built in the United States by private developers since 1920, but among the most important attempts at constructing new communities are Radburn, New Jersey; Reston, Virginia; and Columbia, Maryland.

The earliest of these three major planned communities is *Radburn, New Jersey.* Henry Wright and Clarence Stein conceived of Radburn as a new, planned town near New York City. The City Housing Corporation, a limited-profit group in New York, began development of Radburn in the late 1920s. Initially, Wright and Stein followed Howard's ideas closely but added an innovative "super block" design that built houses facing a large public green space. The rear of the houses faced dead-end streets, thereby limiting the vehicular traffic in residential neighborhoods. These superblocks have proved to be very popular. They now can be found in urban development plans from Adelaide, South Australia, to St. Petersburg (Leningrad in the former USSR).

Radburn was clearly an architectural success, and economically it almost survived the Depression, in part because the emphasis on smaller and fewer streets held down construction costs. In fact, *Business Week* complimented Radburn in 1930 on its apparent immunity to the Depression, but in the long run local communities rarely can resist national trends. In 1934, the City Housing Corporation declared bankruptcy.

When the City Housing Corporation lost control of development, it became clear that Radburn could never become an American version of Howard's garden city. It began as a place where middle-class families could raise their children, and it never changed (Stein, 1957). Early attempts by the City Housing Corporation to attract lower-income residents were unsuccessful. The planned green belt was not completed. Industry never moved to Radburn, and the idea of the community owning undeveloped land remained only an idea. Radburn became not a "garden city," but a "garden suburb" within the larger suburb of Fair Lawn. Radburn is a bit greener and better designed than many suburbs but not qualitatively different from other suburban communities in its local norms and values.

Reston, Virginia, was conceived in the 1960s by developer Robert E. Simon. While it is located only twenty-five miles from Washington, DC, in

Figure 9-2   Wright and Stein's Super Block

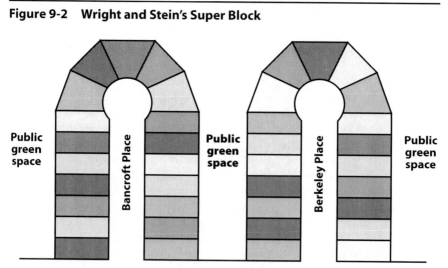

Fairfax County, Virginia (about midway between Washington, DC, and the Dulles Airport), Reston, like Radburn, was designed to have its own industry and thus be more self-sufficient than most suburbs. Simon planned it to have a population of over seventy thousand, living in a decentralized city made up of seven villages separated by the Howard-inspired green belts.

Reston achieved stunning architectural success. With a mixture of various housing types (many designed by famous architects), green belts, office structures, lakes, and industrial sites, it became one of America's most attractive cities. However, it was a financially troubled city almost from the start. Planners assumed that thousands of families would move from Washington, DC, to enjoy the architectural splendor of Reston, even if housing costs were appreciably higher. That was not the case, however, and Gulf Oil, Reston's principal investor, took over the development of the town in 1967 in an attempt to prevent further financial losses. Gulf, then, sold its holdings in Reston to Mobil in 1978.

The two petroleum conglomerates have been successful in bringing economic health to the community. The number of jobs in Reston has surpassed the number of households. It is a largely "white collar" unincorporated community in which modern businesses such as Google and Sallie Mae are especially predominant. Thus, Reston is no longer just a residential suburb for Washington commuters. But some of the architectural quality, while still superior, may have slipped, and Simon's attempt to mix social classes by building middle-class and upper-class housing side by side has been abandoned (Palen 2008). In order to become profitable, Reston became more like other American communities.

Columbia, Maryland, is another planned town built near Washington, DC (midway between Washington and Baltimore), and it, too, hoped to turn a profit while at the same time providing a superior community environment. James Rouse, the developer of Columbia, aimed "to create a social and physical environment which works for people, nourishes human growth, and allows private venture capital to make a profit in land development" (Bailey 1973, 16). Yet Columbia differed from Reston in one major way. While Reston reflected the plans of innovative architects, Columbia reflected the plans of innovative social scientists. While Reston tried to make an architectural statement, Columbia strove to make a sociological one. Columbia's founder hoped to demonstrate that he could provide "a richer sense of community among people if the physical place and the community institutions were all seen as opportunities to support and enable the growth of people" (Rouse 1978, 51). Rouse employed a large group of social scientists as regular consultants in the design of Columbia. While he admits that the social planners "did not produce any brilliant new concepts or sociological breakthroughs" (1978, 53), he does maintain that they developed a plan that "focused on producing a sense of community at various levels from the cul-de-sac or block to the neighborhood, to the village and to the city as a whole." Columbia is more in the tradition of Howard's garden cities in its planning, goals, and development than is Reston.[5]

Rouse planned for Columbia to have a metropolitan population of over 250,000, and yet since its initial development in 1963, it grew to less than 100,000. Like Reston and Radburn before it, Howard's green belt concept is clearly evident in Columbia. Rouse's design attempts to give Columbia more characteristics of *gemeinschaft*, i.e., more decentralization, more focus on neighborhoods, more economic and racial harmony and integration, and less use of the automobile. In some areas Rouse's design has been successful. Subsidized housing is scattered throughout Columbia rather than clustering in one area, neighborhoods have become the basis for a "town hall" type of government, and educational and medical facilities are convenient and of high quality. Still, Columbia has, over time, come to resemble most other American suburbs. Nonetheless, it has been called "the most successful American new town" (Spates and Macionis 1982, 468), and it probably was, at least until the scores of urban communities based on New Urbanism began to appear.

However, one reason that Columbia has been regarded as such a success is because goals for new towns are so much more circumscribed than they were in Howard's day. Howard's plans called for nothing less than a truly new town—new in its architectural design and, most importantly, new in its quality of life, with substantial increases in *gemeinschaft*-like relationships. In these two areas, Columbia has fallen short. Columbia is architecturally attractive, but its design is less harmonious and less innovative than Reston's. The quality of life is perceived by its residents as high, but not much higher than in many other communities (Burby and Weiss 1975). The automobile is still dominant, racial and class antagonisms remain (Palen 1981), and the feeling of *gemeinschaft*-like community is probably no stronger in Columbia than elsewhere (Brooks 1974). In other words, Columbia, like Reston and Radburn, is a fairly typical American edge-city suburb. Columbia is more attractive and better planned than most suburbs—and that is no small achievement—but the similarities of Columbia to other unplanned American suburbs still outweigh the differences. And as we shall discover in the following section, the limited successes achieved by Reston and Columbia are very much like the limited successes from the extremely popular, architecturally-driven experiment in planned communities, New Urbanism.

New Urbanism

The principles of New Urbanism are similar to the principles that produced the planned communities in the preceding section, and Reston and Columbia are sometimes counted as examples of New Urbanism. So, what is different about this approach? Perhaps the best way to view New Urbanism is as a social movement well on its way to institutionalization. The Congress for New Urbanism, founded in 1993 by prominent architects, currently has over three thousand members spread over twenty nations. The Congress articulates design principles, holds well-attended and well-financed annual meetings, grants awards, issues press releases, and participates in all the other activities associated with maintaining a social movement and transforming it into a structured, predictable institution. Its designs have influenced billions of dollars in government-subsidized housing and captured the imagination of the American public, making a huge impact on urban planning movements. Scores of new towns and central city revitalization projects now pledge allegiance to the principles of New Urbanism. These principles borrow from the greenbelt and garden city approaches discussed above and add several assumptions about the desirability of heterogeneous populations and mixed land use from Jane Jacobs's classic *The Death and Life of Great American Cities* (1961).[6] Jacobs argued against urban renewal and defended the urban neighborhoods that planners saw as deteriorated and chaotic. She claimed that the neighborhoods appearing to be chaotic, unsafe, and dilapidated were actually complex, vibrant, avant-garde communities. When urban renewal replaced the dense, redundant, and heterogeneous neighborhoods (e.g., many substandard restaurants or multiple corner groceries, each with high prices and limited selections) with spacious, modern, rational developments, it destroyed community.

So, what are the design principles of this mix of Jan Jacobs and Ebenezer Howard? New Urbanism is a bit fuzzy at the margins,[7] but in general New Urbanist developments are:

- *walkable*, with schools, stores, churches, and businesses within a five-minute sidewalk assisted walk;
- *unfriendly to cars*, with narrow streets, parallel parking (not lots), and garages accessible only through a back alley;
- favorable toward houses with small yards that have *front porches and windows* facing the wide sidewalks and narrow streets; and
- built with *lots of public space*—small parks, walking trails, and town squares.

We can see how these designs play out by looking at two examples of new communities built to New Urbanism standards.

Seaside and Celebration

Arguably, the first and still most famous New Urban development is Seaside, Florida, a planned Gulf Coast community on the Florida panhandle, about halfway between Pensacola and Panama City. Built in the early 1980s according to the designs of New Urbanist architects Duany and Plater-Zyberk, the pastel-painted houses include large front porches, small front yards, broad sidewalks, brick roads (that look quaint but also slow down traffic), and abundant walking paths. While these features were designed to promote community, they also resulted in densities greater than in conventional suburbs, allowing more residents, more structures, and more profit for a relatively small eighty-acre development. Still, it was the architectural quality rather than the ability to turn a profit that drew media acclaim to Seaside. In 1990, *Time* magazine gushed that "Seaside could be the most astounding design achievement of its era and, one might hope, the most influential." In 1998, the movie *The Truman Show* extensively employed Seaside as the utopian and artificial community for Truman's existence and imprisonment. Some critics of Seaside have claimed that the community is too much like the one portrayed in the movie—too perfect, too artificial, too homogeneous. Others have argued that it is too little like *The Truman Show*, with untended lawns, homes left vacant by part-time residents, walking paths too narrow for pedestrians, and cars parked on what should be sidewalks.[8]

Seaside was followed by a score of New Urbanist developments, including the Disney community of Celebration, Florida. Built by the Disney Corporation in the 1990s, Celebration is actually closer to Walt Disney's dream of an Experimental Prototype Community of Tomorrow than the more amusement park-like EPCOT. The unincorporated community is adjacent to Walt Disney World parks and resorts, allowing Celebration residents to drive to WDW without having to use any busy thoroughfares.

Celebration has been well received in the New Urbanist community with its more eclectic (in comparison to Seaside) architectural designs, winning the "New Community of the Year" award in 2001 from the Urban Land Institute. The launch of Celebration was remarkable, as would-be residents lined up for a 1 in 10 chance to buy a home in a price range close to one million dollars. However, the community has come under criticism for its attempt to closely regulate the lifestyles of its residents, with no more than

Celebration homes are characterized by picket fences, large front porches, wide sidewalks, and small front lawns (but, apparently, huge lawn mowers). Source: Preston Mack/Getty Images.

Note Seaside's requisite narrow streets, wide sidewalks, and front porches, all common to New Urbanism. Note also the absence of people in the photo, a common trait in New Urbanist photos due to the emphasis on architecture. Copyright © Steven Brooke Studios.

two people allowed to sleep in one bedroom, all curtains required to be white, and lawns that must be mowed regularly. At one time, Disney had the right to monitor phone calls and Internet activity for residents who signed up for their free communications services (Frantz and Collins 1999).

As the photos of Seaside and Celebration show, the developments produced by the New Urbanist architects are strikingly attractive and resemble a denser version of Reston and Columbia, with a lot more porches. Most New Urbanist developments are suburbs, like Reston and Columbia. However, a few new urban projects borrow more from the ideas of Jacobs than Howard and seek to reenergize central city neighborhoods rather than building new suburbs. Planned neighborhoods such as Atlantic Station in Atlanta, Crossroad in Kansas City, Mockingbird Station in Dallas, and Battery Park in Manhattan are often included as downtown examples of New Urbanism. However, one is much more likely to find Starbucks coffee shops and IKEA-furnished lofts than the eclectic, avant-garde businesses and residences of Greenwich Village so loved by Jane Jacobs (Harvey 2008, Zukin 2009).

Perhaps the New Urbanist developments closest to Jacobs's ideas are the HOPE IV projects, a $6 billion effort by HUD to revitalize and replace failed public housing projects with new facilities based on the principles of New Urbanism (Smith 2002).[9] However, these projects have been criticized in ways similar to urban renewal in that they forcibly relocated poor residents, reduced the number of public housing units (Marcuse 2000), and were dramatically scaled back under President George W. Bush. HOPE IV was granted only a bit of reprieve under the New Choice Neighborhoods Initiative of President Obama, and its future is not promising.

Still, the bottom-line question for New Urbanism is similar to that asked for Reston and Columbia. The primary benefit of New Urban communities is a higher quality of life with the possibility of getting to know your neighbors, forming meaningful relationships within the neighborhood, and most importantly, gaining a sense of place in the community. Do these planned communities offer the enhanced quality of life associated with *gemeinschaft*? The answer is similar to that for Reston and Columbia as well. They are attractive, popular developments that residents enjoy, but they do not build community in the ways proposed by Howard or Jacobs (Talen 1999; Tu and Eppli 1999; Popkin et al. 2004). It seems safe to conclude that architecture's ability to move us back from Wellman's liberated community to a more place-based traditional community is severely limited. Design can make community more attainable, but other social, economic, and technological factors typically matter more.

So, if the effects are minimal, what is the big deal about New Urbanism? Why is it so popular? We find most of the support coming from four categories of boosters, each with a unique reason for promoting New Urbanism:

1. Architects, who gain influence over developers by arguing for the primacy of design over profits;

2. Developers, who can enhance demand by selling the perception of a new and improved quality of life and reduce costs by denser land use;

3. Urban politicians, who see a way to spur reinvestment in decaying central cities; and

4. Environmentalists, who embrace New Urbanism for its potential to stem suburban sprawl.

That each of these four interest groups have different definitions of and goals for New Urbanism does not matter. All support the movement.

Evaluating Planned Communities

How successful, in financial, architectural, and social terms, were these attempts to plan and build new communities? The majority opinion is that they were only partial successes on all three counts. Before the broad acceptance of New Urbanism, financial difficulties always dogged the new towns. In America especially, with new towns almost wholly dependent on venture capital, the inability to turn a profit has been a major obstacle. Accordingly, the profit motive has led to architectural problems. Columbia, for example, has increased its profitability by allowing various developers more freedom in design. John Palen (1981, 325) observed that "architecturally it [Columbia] is less successful; it resembles an ideal supersuburb, largely because the builders of the various sections were given a relatively free hand and built a mixture of their best-selling models." New Urbanist developments are the notable exception here—with a profitable architectural style outside the mainstream as the hallmark of their approval. And given the relatively small influence environment has on community, it should not be surprising that new towns have failed to innovate socially. Residents of American new towns live about the same way and have about the same perceived quality of life as residents in less-planned suburbs (Burby and Weiss 1975; Palen 2008).

Lessons from Attempts at Community Planning

So, what can be learned from these attempts to plan new towns? One lesson concerns the logical contradictions of differences in scale. New towns are scaled to be small, and the concentrations of urban populations are much larger. *If new towns are planned to be limited in their population size, then their effect on urban overcrowding must be limited.* If we believe our cities have several million too many residents (a belief that led to the Mark I and II towns), then a new town of 50,000 or even 500,000 won't make much difference. Taking into consideration that most new towns grow at well below their anticipated rates, it is easy to see how critics like William Alonso (1970) can argue that new towns will have little effect on urban concentrations.

The disappointing growth rates of many new towns brings us to a second lesson—*the necessity of bringing people and jobs together at the same time.* Obviously, new towns have had a hard time providing jobs for their residents, but even if the jobs can be generated, the timing of industrial and residential growth is crucial. John Bardo and John Hartman (1982) point out that when industry was built before housing in Comotara, Kansas, workers settled in places outside the planned community of Comotara. On the other hand, developers in Flower Mound, near Dallas–Fort Worth, built homes before industry and businesses, and Flower Mound became an almost exclusively residential suburb. Moreover, New Urbanist communities like Seaside become communities of second-home vacationers or residential neighborhoods like Celebration.

Another lesson concerns what Roland Warren called the vertical patterns of community (in chapter 4 of this text). For a town to be truly new and different, the social institutions must be new and different. Yet states have strict policies concerning the parameters of local education, government, taxation, and health care. Even local businesses and churches are usually accountable to a larger entity outside the community. *The ability of new towns to experiment, to differ from other towns, is severely limited by their vertical connections.*

The necessity for new towns (in America, anyway) to turn a relatively quick profit is a continuing problem. Community characteristics that enhance private profit are not always the same as characteristics that enhance the public good. An example of this problem is the now-defunct federal program to encourage building new communities with a "proper balance of housing" (the 1968 New Communities Act) by race and income. Thirteen new communities were guaranteed loans, and all but one, The Woodlands (near Houston), defaulted. The failure to turn a profit often was attributed to the required housing mixture. One reason for The Woodlands' success may have been its continued resistance to HUD demands for more subsidized housing. Today, The Woodlands remains more affluent than the Houston metropolitan area. The Woodlands is still typically included on lists of successful New Urbanist communities. Mixed housing may be in the public good, but it may not be profitable.

In sum, new towns are typically small in size and close to a central city for one reason: to increase the chances of short-term profitability. *Planned communities end up looking very much like their unplanned counterparts because both must seek profits.*

The lessons drawn from new towns all seem negative. Together, they tell us that planned communities are hard to build, are too small to do much good, and end up looking much like unplanned communities. Practically, new planned towns don't make much sense. And yet, we do not know what is practical until we try the impractical. In other words, the fact that new towns did not deliver the quality of life Howard and others had hoped for does not allow us to dismiss them as simply impractical, utopian dreams that hold no relevance for the "real" world. Even utopian dreams have a purpose; to paraphrase Goethe, we can attempt the possible only because we have postulated the impossible. Howard postulated the impossible: to create a community sub-

The Woodlands, north of Houston, is among the most successful planned communities in terms of financial strength and population growth. Courtesy of The Woodlands Convention & Visitors Bureau.

stantially different, substantially superior to the society in which it exists. We can now build the possible: modern, attractive, suburban cities like Columbia, Reston, and The Woodlands, and residential communities harmonizing with the local environment like Seaside and Celebration. The impossible dreams of Ebenezer Howard's garden cities led to the practical possibilities of today's New Urbanism.

NOTES

[1] Several major cities existing prior to industrialization reflect attempts at planning: Mohenjo-Daro in the Indus River Valley (2500 BC); Teotihuacan, the forerunner of modern Mexico City (AD 700); Peking, during the Ming Dynasty (AD 1400); Hellenic Athens (480 BC); and Imperial Rome (AD 100). However, planning as an attempt to reverse the growing dominance of *gesellschaft*-like relationships can be attributed to the pioneering works of Ebenezer Howard.

[2] For example, see Engels's descriptions of London quoted in chapter 5 of this text.

[3] The inner green belts are more common than the outer belts, since the outer belts are designed to limit growth. Few communities, even planned ones, want to limit growth.

[4] There were three early unsuccessful exceptions. During the Depression, three green-belt towns were built by the government: Greenbelt, Maryland; Green Hills, Ohio; and Greendale, Wisconsin. In 1949 government support was ended for these towns, and the Howard-inspired green belts that surrounded them were opened to private development. As we will see later in this chapter, the HOPE IV communities represented more recent federal experiments in New Urbanism.

[5] To the degree that the two communities were competitive, it was suggested that one might want to live in Reston out of a sense of "duty," but one would want to live in Columbia because it was "fun" (Michelson 1977b).

[6] As we shall see, however, many New Urbanist developments result in typically homogeneous populations living in new houses, with substantial levels of social conformity.

[7] See, for example, the debate on which communities qualify for true New Urbanist developments (Egan 2002). See Bressi 2002 (2008) for a more detailed list and discussion of the guiding principles.

[8] See Bressi (2002) for a thorough review and response to the various criticisms of Seaside particularly and of New Urbanism generally.

[9] Although HUD was a signatory to the Charter for New Urbanism in 1994, and while New Urbanists typically claim HOPE IV as one of its major accomplishments, HOPE IV was based as much on the design principles of "defensible space" (Newman 1996) as New Urbanism. The "defensible space" approach, with emphasis on fewer common areas and more private space, runs counter to the principles of New Urbanism.

STUDYING THE COMMUNITY

Thus far, we have looked at how to define a community, how to make sense of it theoretically, and how to make communities better places to live. Our treatments of these important topics have been rather broad, with only the most important issues being considered in each chapter. In this section, however, the focus narrows. The goal of this text is more than to encourage an appreciation of the community; it is hoped that the research skills presented in this section encourage an active participation in studying the community as well. And since participation typically requires more detailed information than appreciation, Section III requires more specifics than abstracts.

These last chapters present both research skills and, when applicable, research findings. Most of the focus of chapter 10 (Community Indicators) is on securing and interpreting indicators of the quality of community life. There is only brief mention of research findings concerning which communities offer the highest quality of life. The ratio of skills to findings is even more extreme with respect to community surveys (chapter 11). Here we find a vast body of research techniques but virtually nothing in the way of accumulated knowledge about the community. A more even balance develops in the next two chapters on community power. Chapter 12 reviews the knowledge gained from our studies of local power distributions, and chapter 13 presents a step-by-step guide to measuring community power. The ratio of skills to findings shifts even further in chapter 14 (Field Research: Holistic Studies and Methods), where we see the most significant research findings in all of community sociology. Methodologically, however, we find in these holistic studies a conglomerate of techniques—including all the methods covered in the previous chapters in this section—as well as decidedly individualistic field methods. It is not easy to say exactly how one does a holistic study, but it is easy to see the enduring contribution of their findings.

If Section I sharpened our view of the community and Section II showed us how people have tried to improve the community, then these methods of community study should enable us to do the research that helps raise the quality of community life. But exactly what will the good community be like? Since there are no easy answers to that question, the final chapter considers possible answers in detail. In fact, we have encountered nothing but difficult questions in this text: What is a community? How should it be studied? How can communities be improved? Difficult questions, however, are usually the most important ones, and such questions are what make the study of community both difficult and important.

Community Indicators

The chapters in the preceding section are concerned with the quality of community life. In this section, while the chapters focus more on various community research methodologies, the quality of life remains a concern. Beyond the academic worth of knowledge gained from community research, very pragmatic goals for all the methodologies in this section include analyzing and improving the local quality of life. Indeed, concern with a community's quality of life was the very *raison d'être* for developing the community indicators discussed in this chapter. Community indicators exist largely to indicate the local quality of life.

The Origins and Types of Community Indicators

The concept of *community indicators* is not used as widely as the concepts from which it evolved: economic indicators and social indicators. Generally, anything that indicates the quality of local life can be a community indicator. More specifically, community indicators are typically divided into two types: *objective indicators* that measure actual events such as local crime rates, and *subjective indicators* that measure attitudes about events, such as community surveys on the fear of crime.

Most community indicators have evolved from objective types of measures. Economic indicators, which produced social indicators, which in turn produced community indicators, include objective measures like the gross domestic product, retail sales, earnings reports, inflation rates, and so on. By the 1960s, these objective economic indicators were being combined into econometric models that advised businesses or governments to pursue certain policies, such as cutting taxes that in turn would "reflate" the economy, as measured by the employment rate and gross domestic product. While the predictive success of these econometric models is debatable, their acceptance is not. Thus, the rise of what Otis Duncan (1969) called the "social indicators movement" was an attempt to develop a set of social indicators that might guide public policy in the same way that economic indicators are used currently.[1]

Social indicators also tended to be objective measures, though not as exclusively objective as economic indicators. For example, the US Department of Commerce *Social Indicators* (1973, 1976, 1980) were mammoth compendiums of objective statistics such as unemployment rates, crime rates, divorce rates, health-care expenditures, disability and morbidity data, education levels, household size, and poverty rates, Subjective measures of opinion and perception were virtually nonexistent in the 1973 edition of *Social Indicators*, but there is an acknowledgment (xiii) that they probably should be included if they were "available" and "consistent":

> *Social Indicators* 1973 is restricted almost entirely to data about objective conditions. In only a few instances has information on people's attitudes toward or satisfaction with the conditions of their lives been included. Subjective information has been omitted in large part because it is rarely available on a consistent basis over time. As more attitudinal data become available, however, they will be considered for inclusion in subsequent issues.

And, as promised, the 1976 edition included the results of a few public opinion surveys, but they are a minority of the data, and the 1976 introduction included a lengthy introduction on the "quality" problems with survey data: sampling error, questionnaire design, falsified answers, coding errors, and inaccurate data processing. Still, there was movement toward including opinion survey data. The 1980 volume began each chapter with a survey section entitled "Public Perceptions," suggesting growing acceptance of subjective data. However, the trend toward greater acceptance of subjective data as well as of social indicators themselves was slowed when the social indicators series was discontinued by the Reagan administration. So, the social indicators movement has continued in fits and starts, with growing emphasis on survey-derived subjective measures[2] and health-related objective measures (Sheldon, Cummins, and Kamble 2010).

Community indicators are the logical extension of social indicators. If national statistics can describe the quality of life nationally, then community statistics can be used to describe the quality of life locally (Epley and Menon 2008). As a further extension, just as social indicators are more likely to include subjective measures than are economic indicators, community indicators are even more likely to include attitude surveys than are social indicators.

The reasons for a greater reliance on surveys in assessing the community rather than the national quality of life are pragmatic. Local surveys are easier to do than national surveys, and, conversely, more objective data are available nationally than locally. In fact, some early approaches to community indicators suggested that they would be exclusively surveys (e.g., Rossi 1972), but it is certainly possible and probably desirable to include both objective and subjective indicators in assessing the local quality of life.[3]

There are advantages and disadvantages associated with both subjective and objective local indicators. Surveys have the advantage of directly measuring the state of the community as seen through the eyes of those who live there. And to the degree that the quality of life is a subjective perception of conditions more than the actual state of local conditions, surveys will provide a more accurate assessment of the quality of life. For example, if everyone in the community is afraid to walk the streets at night because of the perceived danger of crime, it may make little difference what the actual crime rate is. It is the *perception* of the magnitude of the crime problem that determines whether we venture out at night.[4]

Although surveys are the most direct measures of local perceptions, they often vary in design and implementation. Thus, they are seldom comparable from one time or community to another since questions and sampling designs differ. We look at proper techniques of survey design in the next chapter, but for now the point is that while surveys are very valuable as local indicators, they also have comparability problems. Comparability, however, is the strong point of more objective indicators.

Objective indicators are usually comparable from one time and community to another because of the impetus from community's vertical ties. The state and national governments require local reports to be comparable with previous reports and with reports filed from other communities. Local businesses, schools, churches, and charities are usually affiliated with extralocal organizations that require comparable standardized reporting. Thus, there are hundreds of measures in each community that are comparable to similar measures in other communities.

Beyond comparability, these objective indicators have other advantages. They are objective (i.e., they report actual conditions rather than perceptions of the conditions). They are unobtrusive (i.e., it's not necessary to "bother" hundreds of people by asking them survey questions). And they are readily available (i.e., it takes relatively little time or money to gather these data). Libraries and websites are full of them.

Objective local indicators are not without their problems, however. One of the difficulties stems from their widespread availability. When hundreds of indicators are available, which ones should be used? And if several are selected, how should they be weighted? For example, if we are assessing the quality of local education, should we include student attendance rates, library size, Internet access, standardized achievement tests, student–teacher ratios, educational expenditures, teacher experience, or teacher education? And if the answer is that all of these indicators should be included in an assessment of local education, then how are they to be combined? Which ones are more important indicators of educational quality than others?

Another problem with using objective indicators is that they are necessarily *indirect* indicators. In the above example, none of the indicators directly and completely measures the quality of local education. Rather, they are a series of proxies—surrogate measures for broader, inherently multidimensional, perhaps unmeasurable concepts. From these indicators, we can infer the level of educational quality, but it is not an inference that is made easily.

So, objective indicators, just like their subjective counterparts, possess attributes and defects. And community research that includes both types of indicators will almost always be superior to research that is restricted to only one. Thus, both objective and subjective indicators are considered in this text: objective measures in this chapter, and subjective measures in the following chapter on community surveys.

The Uses of Community Indicators

Community indicators can be used in three ways: (1) to describe local conditions, (2) to evaluate local conditions, and (3) to prescribe changes for local conditions. A single local statistic can be used as an indicator in any of these three ways. As we shall see, its use depends on the assumptions we are willing to make regarding the community indicator.

Descriptive Indicators

The simplest, most direct use of local data is to describe the local quality of life. We could simply ask a random sample of local residents how they feel about their community. We might ask a special group of local elites to assess the community. Census data can be used to provide local crime and poverty levels. Better yet, all these data can be combined to describe the overall quality of community life.

Yet description, while a necessary step to improving the quality of community life, seldom is sufficient by itself. Suppose we learn that 20% of the community believe it is an excellent place to live; all of the local elites believe more growth is needed; there were 18 murders and 180 stolen bicycles last year; and 10% of the local residents live in poverty. These are important data, and they tell us much about the community. Their interpretation, however, is difficult. How is the community to be evaluated with these data? Should we be pleased that 20% think the community is excellent, or is that percentage shockingly low? Do the elite interviews tell us that more growth truly is needed in the community, or do local elites always want more growth? Do we need to crack down on murders, or on bicycle thieves? Does the community have an alarming poverty problem, or should we rejoice in the 90% who live above the poverty level? Descriptive data, by themselves, cannot answer evaluative questions like the examples above. Evaluative questions require evaluative indicators.

Evaluative Indicators

The missing ingredient that allows descriptive indicators like those in the previous section to become evaluative indicators is a comparative benchmark. Descriptive indicators allow evaluation when they can be compared to other data. If we know that last year only 10% of the local residents felt the community was an excellent place to live, then the more recent 20% figure should please us. Further, if we know that almost all community elite surveys report a desire for growth, that the local murder rate is twice the state's per capita rate while the bicycle theft rate is three times the state average, and that the poverty level is only half the national level, then we can begin to evaluate the local quality of life. In these cases we have benchmarks that allow comparisons with other times, other communities, the state, and the nation.

In these instances, we know where the community is doing well and where it is not; and when such evaluations are determined, the next question is usually *why?* Why do people feel better about our community than they did last year? How can we get the "excellent" percentage even higher? Why are there so many murders and thefts? What can be done to increase the safety of people and bicycles? Is community poverty low because of the strong industries, the strong unions, or the strong impact of United Way? These are questions of cause and effect. Hence, these are also questions about community change, since understanding why local conditions are the way they are should also allow an understanding of how local conditions can be changed.

Indicators for Causal Modeling and Community Change

The supreme use of local indicators is to: (1) explain why the quality of life is at its current level, and (2) prescribe changes in community structure that will improve the local quality of life. If we knew that for every police officer placed on patrol, ten fewer bicycles are stolen and one less murder is committed, then all it would take to make the community safe for people and their bicycles would be putting eighteen more law officers on the streets.[5] This is the way in which one of the progenitors of local indicators—economic indicators—is used. At first, such elaborate models were enthusiastically envisioned for social indicators as well (e.g., Gross 1966; Bell 1969), but it soon became clear that the quality of measurement, the nature of multiple causation, and the controversy of politics combine to move policy making beyond our current capacity (Noll 2004). Still, the effort to construct causal local models continues.

The time may come when mathematical models of social change achieve a precision and acceptance that allows concrete advice about improving the quality of life. Now, however, the thrust of most social indicators remains evaluative (Strine et al. 2007), focusing more on simply comparing social conditions over time and place rather than accounting for changes in those conditions. And the same is true for local indicators. Most attempts to develop and employ local indicators have been pointed toward evaluative goals.

We aim for evaluation, then, because it requires considerably less understanding of local indicators than is required for causal modeling. Still, evaluation is far from easy. It is sometimes difficult to create or locate local indicators. When the indicators are available, it is difficult to choose the best ones. Finally, it is often difficult to compare the indicators across time or communities. Yet comparisons are almost always necessary for the evaluation of the local quality of life. So, in the following sections, we consider techniques for: (1) creating and locating local indicators, (2) choosing the best local indicators, and (3) comparing the indicators for the purposes of evaluation.

Securing Local Indicators

There are two ways to secure the local indicators necessary to evaluate the quality of community life. The most direct way is creating the indicators from scratch, usually with community surveys. The local polling techniques required for community surveys are the subject of the next chapter. Here, however, we consider a more indirect, more unobtrusive way of securing local indicators—using available statistics.

Literally thousands of statistics are available, with the US Census being the major source, and the major source of local census data is the American Community Surveys. These annual surveys of communities of 65,000 or more are available online and have gained wide acceptance due to their relatively large samples and regular annual reports. Communities and neighborhoods smaller than 65,000 can be studied every three to five years, as survey responses accumulate. Also available online, but less well known and perhaps even more valuable, is the *County and City Data Book* (CCDB). Published by the US Bureau of Census, it includes data from the censuses of population, manufactures, governments, wholesale trade, retail trade, service industries, agriculture, other government data from sources such as the Bureau of Labor Statistics, and nongovernment sources such as Moody's Investors Service and the American Hospital Association. These data are combined and presented by nation, region, state, county, city, and place. Thus, one can easily compare a multitude of local data with other communities, the state, or the nation.

Multitude is not much of a hyperbole. There are over two hundred county variables and almost as many at the city level—everything from the proportion of female-headed households to the number of dentists, to the value of residential building permits. And if the CCDB does not provide enough information, the sources that contribute to the book can provide even more. In short, while the CCDB provides an extremely wide range of local information, it still accounts for only a minority of the total data available at the community level, and it is used typically as only a first step in securing local indicators.

Which Indicates What: Choosing the Correct Indicators

Given that hundreds of measures exist for each American community, *finding* local indicators is often easier than *selecting* the most relevant local indicators. So, as a guide, it may be useful to look at some of the indicators' most common uses.

We can distinguish generally between two uses of community indicators: (1) *intra*community comparisons and (2) *inter*community comparisons. The intracommunity studies between neighborhoods were once more common

(Flax 1978), but now, comparing many communities across the country is predominant. The methodology for both types is similar. Both types, for example, rely heavily on census data. So, whether the unit of analysis is the block group, zip code, or tract (for intracommunity comparisons) or cities, urbanized areas, counties, or MSAs (for intercommunity comparisons), the measures are often the same. This means that although the examples that follow are intercommunity comparisons, they can be used as guides for assessing the quality of life between neighborhoods as readily as between cities.

Dividing the Indicators into Groups

Since quality of life is such a broad concept, community indicators are typically grouped into various categories or dimensions of life quality.

An early and influential study by Ben-Chieh Liu (1976) grouped 120 quality of life indicators into five "components": economic, political, environmental, health and education, and social components. Liu weighted each indicator and combined them to give all American metropolitan areas a comparative quality-of-life score on each of the five components. Then, by combining the component scores, the overall quality of life was assessed. So where was the best place to live in America? According to Liu's data, Portland, Oregon, was the very best large metropolitan area. For smaller places, another Oregon community, Eugene, ranked first. These variations in scores reflect a regional pattern throughout Liu's data with the highest overall quality-of-life levels in the West and the lowest in the South.

Other researchers have produced widely different rankings, many of which have become exceptionally newsworthy, though less academic. For example, Boyer and Savageau's *Rand McNally Places Rated Almanac* (1985) identified Pittsburgh as the very best place in which to live and found the very worst to be Yuba City, California.[6] *Money* magazine annually releases a similar list, much to the delight of chambers of commerce in highly rated cities.[7] All of these quality-of-life surveys use similar indicators, but the final rankings differ mostly because different judgments are made about the weights of the various contributors. As an example, a reanalysis of the Rand McNally data showed that 59 cities could be ranked either first or last in quality of life, depending on the weights of the same variables (Becker et al. 1987).

Comparing these various community indicator studies shows considerable overlap in both the general dimensions of life quality and in the specific indicators of those dimensions. Thus, most attempts to estimate the local quality of life should include similar dimensions. Arguably, the best practical example of using multiple indicators to measure basic community quality of life conditions can be found in Jacksonville, Florida (jcci.org). The Jacksonville Community Council uses primarily objective indicators to measure the relative (by time and place) quality of life in Jacksonville over nine dimensions (education, natural environment, social wellbeing, economy, arts and recreation, health, transportation, safety, and government responsiveness) and then strives to improve those rankings. The examples in table 10-1 show some of the most important indicators for Jacksonville and how they have changed over time, but many other indicators and comparisons are used as well.

While the indicators in these studies can provide an excellent point of departure, hundreds of other possibilities remain to be explored. For example, suppose it is important to assess the problem of alcohol abuse in the com-

Table 10-1   Community Indicators to Measure Quality of Life

The Quality of Life Progress Report at a Glance

Key Indicators

Indicator (Year)	Data	Trend
Achieving Educational Excellence		
Public high school graduation rate (2008-09)	69.6%	up
Kindergarten Readiness (2008-09)	85.5%	up
Growing a Vibrant Economy		
Total employment (2008)	456,448	down
Unemployment rate (2008)	6.1%	up
Per capita income (2007)	$39,749	up
Preserving the Natural Environment		
Days the Air Quality Index is "good" (2008)	312	up
Average daily water consumption (gallons) (2008)	187	up
Promoting Social Wellbeing and Harmony		
Is racism a local problem? (2009)	55%	*
Births to single mothers (2008)	48.2%	up
Enjoying Arts, Culture, and Recreation		
Public and private arts support per person (2008)	$32.75	down
Public performances and events (2008)	501	down
Sustaining a Healthy Community		
Infant mortality rate per 1,000 (2008)	9.7	up
White (2008)	7.1	up
Black (2008)	13.9	up
People without health insurance (2008)	17%	*
Maintaining Responsive Government		
Voter turnout (2008)	78%	up
Satisfaction with basic city services (2009)	83%	up
Moving Around Efficiently and Safely		
Commute times of 25 minutes or less (2009)	67%	stable
Average weekday JTA bus ridership per 1,000 (2008)	42	up
Keeping the Community Safe		
People feel safe in their neighborhood (2009)	60%	up
Index crimes per 100,000 people (2008)	6,436	up

*Signifies a trend that is not easily classified but bears watching.
Source: Jacksonville Community Council, 2009 Quality of Life Progress Report, Indicator Index, http://jcci.org/jcciwebsite/documents/10%20QOL%20Summary%20Document.pdf

munity. None of the Jacksonville health indicators relate directly to alcohol abuse, but several indicators do exist (e.g., arrest rates for crimes such as driving under the influence of alcohol, public intoxication, and other liquor law violations, and medical records for alcohol-related diseases such as cirrhosis). Searching for such indicators is often difficult and always time consuming, but it is also an intellectually intriguing search that combines library, statistical, and political research skills. The skills of a reference or government documents librarian are an immense aid in determining what is available and how to find it. Statistical skills associated with the particular measure are required to select and interpret the correct indicator.[8] Politically, it often requires authority or influence to obtain the needed data. Not all records are in the public domain, and even those that are legally available may not be practically accessible without the assistance of a willing bureaucrat. So, while there are indicators for almost any local phenomenon imaginable, finding and selecting the best indicators is typically a difficult task.

Interpreting Local Indicators:
The Necessity for Comparisons

Data do not speak themselves, and that is especially true for community indicators. Even when the correct indicators are selected, their interpretation requires comparison with similar indicators from a different time or place. Thus, a necessary step in assessing the quality of life with local indicators is comparing those indicators with similar indicators from another neighborhood (usually a census tract), another community (selected perhaps because it is similar in size, racial composition, economic structure, etc.), or a state or national average.[9]

A general rule is "the more comparisons, the better." If the assessment is directed toward a census tract, compare the indicators with all other tracts in the community, with similar tracts in other communities, with state and national indicators, and with indicators from earlier time periods. For example, if unemployment is 10% in one tract, is that higher or lower than other tracts, than other communities, than the state and national average? Over the last ten years, is unemployment a growing or shrinking problem in this tract? How does it compare with national unemployment data? Are the trends the same?

It is possible, perhaps, that such comparisons are unnecessary if an absolute benchmark exists. If one decides that nothing less than zero unemployment is acceptable, then comparisons are not needed. The single indicator is sufficient. But most of us are willing to settle for levels of unemployment, or crime, or alcohol abuse that are simply lower than those of other communities or lower than last year's, and that requires comparisons. A strength of the Jacksonville quality-of-life measures mentioned earlier is that they allow comparisons with multiple times and places.

Conclusion: Community Indicators and the Quality of Life

In most cases the objective indicators of life quality discussed in this chapter need to be supplemented with subjective indicators. Most of us would not choose to dwell in a particular city based solely on objective rankings from *Money*. We would still want to visit and subjectively/personally experience the city before deciding to move, just as most college students do not rely solely on *U.S. News and World Report* rankings but rather choose to visit and experience several campuses before enrolling. Likewise, the description and evaluation of the local quality of life is often only an intermediate step, with improvement being the final goal. If one finds that a particular community has relatively high levels of poverty, then consideration of increased social services and economic development will likely follow. Thus, while local indicators are closely related to concerns with the quality of life, they are insufficient for a satisfactory analysis without: (1) more subjective indicators based on community perceptions and (2) an understanding of the local political conditions that must be dealt with to improve the quality of life. For example, if we learn that poverty is much worse in our community than in other communities, it is also important to learn if the community is aware of and concerned about the problem and if those in power are willing to address the problem. The next three chapters consider these more subjective aspects of the quality of community life.

NOTES

[1] Interestingly, scientists at NASA were among the early proponents of social indicators, hoping for a better understanding of the social consequences of our space program (Land 1983).

[2] See Campbell, Converse, and Rodgers (1976) for the origins of subjective quality-of-life indicators and Cummins (1996) for a summary of much of the research.

[3] Some analysts still champion exclusive use of objective indicators (Cobb 2000; Veenhoven 2000), but in the United States, with its individualistic culture, subjective assessments are increasingly common (Noll 2004).

[4] Numerous studies (e.g., Chadee, Austen, and Ditton 2007) have shown that fear of crime tends to be higher among those who are less likely to be victims of crime.

[5] For a less hypothetical example of accounting for changes in crime rates and projecting future changes, see Levitt (2004).

[6] For annual updates, see placesrated.expertchoice.com.

[7] See McCann (2004) for a discussion of effects of these rankings generally and of the *Money* rankings specifically.

[8] As examples, *age-specific* cirrhosis data is preferred because a community with a high proportion of elderly will usually have a high cirrhosis rate regardless of the level of local alcohol abuse, since it is a disease that results from continued abuse over a number of years. There is no similar adjustment for variations in legal definitions of alcohol-related crimes, and enforcement often varies more than the definitions.

[9] Comparing the most widely accessible indicators, the kind published by *Money* and many others are used by the "Growth Machine" (chapter 13) as part of an intercommunity competition for growth (Cochrane 1999; McCann 2004), a competition that is resulting in more entrepreneurial growth in cities around the world (Harvey 1989).

chapter eleven

Community Surveys

While the social indicators in the preceding chapter allow objective, indirect community assessment, a more direct approach is simply to ask local residents about their perceptions of the community. For example, rather than relying on test scores, dropout rates, attendance levels, and other "indirect" indicators of the quality of local education, one can "directly" ask teachers, parents, students, and school district residents how good they believe the local schools are. And directly measuring subjective views of school quality can be as important as uncovering more objective indicators. The outcome of a school's bond election will hinge more on the *perception* of local education's quality than on its *actual* quality.[1] This means, then, that community surveys can add important supplements to the information provided by community indicators.

In addition to being more direct and subjective, data from community surveys differ from community indicators in another way. Unlike social indicators, survey data are not as comparable to data from other communities. For example, crime rates, levels of unemployment, and standardized test scores are comparable from one to another and, accordingly, a considerable body of knowledge is built on such comparisons. However, there are no cross-community comparisons of how school quality or fear of crime or expectations of job security are perceived via local surveys. Such comparative data exist only at the national level.

One reason for this lack of comparative community surveys can be attributed to the mass society view of America. When it became methodologically possible to survey a sample representing all of the United States, the use of the community as a sample of American perceptions virtually disappeared. Why study the opinions of Middletowners when with a similarly sized sample one can study the opinions of all Americans?

The position taken throughout this text is that researchers need not always choose between community and society. Rather, surveys should be made of local *and* national perceptions since both are important. Unfortunately, however, the same question is seldom asked in the same way in several communities. Thus, no cumulative body of knowledge concerning cross-community variations in local perceptions exists.[2]

Clearly, the production of cross-community information on local perceptions is a sorely needed addition to our knowledge of American communities. Some promising steps are being made in the direction of greater comparability: More questions asked locally are now being phrased identically to those in national surveys, and attempts are being made to catalogue the various local surveys administered each year (e.g., the American Public Opinion Index). For now, though, the absence of such information means that rather than including a cumulative body of knowledge gleaned from local surveys, this chapter must focus only on the techniques necessary to survey a community—techniques that sometimes differ from those of national surveys.

Designing a Community Survey

A variety of reasons exist for surveying a local population. Pragmatic concerns, such as assessments of community needs (Is there a demand or perceived need for a local service?), determining the local perceptions of community agencies and institutions (e.g., Do residents believe their police protection is adequate?), and estimates of the support for various community plans (e.g., Will the public support a bond issue?), often result in community surveys. Less often, traditionally academic concerns, such as disaster research (Hong and Farley 2008), neighborhood deterioration (Kruger 2008), or community satisfaction (Grogan-Kaylor et al. 2007), result in community surveys. Regardless of the areas of interest, researchers select their methodology from a small set of survey techniques.

Choosing the Technique

There are four general techniques commonly used for community surveys: (1) face-to-face, (2) mail, (3) telephone, and (4) Internet. For many years, the face-to-face interview was the exclusive choice of survey researchers, but more recent improvements in mail, telephone, and Internet methodologies have made all these options viable.

Face-to-face interviews. Although there are several types of face-to-face interviews, the most common type is a relatively structured questionnaire administered by one interviewer in the physical presence of the respondent. Since the interview usually occurs in the respondent's home, face-to-face surveys require a larger investment of time, personnel, and money than the other two techniques. These investments, however, are much less for a community than for a national survey. Still, in spite of the costs, the face-to-face interview remains a common technique. It is probably the most likely to come to the public's mind when surveys or polling is mentioned, and even in many academic circles it remains the preferred technique.

Much of this popularity reflects its traditional preeminence, but another reason face-to-face interviews maintain a favored position among surveyors is that certain questions are especially well suited to face-to-face interviews.

For example, demographic questions such as race or housing quality, which can be verified by the interviewer's observations, are less susceptible to error. And questions requiring the respondents to rank a series of statements typed on cards, to respond to pictures or products, or to consult their records or other family members work well with face-to-face interviews.

Mail interviews.   Mail interviews are sometimes referred to as self-administered surveys since the respondents must go through the questionnaires themselves and, in effect, interview themselves. This is their chief disadvantage since there is no one to explain the questions, probe for additional responses, or ensure that the desired respondent is actually the person completing the questionnaire. Additionally, complicated "skip patterns" do not work well. Hence, this self-administered approach to surveys now probably ranks well behind telephone surveys in popularity. Nevertheless, this approach does have the advantages of allowing respondents to answer at a time of their own choosing, to consult records, or to check with someone else who might assist in answering the questions. For this reason, many surveys of organizations (rather than households) are conducted by mail because organizational surveys typically require complex numerical data that may require the investigation of several people. A self-administered survey allows respondents to gather the information at their convenience and when the survey is done correctly, the response rates can sometimes exceed those of telephone surveys.[3] Many of the advantages and disadvantages of mail surveys are shared with Internet surveys.

Telephone interviews.   In recent years, telephone interviews have become increasingly popular. Naturally, a major advantage is reduced time and cost, but technological changes (e.g., the proliferation of residential phones) and methodological advances (e.g., random-digit dialing) have combined to make telephone surveys as reliable as face-to-face interviews. And cultural changes associated with *gesellschaft,* such as respondent reluctance to admit interviewers into the home and interviewer reluctance to enter certain neighborhoods at certain times, have made the telephone survey an attractive alternative to face-to-face interviews. The quick turnaround makes it attractive in comparison to mail surveys.

Internet surveys.   Technological advances and the increased use and availability of the Internet have ushered in the web survey. Internet or web surveys have decreased costs and allow researchers to survey a much larger sample than other traditional methods. Web surveys also provide the privacy and convenience of a self-administered survey with the feedback timeline of an interviewer-assisted survey. Web surveys have the added benefit of easily being able to include color, graphics, and other visual cues to aid respondents, as well as the potential to correspond in real time with a trained interviewer. Web surveys have some of the setbacks of other traditional self-administered surveys, including the potential for distraction during the survey and the lack of support for respondents who have questions about a specific probe. However, these difficulties are minor compared to the fundamental, and as yet intractable, problem for web surveys—sampling bias. Only two-thirds of Americans have Internet access from home (Pew Internet and American Life Project 2010). Although this number is likely to climb to levels associated with telephone coverage in the future, the level of penetration has currently plateaued (Jones and Fox 2009) and there is no sample frame of local e-mail addresses, nor is one on the horizon. Thus, while Internet surveys may work well for specialized groups with known e-mail addresses (e.g., students at a particular university), for community surveys their use is severely limited.

Comparing the techniques.   No "best" survey technique exists, but some are more appropriate than others. Depending on the research question and the resources of the researcher, one technique will usually be most appropriate. As the comparison in table 11-1 indicates, if funds are limited, face-to-face interviews are probably out of the question; if visual aids are necessary, telephone surveys are inappropriate; and should it be important to probe for additional responses, self-administered questionnaires cannot suffice. And while almost everyone believes that web-based surveys are the wave of the future, the sampling issues remain a major problem. Each technique has strengths and weaknesses, and no technique can be categorically rejected as inferior to another.

Still, telephone polling has proved to be the most *generally* applicable technique for community surveys. It is about as reliable a survey instrument as traditional face-to-face interviews, it can be based on effective sampling techniques that often exceed mail[4] and Internet approaches, and it is consid-

Table 11-1   Comparison of Four Basic Community Survey Techniques*

Area of Comparison	Face-to-Face	Mail	Telephone	Web
Cost	4	2	3	1
"Turnaround-time" from initiation of polling to analysis	3	4	2	1
Response rate	1	3	2	4
Ability to probe	1	4	2	3
Ability to ask complex questions	1	4	2	3
Ability to use visual aids	2	3	4	1
Ability to allow respondent to seek additional data	3	1	4	2
Ability to use long questionnaire	1	4	3	2
Assurance that desired respondent completes questionnaire	1	4	2	3
Ability to monitor interview process	4	2	1	3
Representative sampling frame	2	3	1	4

*Categories are ranked from 1 to 4, with 1 being the best and 4 being the worst.

erably quicker than mail-out surveys and less expensive than face-to-face interviews. Thus, the methodology that follows applies more specifically to telephone surveys than to web, face-to-face, or mail techniques.

Designing the Questionnaire

Unlike the sampling procedure and data analysis techniques associated with survey research, questionnaire design remains more art than science. While there are a number of excellent overviews of questionnaire design (e.g., Schaeffer and Presser 2003), not all of the general principles or hints are based on theory or on systematic replications. The following prescriptions for questionnaire design, then, can and should be modified when circumstances dictate.

The introduction: "setting the hook." Most respondent refusals occur during the introduction phase. But if this phase is successfully completed, there is a very good chance that the entire questionnaire will be completed as well. This applies more to phone surveys than to web surveys, where "survey break offs" are more common (Peytchev 2009). In framing an introduction, it is a good idea to put yourself in the place of the respondent: the unanticipated call, the unknown caller, the anticipated sales pitch, the natural suspicion. The introduction must allay the respondent's fears and skepticism by providing assurances of legitimacy and, most important, the introduction must make the respondent willing to participate in the survey. Otherwise, it makes no difference how well designed the questions are, how carefully the sample respondents are selected, or how sophisticated the data analysis is.

Surveyors disagree as to how much information should be included in the introduction, but it should always include: (1) the full name of the interviewer, (2) the research organization and/or its sponsor, (3) the general topics of the survey, (4) the selection procedure, (5) a screening technique, and (6) an assurance of confidentiality. It might also include: (1) the approximate length of the interview, (2) an opportunity to ask questions, and (3) an opportunity to refuse to participate.[5] In most cases this additional information is not needed in the introduction. Naturally, the interviewer needs to be prepared to answer inquiries such as "How long will this take?" or "Why did you pick me?" However, it is not necessary to provide such information if it is not requested. Box 11-1 illustrates an introduction that includes only the required information. It is the type of introduction most successful in increasing the response rate while still producing a sample with minimal demographic bias.

Box 11-1   A Brief Introduction to a Community Telephone Survey

Hello. My name is (*interviewer's full name*). I'm conducting a survey for the Baylor Center for Community Research. This phone number was selected by a computer, and I would like to get your opinions on some important local issues. Of course, your opinions will be kept confidential. In fact, I don't know your name or address. So, first of all, are you eighteen years of age or older?

Borrowing questions: It's better and easier.   After the introduction comes the reason for the survey—asking questions. Whenever possible, don't write your own; use the same questions asked in other surveys. Borrowed questions have two important advantages. First, valid questions are difficult to write. If other researchers have already wrestled with how to ask a person if s/he feels alienated and then have tested, revised, and retested those questions, why not profit from their labors? The Survey Research Center at the University of Michigan, the National Opinion Research Center at the University of Chicago, the General Social Surveys, various commercial polls, and hundreds of academic and marketing articles are excellent sources for questions.[6] If you borrow questions from research articles previously published in academic journals, remember to obtain permission from the author(s) before using the questions and to credit your source(s).

A second advantage of borrowed questions is comparability. When a question asked nationally or in one community is also asked in exactly the same way in other communities and at the state and national level, it is possible to analyze the responses in a relative context. For example, if we learn that 20% of the local residents express some feelings of alienation, is that a high percentage, low, or about as expected? If data are available from identical questions asked in other communities, then the local percentage becomes more meaningful.

Developing original questions.   In spite of the advantages of borrowing, local issues are often unique to a community, and it is usually necessary to custom-design questions. In designing your own questions several general rules apply:

1. *Vocabulary should be aimed at the "lowest common denominator."* Since questionnaires are typically the result of formally educated researchers interacting with similarly educated community leaders, there is a tendency for the vocabulary of the questions to include terms such as *tax abatement districts, discriminatory intent, self-actualization, feasibility, central city, MSA,* and so on. Needlessly long words, complex phrases, and technical jargon will greatly limit the applicability of the survey.

2. *The questions should be conversational, not condescending.* Questions should be asked at a conversational level. While it is important to be "natural" in vocabulary choices, it is not necessary to "talk down" to the respondent. One can usually assume, for example, that local residents understand what a mayor is. Thus, an explanatory phrase such as "The mayor, *who is the top elected official in our city,* recently suggested . . ." should be avoided.

3. *Avoid "double-barreled questions" that ask for opinions on two different issues in one question.* For example, "How satisfied are you with the performance of our local police and fire departments?" will produce responses that are difficult to interpret. What if the respondent is posi-

tive toward police protection but negative toward fire protection? Ask two separate questions instead.

4. *Be specific.* Asking "Are local taxes too high?" will yield little useful information (and, usually, a strong affirmative response). What is too high: the sales tax, the property tax? Or is it too high for the respondent (who typically views him- or herself as middle class) but too low for the rich?

5. *Avoid extreme terms such as "always," "never," "racist," "exploitation," and so on.* You may indeed want to measure "exploitation" or find if the respondent "always" acts in a certain way, but such terms are typically so extreme as to bias the response. For example, levels of agreement with "Local businesses always exploit women workers" will be so low that they will probably be of no value; but a rewording of the statement to "Local businesses often take advantage of women workers by paying them less than men workers in the same jobs" will produce higher levels of agreement and specificity (i.e., the kind of exploitation is defined).

6. *Make it difficult for the respondent to acquiesce to statements.* For a variety of reasons, respondents are likely to agree with statements presented to them (Krosnick and Fabrigar 2003). Thus, when possible, a forced-choice question is preferable to agree-disagree versions, especially for face-to-face and phone surveys (Dillman et al. 2009). For example, when presented with a statement such as "The city should raise property taxes to build a new library" and asked if they agree or disagree, some respondents will agree for reasons other than supporting higher taxes for a library. If the question is reworded to force a choice such as "Should the city raise property taxes to build a new library or leave property taxes at their current level and do without a new library?" there is less chance for a biased response. When forced-choice questions are not possible, then increasing the variation of agreement (e.g., "strongly agree," "agree," "disagree," "strongly disagree") will help minimize acquiescence-response bias.

7. *Finally, be careful to structure the questions logically, grammatically, and precisely.* There could be a dozen more "rules" or "hints" to effective question construction, but, generally, the carefully and thoughtfully constructed, pretested questionnaire will also be a valid and useful questionnaire.

Response sets: Open- versus closed-ended. Questions naturally elicit answers, so as much care should be given to the structure of potential responses to questions as to the questions themselves.

There are two broad types of answers: open-ended and closed-ended. Open-ended answers allow the respondents freedom to answer in any way they wish (e.g., "What do you believe are the major contributors to the overall quality of life in our community?"). Closed-ended answers require the respondent to choose between predetermined responses, such as "Which do you believe is the most important contributor to the quality of life here: (1) the local economy, (2) the climate, or (3) the size of the population?"

The open-ended answer appears, at first glance, to be clearly superior. It allows the respondent to answer with less bias from the interviewer; qualifications and specifications impossible with closed-ended answers can be attached to the responses; and an open-ended response requires more focused attention by the respondent. However, there are some less apparent disadvantages associated with an open-ended answer. For example, it takes much longer to answer, since a typical respondent will verbalize the thought process that produces the answer as well as the answer itself.

> *Interviewer:* What do you believe are the major contributors to the overall quality of life in our community?
>
> *Respondent:* I don't know. I guess there are a lot of good things about Waco. The lake is pretty, but I don't know if it's actually in Waco. Is it okay to mention it as a good point?
>
> *Interviewer:* Yes. Our community includes the entire Waco/McLennan county area.
>
> *Respondent:* Well, then, the lake, but we really don't go there that much. It's hard to say; I guess the park is awfully nice, and we probably go there more than to the lake. Of course, my job is the main reason we live here; can that be a good point?
>
> *Interviewer:* Yes, it can.
>
> *Respondent:* Well, let's make that one of them. How many do I have so far?

How many indeed! Does the interviewer include the lake and the park? In addition to being time consuming, the responses are difficult to record and interpret.

Since all the open-ended responses must be categorized eventually, and since the opportunities for subjective error in that process are considerable, why not let community respondents code their own answers from a list of categories? That is, why not use closed-ended answers exclusively? In practice, this isn't a bad rule to follow. *Most of the time, most of the questions should have closed-ended response sets.* Open-ended responses should be included in community surveys only when there is little agreement before the survey as to what the most common responses will be or when there is a clear need to probe for further analysis ("Why do you feel that way?" or "Why did you choose this over another?")

Ordering the questions.   Order the questions in the following ways: "easy" first and last, "sensitive" last, and "transitions" in between. The initial question should be: (1) related to the introduction, (2) interesting, (3) closed-ended, and (4) easy to answer. For example, if the introduction refers to important local issues, questions about threats to world peace or relatively trivial city zoning changes are inappropriate.

Subsequent questions should be grouped by subject, and the interjection of an occasional opportunity for an open-ended response will not only give the respondents chances to express themselves more fully but also provide an effective change of pace.

Particularly difficult questions (e.g., those requiring open-ended responses, choosing from long lists, or making difficult choices) should be placed toward the front of long questionnaires to reduce the effects of respondent fatigue. Easier questions (e.g., demographics, such as age or education) can be asked toward the end when fatigue is not so serious a bias. Potentially sensitive questions (e.g., income, candidate preferences) are also best asked toward the end of the questionnaire. Hopefully, sufficient rapport and trust will have been established with the respondent to overcome any hesitation, but in the worst case—the respondent terminating the interview—enough information may have been gathered by then to include it in the sample.

Transition statements (e.g., "Now I would like to ask you some questions about education") aid in the movement from one group of questions to another. They can also ease the movement from one response set to another (e.g., "Now I am going to read a series of statements about the local quality of life and would like you to tell me the extent to which you agree or disagree with them"). In either case, when the questions are grouped and ordered, transition statements will aid in moving the respondent from one part of the questionnaire to another.

Length of the questionnaire. Since considerable time is devoted to choosing the sample, training the interviewers, and contacting desired and willing respondents, one naturally tends to try to get as much return on that investment as possible—in other words, to ask as many questions as possible. However, there is a point at which respondent fatigue makes further questioning unreliable; but what, exactly, is that point—ten minutes, an hour? The answer, typically, is "It depends." It depends largely on the difficulty and interest of the questions. If we are asking complicated questions that hold little perceived relevance to the respondent (e.g., asking a random sample of community residents to choose between five different ways of treating sewage), try to keep the average interview under ten minutes. If we are asking relatively simple and overtly relevant questions (e.g., asking a sample of teachers if their classes are overcrowded), then the average interview might go as long as thirty minutes.

It can be argued that community surveys need to be briefer than state or national surveys because the resource (potential respondents) is so much smaller locally and, therefore, more likely to be used up. If a community has 100,000 adults who are sampled four times per year (with a sample size of 1000), after five years we would expect that in our next sample approximately 20% of the respondents will have participated in previous local surveys, and about 20% will live in a household that has been previously surveyed. (Given the movement of people into and out of the community, the exact level of overlap is impossible to predict.) If the respondent's previous interview was tiring, boring, or in some other way unpleasant, he or she will be less likely to participate a second time.

In general, then, it is advisable to keep community surveys shorter (and less threatening and more interesting) than national surveys. If the community is surveyed regularly, the people you interview are more likely to be interviewed again, and, perhaps even more important, they are also more likely to know the surveyor or the client organization on a personal basis. Thus, long, boring, threatening questionnaires can do considerably more damage locally than nationally.

Pretesting the questionnaire.   The questionnaire is so important that everyone agrees it ought to be pretested, but not everyone agrees on exactly what constitutes an adequate pretest (Presser et al. 2004). While some researchers engage in vigorous test and retests (Beatty 2004), given the resources typically available for community survey, a field test of twenty or thirty interviews is probably sufficient. One new and novel approach from the University of Memphis is the Question Understanding Aid (QUAID), a free, online assessment of potential questions based on cognitive psychology.[7] A technique like QUAID would typically be applied before the field test and then again after the field test uncovers problems.

Choosing the Sample

Sampling is the cornerstone of the community survey because it makes feasible an accurate estimate of local opinion without asking for the opinion of each and every community resident. We take this marvelous shortcut for granted now, but systematic, representative sampling is a relatively new addition to social science methodology. As examples, Robert Woodbury (1934, 364) concluded that "it is so difficult to insure the representativeness of the sample that . . . complete enumeration is preferred,"[8] and even in the 1960s, Gerhard Lenski (1963, 12) referred to survey sampling as "a new research technique." By the 1980s, however, this "new research technique" had been developed quite extensively for local research, especially in light of advances in telephone surveys. This section, then, provides an overview of the community sampling techniques necessary for an accurate local telephone survey.

Fortunately, community surveys typically require only the simplest, most basic, and most accurate form of sampling: *simple random sampling.* This means that while state and national surveyors must build complex modifications of simple random sampling methodology (e.g., stratified samples, cluster models, multistage designs), local telephone surveys possess one key element that is missing in national and even state surveys, the one element that always makes simple random sampling possible: a list of all units in the universe from which we wish to sample. In this case, of course, the all-important list is the local telephone directory.

Using the Directory

The community is one of the largest groups for which a reasonably complete and accurate list of all members (or, more precisely, all members' households) is available. There are no such lists, or sampling frames, for states or nations. The presence of this list, then, is the reason a reliable community sample is so much simpler to obtain than a similar state or national sample. However, the phone directory does not solve all our problems. We cannot simply call every nth number in the book until we get our sample. Actually, if we did, the sample wouldn't be too bad, but there are better ways.

Why not rely completely on the directory? The most serious drawback for randomly selecting numbers from the directory is unlisted numbers. Numbers are not listed in the directory for two reasons: (1) the person has recently moved into the community and is not yet in the directory, or (2) the person has chosen to have the number unlisted. In both instances, this can seriously bias the sample since these unlisted numbers have no chance to be selected. Combined, these two problems mean that a local directory will not list from a fifth to a third of the current households in a community.

Fortunately, however, a methodology exists that enables telephone surveyors to reach new residents and even households with unlisted numbers: random-digit dialing (substituting the last digits of each number selected from the directory with a randomly selected set of digits).

Random-digit dialing (RDD) based on a telephone directory. While a number of firms sell high-quality lists of numbers for telephone interviews, in many cases a local phone book and a computer can produce the calling list. Assuming that the telephone directory includes numbers that have the same geographic boundaries as your community,[9] drawing a representative sample from the directory requires:

1. Choosing a sampling interval (n) that will move through the phone book and produce a sufficient amount of numbers to build upon (usually 500 is sufficient).
2. Determining a random starting point.
3. Proceeding through the directory taking every nth residential number.

After the sampling interval is determined, start with the third, fifth, eighth (or whatever) phone number and then select every nth listing thereafter until approximately 500 telephone numbers are selected.

At this point the 500 telephone numbers, while representative of the listed residential numbers, do not include unlisted numbers (or cell phone numbers, which are discussed in the following section), and they are not nearly enough numbers to complete the survey. To catch unlisted numbers and increase the count of phone numbers, replace the last two, three, or four digits of each phone number with random numbers. How many digits to replace is a judgment call. Replacing the last four digits is the most likely way to pick up banks of new numbers and unlisted numbers, but it is also the most likely way to pick nonresidential and nonworking numbers. A two-digit replacement, conversely, minimizes the incidence of nonresidential and non-working numbers but maximizes the chances of missing new numbers and numerically distant unlisted numbers. Since communities vary substantially in the degree to which new numbers are opened, the proportion of unlisted numbers, and the numerical distance nonresidential and unlisted numbers are from listed residential numbers, there is no substitution level that is appropriate for all communities. A general strategy might be to begin with a four-digit exchange. If that produces an intolerably large number of nonresidential and nonworking numbers, substitute only the last three on the next survey, and go down to a two-digit exchange, if necessary, on the third survey.[10] Using any spreadsheet software, an almost infinite list of random phone numbers can be created from the 500 or so numbers from the pages in the phone book.

Cell phones and directory-based RDD.   While some problems are endemic to all telephone surveys (e.g., increased refusal levels, individuals without phone service), one growing problem is unique to directory-based RDD samples: cell phones. The growing use of cell phones *per se* is not a problem, but the growing number of potential survey respondents who do not have land lines and are reachable only by cell phones seriously threatens all RDD techniques. The percentage of cell-phone-only households is about 25% and climbing (Christian, Keeter, Purcell and Smith 2010). These cell-phone-only users tend to be younger and unmarried, and missing them can bias the survey.

The most common and defensible solution is to use a sample of landline numbers based on a directory and also draw potential numbers from a sampling frame of cell numbers, and this is increasingly the norm for state and national telephone surveys. However, for community surveys that is an unworkable solution. Cell phone numbers do not have to reflect a residential location, and even when a cell phone area code is tied to a geographic area, number portability means that over time geographic correspondence may disappear. Recent research suggests that in a local sample of cell phone numbers, 40% will not correspond to the current residential address (Christian, Dimock, and Keeter 2009). For most state and all national polls, the lack of geographic mismatch is less than 10%, so this is a uniquely community problem.

While some community survey solutions to this cell-phone problem exist, such as using a mail survey (Link et al., 2008), an Internet survey (Gosling et al., 2004), or some mixture of modes (Dillman et al. 2009). For now, and for the foreseeable future, RDD remains the preferable approach in most instances.

So, how does one correct for cell phones in RDD community surveys? *Weighting* is a technique that hides a multitude of sins. Typically, the demographics of completed calls are compared with census data. Then, most statistics programs can weight the sample to correct for the likelihood that cell-phone-only users are younger and less likely to be married or homeowners. The weighting appears to virtually eliminate measurable bias in responses to attitudinal or behavior questions (Christian, Keeter, Purcell, and Smith

2010). Still, as the cell phone-only population continues to climb, there may come a time when, paradoxically, it is easier to do a national survey than a community survey.

Callbacks.   Not every RDD number on the list will result in a completed interview. Some will be business numbers or nonworking numbers and are not really a part of the sample anyway, but some numbers will not answer, will be busy, or the person you need to interview will not be home. What is to be done with these numbers? Move on to another number? Try again later? Yes, to both questions: Move on, but also call back at a later time. Considerable bias can be introduced into the sample if there is not a strong attempt to reach such numbers. If the caller moves on to the next number on the list and never returns to the busy or nonanswering number, then those people most likely to be talking on the phone or to be away from home will not have a chance to be interviewed equal to that of people who rarely talk on the phone or usually stay at home. The only way to equalize their probability of being interviewed is to call back.

Again, there is a judgment call to be made here. It's generally advisable to complete a community survey as quickly as possible so that local events won't occur during the survey to bias those who answer after the intervening event. On the other hand, if the survey is completed in one night, there will be little opportunity to reach respondents through callbacks. So, if the survey lasts two or three days, the callbacks should be equally distributed over the remaining time.

Screening within the household.   The numbers selected by the techniques described above represent *households* rather than *individuals*. Since we are usually interested in individual opinions rather than household opinions, we must systematically sample among the residents in each household called during the survey. Usually the surveyor is interested in adults, and there are several methods available to screen or filter the household for the desired adult respondent. The initial attempts at screening (e.g., Kish 1949, 1965) were designed to systematically select by age and sex within each household so that every adult in each sampled household would have an equal probability of being selected. The screens were successful, but they were also time consuming, cumbersome to administer, and better suited to face-to-face interviews than to telephone surveys. Subsequent modifications have typically sacrificed some degree of probability of equal distribution in selection for an increase in ease of administration. This has been particularly true in telephone surveys, where the traditional screening questions about the number of adult males and females living in the house were sometimes seen as threatening and too personal by the people being interviewed.

There has been a series of modifications in screening procedures for telephone surveys (Troldahl and Carter 1964; Bryant 1975; Groves and Kahn 1979; Hagen and Collier 1982), and, generally, they have moved toward less time-consuming and less intensive methods of selecting respondents. An

example of such a screen in figure 11-1 lists a set of questions used to minimize respondent resistance (as measured by refusals to be interviewed) and to
maximize representativeness (as measured by comparisons with census
data). Theoretically, it is not as rigorous as it should be in systematically sampling by age and sex, but, practically, it works.

The screening questions in figure 11-1 assume that (1) no serious bias is
introduced by not systematically asking for the youngest or oldest adult; and
(2) women are more likely to answer the phone and participate in the interview. Comparisons of the age and sex distributions of samples with census
data from the same communities indicate that these two assumptions are
sound. Again, trade-offs are involved. Most screens are more systematic than
the one in figure 11-1, but they are also more likely to increase the refusal rate.

Figure 11-1   Telephone Survey Screen

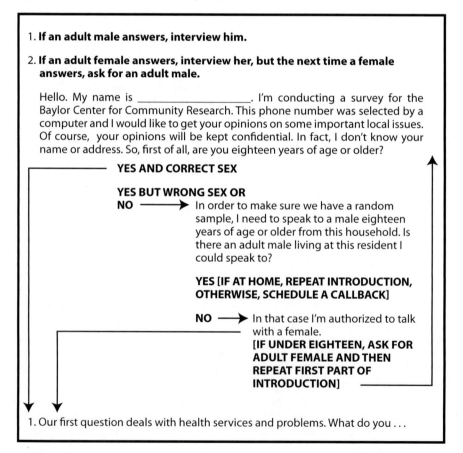

1. **If an adult male answers, interview him.**

2. **If an adult female answers, interview her, but the next time a female answers, ask for an adult male.**

Hello. My name is _____. I'm conducting a survey for the Baylor Center for Community Research. This phone number was selected by a computer and I would like to get your opinions on some important local issues. Of course, your opinions will be kept confidential. In fact, I don't know your name or address. So, first of all, are you eighteen years of age or older?

YES AND CORRECT SEX

YES BUT WRONG SEX OR
NO ⟶ In order to make sure we have a random sample, I need to speak to a male eighteen years of age or older from this household. Is there an adult male living at this resident I could speak to?

YES [IF AT HOME, REPEAT INTRODUCTION, OTHERWISE, SCHEDULE A CALLBACK]

NO ⟶ In that case I'm authorized to talk with a female.
[IF UNDER EIGHTEEN, ASK FOR ADULT FEMALE AND THEN REPEAT FIRST PART OF INTRODUCTION]

1. Our first question deals with health services and problems. What do you . . .

How Big Should the Sample Be?

Usually the first questions asked about any survey concern sample size: "How large is the sample?" "Why is it that size?" "How large should the sample be?" These questions are not as important as those concerned with the validity of the questions, the selection procedure for the telephone numbers, and the efficiency of the screening questions. If these matters are not properly attended to, the sample size will make no difference. The survey will be scientifically useless as a measure of community opinions. Conversely, if the questions are reasonably valid, if the numbers are selected in a random and representative manner, and if the screen systematically samples respondents within the household, it doesn't make much difference whether the sample size is one hundred or one thousand; the survey will be a reasonably accurate measure of community opinion. Sample size is not as crucial a component of a community survey as it first appears. Still, it is an issue. How big should the sample be?

Confidence levels and intervals.   One of the major considerations in determining the size of a community sample is how precise one must be in estimating local opinion. If 60% of the sample believes the community is a good place to live, how sure can we be that 60% of the entire community feels that way? Naturally, it would be nice to be absolutely sure, but most surveyors practically settle for a 95% *confidence level* (i.e., we are willing to accept five chances in one hundred of being wrong).

When a confidence level is specified, typically at 95%, it is then possible to specify a *confidence interval,* which is the range around the sample's response within which the community's response can be expected to lie 95 times out of 100. If the confidence interval was ±4%, the confidence level 95%, and the sample response of 60% says the community is a good place in which to live, then there would be a 95% probability that between 56% and 64% of the community believes it is a good place in which to live.

The computation of a confidence interval is relatively straightforward for community surveys because, unlike national surveys, local surveys typically use a form of simple random sampling; and the statistics for computing a confidence interval for simple random samples are much simpler than for other forms of samples.

The formula for computing a confidence interval is based on the proportion of responses (A and B in the formula below) to the question, the confidence level (always 1.96 for 95%, since 95% of a normal distribution falls within 1.96 standard deviations around the distribution's mean), the number of potential respondents in the community (C), and the sample size (S). If, for example, 60% of a sample of 500 respondents from an estimated 100,000 adult community residents believe the community is a good place in which to live, the confidence interval would be between 56% and 64% (60% ±4%). A and B can be equal when 50% choose one response and the other 50% choose another response. Usually, it is 60%–40% or 80%–20%, not a 50%–50% split.

$$\text{Confidence Interval} = 1.96 \sqrt{\left(1 - \frac{S}{C}\right) \frac{A \times B}{(S-1)}}$$

$$= 1.96 \sqrt{\left(1 - \frac{500}{100,000}\right)\left(\frac{60 \times 40}{499}\right)}$$

$$= 4.29$$

$$= \pm 4\%$$

If you experiment with various values in this formula, it will become clear that the size of the community doesn't matter very much, the proportion of the responses matters a little, and the size of the sample matters a great deal (up to a point). For example, if the number of adults in the community increased tenfold to 1,000,000, the confidence interval would increase to only ±4.3; or, in effect, it would often still be reported as ±4% and not change at all! Thus, sampling in a community is not much more efficient than sampling an entire state or nation.[11]

Further experimentation will show the effects of variation in response proportion to the questions asked on the survey. The worst possible case is a 50-50 split, where the confidence interval would increase to ±4.4. Narrower margins result from more uneven response levels, with a 90–10 split producing an interval of only ±2.6%.

Finally, experimenting with sample size shows that a sample of only 100 produces a confidence interval of ±9.6%, a sample of 500 = ±4.3%, a sample of 1,000 = ±3.0%, 5,000 = ±1.3%, and 10,000 = ±.9%. Increasing the size of the sample will narrow the confidence interval, but the law of diminishing returns soon asserts itself. Note, for example, that adding 400 respondents to an original sample of 100 cuts the confidence interval in half, but adding 5,000 more to an initial sample of 5,000 hardly narrows the interval at all.

So, what do all these statistical exercises tell us about how large the sample should be? Simply this: *If a specific confidence interval is desired for the survey, adjust the sample size accordingly.* Assume a 50-50 split on the response proportion to the question (any deviations from that even split will narrow the interval) and determine the number of respondents necessary to reach ±3%, ±5%, or whatever confidence interval is required. As a general guide to selecting a sample size, the relationships in table 11-2 should be helpful.

Subsample analysis.   Another equally important consideration is the need to analyze the responses of various groups within a sample. For example, it may be particularly important to separate and analyze the responses of males over the age of sixty-five to a question on a proposed retirement center; but if only 5% of the adult community fits that category, then only about fifteen male respondents over sixty-five will come from a sample of three hundred. That produces a virtually useless confidence interval of about ±26%! Unless there is a special procedure to oversample the older males, the entire

Table 11-2   Approximate Relationship between Sample Sizes and Confidence Intervals

Sample Size	Confidence Interval*
10,000	±1.0%
1,500	±2.5%
1,000	±3.0%
800	±3.5%
600	±4.0%
500	±4.5%
400	±5.0%
300	±6.0%
200	±7.0%
150	±8.0%
100	±10.0%
50	±14.0%

*Rounded to nearest .5%, assuming a community size ranging from 50,000 to 1,000,000 and a 50–50 division on the responses.

general sample will need to be increased. For example, a general sample of 600 would reduce the confidence interval in this case to ±18%, and a general sample of 1,500 would bring it down to ±11%.

A subsample of only 5% is an extreme case, and in most instances (e.g., race, sex) the subsample will be proportionately larger, but the point should be clear: The sample must be large enough to allow required subsample analysis with reasonable confidence intervals. How large should a sample be, then? It should be large enough to be: (1) precise in its confidence interval for the entire community and (2) reasonably precise in the confidence intervals of relevant subsamples. The precision required to be "reasonable" depends on the researcher.

Administering the Survey and Analyzing the Results

After the questionnaire is developed and the telephone numbers are selected, the remaining tasks include scheduling the times to call, training and monitoring the interviewers, coding the responses, and finally, analyzing the results. These administrative jobs are sometimes shortchanged for the more "visible" or "sophisticated" tasks of sampling or questionnaire design, and there are fewer published guides to some of these "nuts and bolts" methods; but each administrative or analytic task is crucial to the successful completion of a community survey.

Scheduling the Calls

Obviously, not all days and times are equally well suited for telephone interviews, but which days and times are best for calling? That is, when will calls produce the most responses and the most representative responses? Usually, weeknights between 6:00 PM and 9:00 PM are best; while weekends typically do not produce as many interviews per hour, they are necessary to reduce sample bias. Saturdays from 10:00 AM to 5:00 PM are typically used for weekends.

Since communities do vary, these times should be seen only as rough guidelines. Calls in a farm community may need to be stopped earlier at night than in an urban community. Special events such as sports or weather conditions can also affect surveys. One of our worst calling periods in Texas occurred when the Dallas Cowboys appeared on Monday Night Football; our best ever was when the community was snowed in.

Training the Interviewers

Telephone interviewing is not an easy job, and many people are not well suited for it. Not everyone has (1) the tonal qualities of voice, (2) the ability to read precisely but also conversationally, (3) the mental "quickness" necessary to handle unanticipated respondent questions or comments, and (4) the tact and self-confidence to deal with refusals. But even potential interviewers who are ideally suited for telephone surveys will not do well without training and practice.

If the interviewers have no experience, the training process typically goes through three stages: (1) a general overview of telephone survey methods (open versus closed responses, probes, etc.); (2) question-by-question instructions on the actual questionnaire; and (3) a practice time when interviewers can actually go through the questionnaire and code the responses. If the interviewers have participated in previous surveys, much of the initial steps in the training process can be omitted, but in all cases some training and practice are required before actual calls are made into the community. In fact, interviewer training is arguably more important for local surveys than for national ones since community surveys are more likely to encounter respondents who have participated in previous surveys or who know the interviewer, the research organization, or the client sponsoring the survey. Poorly trained interviewers can be more than just a threat to the reliability of survey results; for community surveys, they will damage the public image of the research organization and the sponsoring organization.

Monitoring the Calls

Interview training does not stop when the calling begins. Even interviewers who have gone through extensive training prior to the calling should be monitored during the interviews. There is some difference of opinion on whether it is a breach of confidentiality to "listen in" on the interview, but all agree that either one or both sides of the interview should be monitored.

Monitoring is possible only with a phone bank that centralizes the calling. The centralized facilities give phone surveys a distinct advantage in quality control over face-to-face interviews. Telephone interviews made from a central location can be checked to be sure the right people are asked the right questions in the way they were intended to be asked. Because face-to-face interviews are scattered throughout the community and because mail interviews are completed in isolation from an interviewer, telephone surveys are clearly superior here. A centralized facility, then, is the key to monitoring the interviews, and monitoring is one of the strongest links in the methodological chain of a telephone survey.

Coding the Responses

Just as almost all calls are now made from a centralized location, all responses are now coded for eventual entry into a computer. In fact, state-of-the-art telephone survey methods allow for *immediate* entry into the computer. Computer-assisted telephone interviewing (CATI) bypasses traditional pencil-and-paper techniques by having questions read from a video screen and directly keying the response into the computer as the respondent answers (Groves 1990). Once used only for well-funded national surveys, CATI systems are now increasingly the norm for community surveys. In addition to immediate data entry, CATI systems also allow much more complicated skip patterns than pencil-and-paper questionnaires can support. With appropriate software, most university computer labs can be turned into CATI labs.

Analyzing the Responses

Relatively simple descriptive statistics are sufficient for most research questions, especially for those asked by nonacademic clients. That is, for the pragmatic questions of *who* feels *how* about *what,* computations of mean and modal responses (perhaps broken down by demographics such as age, sex, or neighborhood) will suffice. And all computers will run software that can quickly and easily provide such information. Only for more complex issues (such as causal modeling or analyzing latent structures) are sophisticated statistical packages such as SPSS or SAS necessary.[12]

With the completion of the data analysis, it will be possible to answer those pragmatic community questions referred to earlier in this chapter. However, full pragmatism must include recognition that improving the local quality of life requires more than compiling a public "wish list," no matter how accurately compiled. Discovering that the elderly want more public transportation or that the community as a whole supports the idea of a new park does not mean that the desired community changes will occur. There is a complex political process that must be successfully negotiated—a process in which the opinions of some people are much more important than those of other people. And it is to the areas of unequal local power and community politics that we now turn.

NOTES

[1] This type of argument is based on W. I. Thomas's famous dictum: "If men define situations as real, they are real in their consequences" (Thomas and Thomas 1928, 572).

[2] This absence of published information from local surveys is especially striking when compared to the following chapter on community power. While hundreds of local elite studies have been published, widely analyzed, and intensely debated, there are no comparable publications or analyses for local surveys of the general community population. The great popularity of the local elite surveys in chapter 12 is due in part to the methodological difficulties associated with national elite surveys. That is, power has been studied at the community level almost by default since, in spite of pioneering work by Mills (1959) and Domhoff (1978), few national studies exist.

[3] Done poorly, the response rates are very low. See Dillman (2000) for an exceptionally thorough and practical approach to mail surveys that increases response rates.

[4] A new product from the US Postal Service, Delivery Sequence Files (DSF), appears to have reduced sampling problems for mail-out surveys (Iannacchione, Staab, and Redden 2003).

[5] Some federal agencies require surveyors to inform each potential respondent that participation is not required and that the contents of individual responses will not be released except as required by law.

[6] One exception to the "borrowing is better" rule: Questions designed for other survey modes (e.g., paper or web) may not be appropriate for phone surveys (Dillman and Smyth 2007).

[7] Psychologists are now among the most active researchers in questionnaire construction (e.g., Tourangeau 2003), displacing statisticians and sociologists. See Graesser, Cai, Louwerse, and Daniel (2006) for an empirical assessment of QUAID.

[8] The classic debacle of the *Literary Digest* predicting a victory by Alf Landon over Franklin Roosevelt shows that Woodbury's assessment of sampling techniques was indeed correct for that time.

[9] If the community is a small subset of those numbers listed in the directory or if it is a subset of two or more directories, then sampling based on cross-reference directories is required in order to focus more efficiently on those numbers within the community. These directories are a valuable tool for many types of community research. The International Association of Cross-Reference Directory Publishers produces an annual catalog of these directories. They may become even more valuable if local "white pages" are no longer published.

[10] Another strategy for selecting the most efficacious exchange level is to peruse a cross-referenced municipal directory and determine the degree to which nonresidential numbers are separated from residential numbers. That is, are most business members separated from most residential phones by two, three, or four digits?

[11] Actually, the formulas used to compute community and national samples are identical, even though communities should have more homogeneous populations and therefore less element variance. In other words, although community and national surveys may report identical confidence intervals, the community's confidence interval is probably narrower than the nation's, but it is impossible to estimate how much narrower.

[12] Since statistical analysis is the same at the local and national levels, there is no need for this text to explore either simple or complex methods of statistical analysis, especially since scores of excellent texts exist.

chapter twelve

Community Politics

With the development of reliable methodologies for questionnaire construction, sampling, and interviewing outlined in the preceding chapter, it has become possible to measure the desires of the community. The ideology behind this community polling is democratic, perhaps naively so: If the will of the community is more clearly understood, then it can be followed more closely. This implies that all in the community are equal and that all "wills" are equally likely to be implemented. Of course the Lynds' description of the X family in Middletown illustrates the fallacy of that implication. Everyone is not equal. Some have tremendous amounts of power; some have none, and most are in between. Any successful attempt to improve the local quality of life must be cognizant of local politics and the unequal distribution of community power. In fact, the first systematic study of community power began with an attempt to improve the local quality of life.

Floyd Hunter's *Community Power Structure*: The Reputational Approach to Measuring the Distribution of Community Power

As noted in chapter 1, Hunter's *Community Power Structure* (1953) is generally acknowledged as providing the initial impetus for community power research. What has not been generally acknowledged is that Hunter's reason for studying community power was to improve the local quality of life by describing more clearly the processes by which important local policies are conceived:

> It has been evident to the writer for some years that policies on vital matters affecting community life seem to appear suddenly. They are acted upon; but with no precise knowledge on the part of the majority of citizens as to how these policies originated or by whom they are really sponsored. Much is done, but much is left undone. Some of the things done appear to be manipulated to the advantage of relatively few. (Hunter 1953, 1)

Hunter set out to discover the "real leaders" and determine how they were able to foist their will upon the community. His premise was that until the local power structure becomes visible, the chance for meaningful change remains remote:

> If the basic issues which confront individuals and groups in the community are to be adequately met, it would seem necessary for the citizenry to be fully aware of who their real leaders are and how they are chosen. This would seem to be a first order of business for any individual who is interested in civic issues. (Hunter 1953, 260–61)

But how can one discover who these "real" leaders are? Hunter's answer was a technique for uncovering the local leadership that came to be known as the *reputational approach*. He began with a list of 175 people who held positions of power in Regional City (his pseudonym for Atlanta). That list was submitted to the scrutiny of fourteen local informants. These informants, who were described as knowledgeable of local affairs and representative of various segments within the community,[1] were asked to select the ten persons from the list (or choose unlisted names) who they felt were among the most powerful. This produced a group of forty reputational leaders who were subsequently interviewed by Hunter. In the course of the interview, each of the forty was asked the same principal question: "If a project were before the community that required a decision by a group of leaders—leaders that nearly everyone would accept—which ten on this list of forty would you choose?" The forty reputational leaders named twelve men consistently enough to convince Hunter that these twelve represented the top echelon of the community power structure in Atlanta. None of the twelve top leaders held a public political office. In fact, only four of the original forty reputational leaders held a public office of any sort. Most were businessmen in the fields of banking, insurance, and manufacturing. Although these elite leaders held no political office, Hunter concluded that they managed to effectively control the local government:

> It is true that there is no formal tie between the economic interests and the government, but the structure of policy-determining committees and their tie-in with other powerful institutions and organizations of the community make government subservient to the interests of these combined groups. The government departments and their personnel are acutely aware of the power of key individuals and combinations of citizens groups in the policy-making realm, and they are loath to act before consulting and "clearing" with these interests. (Hunter 1953, 100–1)

Hunter then described a class-structured distribution of power in Atlanta that was very similar to the Lynds' earlier description of Muncie. When Robert and Helen Lynd wrote of Middletown's politicians as "men of meager caliber, [whom] the inner business group ignore economically and socially and use politically," or when they used "the pervasiveness of the long fingers of capitalist ownership" to describe how the business elite maintained their local control, the Lynds could have been describing Hunter's Regional City as easily as their own Middletown. In both communities there was a ruling class that used its economic dominance to structure the local cultural and political values and actions for their own advantage.

Hunter → reputational

Dahl → decisional

Robert Dahl's *Who Governs?*
The Decisional Approach to Measuring
the Distribution of Community Power

Considerable response greeted Hunter's *Community Power Structure*, much of it critical. His techniques were questioned on scientific grounds, his findings on ideological ones. Political scientists, generally more conservative than sociologists and viewing Hunter and other sociologists as invaders of their academic turf, were among the most critical. This is hardly surprising since Hunter's findings could be construed to imply that: (1) democracy was not working well, if at all, on the local level; and (2) by studying local politicians, political scientists were missing the true leaders and focusing, rather, on lower-level functionaries. Yet, it was not until Robert Dahl's *Who Governs?* was published in 1961 that an organized set of criticisms accompanied by an alternative theory of community power was presented as a response to Hunter's thesis. Dahl and his colleagues (Nelson Polsby and Raymond Wolfinger) in the Political Science Department at Yale University authored major criticisms of the reputational-elitist approach to community power, and *Who Governs?* was the theoretical and methodological linchpin.

The methodology for answering the question of *Who Governs?* in New Haven, Connecticut (this time, thankfully, there was no pseudonym for the community being studied), was based on the detailed analysis of political decisions. While Hunter's focus was directed largely toward top *leaders*, with specific decisions analyzed only tangentially, Dahl focused primarily on what he felt were key *decisions* in New Haven and who made them.

Dahl, employing what came to be known as the *decisional approach*, analyzed decisions made in three areas: public education, political nominations, and, especially, urban renewal, which was "by most criteria the biggest thing in New Haven" (Polsby 1963, 70). He found an elected official, the mayor, to be the driving force behind urban renewal, and, with the exception of the mayor, leaders making decisions in one issue area were not found to be particularly influential in another. Dahl discovered an essentially pluralistic local power structure, with only the mayor able to move from one competing group to another and from one issue to another. In short, representative democracy was alive and reasonably well in New Haven:

> For more than a century, indeed, New Haven's political system has been characterized by well nigh universal suffrage, a moderately high participation in elections, a highly competitive two-party system, opportunity to criticize the conduct and policies of officials, freedom to seek support for

one's views among officials and citizens, and surprisingly frequent alter-
nations in office from one party to the other as electoral majorities have
shifted. (Dahl 1961, 311)

Methodological Debate and Compromise

Although a careful comparison of *Who Governs?* with *Community Power
Structure* will show considerably more agreement than the subsequent literature would suggest, it is possible to find in the works of Dahl and Hunter the
beginnings of the polar extremes for the pluralist-elitist debate. Hunter analyzed local *opinions* to discover a largely elitist power structure based on *economic class structure.* Dahl analyzed local *behaviors* to discover a largely
pluralistic distribution of power based on *formal political structure.*

The Debate

The resulting debate between the elitists (typically and somewhat incorrectly conceptualized as sociologists employing reputational approaches) and
pluralists (political scientists employing decisional approaches) was a decade-
long epistemological phenomenon. In addition to competing methodologies,
the debate was seen as including interdisciplinary and ideological competition as well.[2]

Based upon the contention that studying beliefs about community power
is a poor substitute for actually studying the exercise of power, pluralists (see
especially Wolfinger 1962 and Polsby 1963) pointed out, quite accurately, that
the reputational approach measures the reputation for power rather than
power itself. They argued that power can be measured only by the careful analysis of important decisions made in key community issues (i.e., the decisional
approach). Thus, the way to determine who has power is to study local decisions and find out who dominated those decisions. Otherwise, the researcher
is dependent upon gossips who "distort reality" and "accept gossip as gospel
and pass it on as the latter" (D'Antonio, Ehrlich, and Erickson 1962, 849).

In the early 1960s, then, the pluralists were clearly on the offensive, largely
due to the apparent superiority of the decisional approach to community
power. It was during this decade, however, that the shortcomings of the decisional approach began to surface. Robert Presthus (1964) found that the decisional method identified several government officials as powerful when a more
accurate and complete interpretation including a reputational method showed
them to be only highly visible front men with very little decision-making power.

Another criticism involved the absence of criteria by which the key local
issues were selected (Dye 1970). Obviously, the selection of specific issues
influences the findings since other local issues might produce entirely different findings. For example, leadership patterns for urban renewal issues may
be very different from leadership patterns for public education issues. Yet,
there is no clear method for selecting the correct issues for analysis.

Still another, and very pragmatic, drawback of the decisional approach became recognized during this time: It is extremely time consuming. In order for Dahl to write *Who Governs?*, Wolfinger (who was a graduate student at Yale at that time) camped in an amazingly gracious mayor's office for a year. Other researchers employing decisional approaches (e.g., Burgess 1962; Agger, Goldrich, and Swanson 1964) devoted even longer amounts of time to observing and analyzing community politics.

Perhaps the most telling criticisms of the decisional approach came from Peter Bachrach and Morton Baratz (1970). They argued that the decisional approach focuses too narrowly on formal, overt decision making. Using examples from race relations in Baltimore, they show that formal decision making, the kind analyzed by the decisional approach, is typically limited to "safe" choices that benefit vested interests. Key issues that might challenge dominant groups are never raised.

Just as measuring the reputation for power can bias the findings toward elitism, focusing on formal decision making can overestimate the role of public officials and the degree of pluralism. In short, both the reputational and decisional approaches to community power possess inherent methodological problems. Fortunately, however, many of their shortcomings can be offset by combining the two approaches.

Compromise and Combinations

In the late 1960s, the mutual condemnation society of the elitists and pluralists disbanded. In its place, a movement toward combining the reputational and decisional methodologies emerged. Typically, this approach involved reputational questioning, supplemented with a focus on specific decisions. Terry Clark's (1968, 1971) "ersatz decisional method" was a leading example of this type of combinational approach:

> Attempting to collect as much information as possible but to maximize reliability and validity while minimizing costs, we decided to interview eleven strategically placed informants in each community . . . [T]hese same informants were interviewed about the same four issues: urban renewal, the election of the mayor, air pollution, and the antipoverty program. These four particular issues were selected because they tend to involve different types of community actors in differing relationships with one another. . . . For each area we posed a series of questions inquiring essentially:
>
> 1. Who initiated action on the issue?
>
> 2. Who supported this action?
>
> 3. Who opposed this action?
>
> 4. What was the nature of the bargaining process; who negotiated with whom?
>
> 5. What was the outcome? Whose views tended to prevail? (Clark 1971, 296–97)

Clark's inclusion of specific issues in the reputational approach is clearly a methodological improvement that incorporates one of the major tenets of the pluralist position. For example, in *Who Governs?*, Dahl (1961, 169) observed that "probably the most striking characteristic of influence in New Haven is the extent to which it is specialized; that is, individuals who are influential in one sector of public activity tend not to be influential in another sector." Unlike many reputational techniques, Clark's methodology can easily reflect such a segmented and specialized distribution of power. In other words, there should be little bias toward elitist findings with this combinational approach.

The similarities between the reputational and decisional approaches. It is not very surprising that the study of community power moved to a complementary combination of the reputational and decisional approaches, like that developed by Clark. In spite of the polemics on both sides of the debate, the methods of the reputational approach are quite complementary with the decisional approach. For example, a comparison of Hunter's (1953) methodology with that of Dahl (1961) will show that both make extensive use of interviews, historical documents, current news reports, and subjective impressions. Further, both approaches, in the final analysis, rely on someone's opinion about the distribution of power. In sum, since their methodologies are hardly mutually exclusive, attempts to combine them did not prove inordinately difficult.

As noted earlier in this chapter, the methods and findings of the two camps were more alike than one would suppose from the ensuing debate and controversy. Rather, the fundamental differences between *Community Power Structure* and *Who Governs?* lie in the interpretation and implication of their findings. It is not so much a question of who governs (in New Haven, Atlanta, or wherever)—rather, it is why, how, for whose benefit, and what (if any) difference the distribution of power makes in the community. In order to answer questions such as these, some community power researchers moved from case studies of single communities to comparative research based on large samples of communities.

Comparative Research: The Causes, Characteristics, and Consequences of Community Power

As long as community power research consists of case studies, it is virtually impossible to validly generalize about the nature of local decision making. Generalizations were made, of course, but with questionable validity. Philip Trounstine and Terry Christensen, in a review of community power research, made the following observation:

> Power was studied community by community. From each case researchers strove to generalize about power to the universe of communities. The

> effort to generalize is apparent in the researchers' choice of titles for their works: The Lynds called their book *Middletown*, not "Uniquetown"; Hunter titled his *Community Power Structure*, not "Atlanta's Power Structure"; and Dahl wrote *Who Governs?*, not "Who Governs New Haven?" But even if we accept the reliability of each researcher's methods, are we willing to accept that all communities function like Middletown or Atlanta or New Haven? Would a biologist generalize from a single fruit fly to the species? (Trounstine and Christensen 1982, 37)

Naturally, one fruit fly is not enough, but fruit flies are considerably easier to collect and study than communities. Trounstine and Christensen (1982, 38) ask, "How could social scientists study enough communities to get a valid sample for generalization?" Their answer is direct and disappointing: "The simple fact is, it can't be done."

Fortunately, Trounstine and Christensen's position is slightly overstated. Studying the distribution of power in enough communities to provide a meaningful sample is indeed difficult, but not impossible. There were several attempts to create such samples, with varying degrees of success.

Comparative Community Power Samples

Hawley's MPO.   The first attempt to measure the distribution of power in a large number of communities was an ingenious ecological approach developed by Amos Hawley (1950, 1968) that computed a ratio between the total number of *M*anagers, *P*roprietors, and *O*fficials (positions of potential power) in a community and the size of its local labor force. The smaller this MPO ratio, the smaller the number of leadership positions, and, therefore, the more elitist or centralized the community power structure.

Since the necessary labor force data are available on virtually all communities at all times from the US Census, the problem of securing an adequate number of communities for comparative research no longer existed. Thus, the ease of measurement and resultant wide availability of Hawley's measure appeared to be significant advances in community power research. Unfortunately, however, the MPO ratio proved to be of little use.

Aiken (1970) and Williams (1973) both found that when the MPO ratio was computed for communities in which the distribution of power had been measured by the more traditional reputational or decisional approaches, the relationships were opposite to Hawley's propositions. The MPO ratio measured only the local proportion of managers, proprietors, and officials rather than the nature of community power.

Walton's secondary analysis.   The major advantage of Hawley's ecological approach was that it was easily administered. Since the usual case study approach to community power typically took months or even years, Hawley's ability to quickly measure the distribution of power in a large number of communities appeared to be a decided improvement. Another technique developed by John Walton promised to provide similar ease of measurement, but without the validity problems of the MPO ratio. Walton (1966, 1970) reviewed the community power literature and selected thirty-three studies containing information on fifty-five communities. In this way, Walton was able to produce a relatively large sample of communities that were measured with intensive reputational and decisional techniques. Additional case studies were added to the sample by Walton and other researchers (Walton 1970; Curtis and Petras 1970; Aiken 1970) so that by the early 1970s this secondary analysis approach to community power seemed to have the best of both worlds. It produced relatively large samples with almost as much ease as Hawley's ecological approach, and it possessed the in-depth, direct measure of community power found only in time-consuming case studies.

Walton's secondary analysis technique, much like Hawley's earlier MPO ratio, seemed almost too good to be true; and just as we found for Hawley's ecological approach, it was. Nelson (1974) wrote to the original researchers of the case studies and asked them to classify the distribution of power in the communities they studied. In Walton's sample, Nelson found eighteen of thirty-three communities were classified differently by the original researcher than they were by Walton. For Curtis and Petras it was even worse, with thirty of the forty communities incorrectly classified. If that were not discouraging enough, there were even cases where the senior author of a case study would provide a different local power classification than a junior author of the same study! Nelson concluded that because community power is an extremely elusive, multidimensional concept, it is difficult if not impossible to group the various case studies into a single scheme such as the one developed by Walton.

The problems associated with the ecological and secondary analysis "shortcuts" imply that the only way to produce an adequate sample of community power structures is the hard way—that is, to directly measure the distribution of power in a large number of communities with the same research methods and theoretical definitions in each community. Hard enough that only one national sample was ever created, by Terry Clark, at the University of Chicago.[3]

Because Clark's ersatz decisional method (discussed earlier in this chapter as an example of a combinational approach) was relatively quick and easy, he was able to administer it to a total of fifty-one communities that comprise part of the Permanent Community Sample of the National Opinion Research Center (Rossi and Crain 1968). The distribution of power (or, in Clark's terms, the degree of decentralization) in table 12-1 shows a pattern of wide variation.

Although only eleven respondents must be interviewed in each community with Clark's technique, a sample of this size and diversity still requires substantial effort and costs; thus, the opportunities of a magnitude similar to Clark's project are limited. Considerable analysis and reanalysis has been made of Clark's data. Such intensive analysis is appropriate since it represented our only collection of "fruit flies." It was our best opportunity for comparative research into the "whats," "whys," and "effects" of community power.

Table 12-1   The Clark Sample and the Distribution of Community Power

Community	Number of decision makers per issue	Community	Number of decision makers per issue
1 Waco, Texas	3.25	27 Saint Petersburg, Florida	6.75
2 Amarillo, Texas	3.33	28 Euclid, Ohio	6.93
3 Bloomington, Minnesota	4.45	29 South Bend, Indiana	7.00
4 Long Beach, California	4.75	30 Salt Lake City, Utah	7.13
5 Manchester, New Hampshire	4.97	31 Boston, Massachusetts	7.25
6 Cambridge, Massachusetts	5.00	32 Akron, Ohio	7.50
7 Duluth, Minnesota	5.25	33 Seattle, Washington	7.50
8 Pasadena, California	5.50	34 Irvington, New Jersey	7.67
9 Warren, Michigan	5.50	35 Tyler, Texas	7.67
10 San Jose, California	5.63	36 Waukegan, Illinois	7.67
11 Schenectady, New York	5.75	37 Hammond, Indiana	7.75
12 Birmingham, Alabama	5.88	38 Milwaukee, Wisconsin	7.75
13 Clifton, New Jersey	5.90	39 Phoenix, Arizona	7.75
14 Berkeley, California	5.92	40 Pittsburgh, Pennsylvania	7.75
15 Hamilton, Ohio	6.00	41 San Francisco, California	7.75
16 Charlotte, North Carolina	6.25	42 Minneapolis, Minnesota	8.00
17 Jacksonville, Florida	6.25	43 Saint Louis, Missouri	8.00
18 Santa Monica, California	6.33	44 Tampa, Florida	8.25
19 Memphis, Tennessee	6.38	45 Malden, Massachusetts	8.50
20 Fullerton, California	6.45	46 Saint Paul, Minnesota	8.50
21 Atlanta, Georgia	6.50	47 Buffalo, New York	8.67
22 Palo Alto, California	6.50	48 Waterbury, Connecticut	8.75
23 Santa Ana, California	6.50	49 Indianapolis, Indiana	9.00
24 Albany, New York	6.63	50 Newark, New Jersey	9.13
25 Fort Worth, Texas	6.75	51 Utica, New York	9.38
26 Gary, Indiana	6.75		

Source: Terry Clark (1971). "Community Structure and Decision-Making, Budget Expenditures, and Urban Renewal in 51 American Communities." In *Community Politics*, edited by Charles M. Bonjean, Terry Clark, and Robert Lineberry. New York: Free Press.

The Characteristics of Community Power

What are the characteristics of community power? Is it largely an elitist phenomenon similar to the descriptions of Hunter and the Lynds, or is it more commonly found in relatively pluralist patterns, such as that described by Dahl? The answer is, as you might suppose, "It depends." It depends on both the definition of power and the community studied. However, it is possible to find agreement on at least one basic characteristic of community power.

Communities vary substantially in the distribution of local power. Clark's sample shows wide intercommunity variation in power structures. This means, then, that the earlier debate over whether American communities are largely elitist or pluralist was misguided. Some communities were very elitist (e.g., Bloomington, Indiana; Waco, Texas). Others were more pluralistic (e.g., Charlotte, North Carolina; Newark, New Jersey). This time the differences cannot be ascribed to the discipline of the researcher or the type of methodology.

The Causes of Community Power

When we find that some communities are much more pluralistic than others, the obvious question is: "Why?" Based largely on published analysis of the Clark sample, three causes of variation in community power are presented:

1. *The larger the population size of the community, the more pluralistic the power structure.* Larger cities are more likely to have multiple groups with opposing interests competing for power (Clark 1971; Grimes et al. 1976). Similarly, as communities grow, it should become more difficult for one or two groups to dominate local decision making.

2. *The more economically diversified the community, the more pluralistic the power structure.* The logic here is similar to the proposition above. Economically diverse communities will be particularly difficult to dominate to the degree the X family was able to do in a one-factory town like Muncie (Clark 1971; Grimes et al. 1976).

3. *The more "reformed" the formal political structure of the community, the more elitist the power structure.* City governments that include nonpartisan elections, a city manager, and at-large representation are more likely to have dimensions of elitism (Clark 1971; Lyon 1977a, 1977b). Political scientists (Lineberry and Fowler 1967) have found that the reform movement that transformed many cities of the South, West, and Midwest into more "businesslike" governments also insulated them from the demands of the public they represented. This lessening of public accountability appears to have increased the possibility for elitist power structures.

The Consequences of Community Power

After examining some of the contributors to the different characteristics of community power, the next logical consideration concerns the effects of variations in community power structure. That is, what difference does it make to the community for its power structure to be pluralistic or elitist? Often, the answer may be that it makes very little difference. For many local phenomena, political elitism or pluralism is not very important (Lyon and Bonjean 1981). This appears to be because many local decisions (e.g., most municipal budget expenditures) are incremental in nature and more likely to involve mid-level administrators instead of top-level community leaders. Only the most visible or important local issues are likely to produce the active involvement of community leaders. Of course, what is important in one community may not be important in another. However, there is at least one issue that is crucial to virtually all local leaders: community growth. And that issue ushered in major changes in community power research.

The Community as a Growth Machine

Harvey Molotch (1976, 313), in a provocative article entitled "The City as a Growth Machine," maintained that

> this organized effort to affect the outcome of growth distribution is the essence of local government as a dynamic political force. It is not the only function of government, but it is the key one and, ironically, the one most ignored. . . . This is the politics which determines who, in material terms, gets what, where, and how.

Molotch argues that in virtually all communities, a business-oriented elite exists that has population growth as a major goal. And a subsequent analysis of the relationship between community power and population growth in the Clark sample found a strong causal link between the power of local business leaders and population growth that was independent of environmental factors such as region of the country or size of the city (Lyon et al. 1981). Thus, we can list the following outcome of community power: *Communities in which business leaders have high levels of power are likely to experience relatively high levels of population growth.*

Community growth may be a very special local phenomenon that is an important issue in virtually all American communities. This would help to account for the fact that while community power is linked to growth, it does not appear to be closely associated with many other local phenomena. Most local issues are routine or administrative in nature and therefore of little concern to local leaders, and, equally important, an issue that may be very important in one community may be of little consequence in another. So with few exceptions (such as growth), those issues that are important enough to involve top local leaders will vary by community. In sum, *the structure of community power matters most for those issues that matter most in the community, and those issues typically vary from one community to the next.*

Since the degree to which local leaders influence community phenomena typically varies by both issue and community, it follows that the practical applications of community power measurement techniques should be issue-

and community-specific as well. While there may be a few local issues, such as population increase or economic growth, that are important in virtually every community, the more common situation is for local issues to vary in importance by place and time. Thus, it may be that the major lesson to be learned from comparative community power research is that much of community power is a locally unique phenomenon and that the causes and consequences of community power will vary accordingly. This would indicate, then, that the proper study of community power should once again be based on the case study approach. As sociologists and political scientists moved back to case studies, a common concern with economic growth resulted that reflected the influence of the *growth machine* conception of community power (Logan and Molotch 1987).

From Comparative Research Back to Case Studies

While it may seem that more methodological heat was generated than meaningful light, the half-century of research that followed Hunter was not without merit. Political scientists and sociologists returned to the case study approach with a considerably more sophisticated understanding of community power and its measurement than existed in the 1950s. As we shall see, *power* is now defined with more nuance, usually with a broader, systemic emphasis on a coalition rather than a ruling elite. Likewise, the overemphasis on techniques of measurement receded, replaced by more holistic approaches similar to the Lynds' and avoiding the inherent difficulties in any single method.

A Return to the Case Study Approach in San Jose

A particularly interesting example of the post-growth Growth Machine case studies is *Movers and Shakers: The Study of Community Power* (1982), a joint effort by journalist Philip Trounstine and political scientist Terry Christensen. One of the goals of their case study of San Jose, California, was to increase local citizens' understanding of how the "movers and shakers" control community events and, thereby, increase the local residents' ability to form more responsive power structures. In addition, Trounstine and Christensen also attempted to insure a wider dispersion of information about community power.

A major finding, not surprisingly, was that "San Jose and other cities of the Sunbelt have functioned as 'growth machines.'"

> The combination of aggressive annexation, lenient zoning, eagerly supplied capital improvements, and the sewage monopoly sped growth on its way. San Jose was a paradise for developers, who maintained good relations with the city council through the Book of the Month Club and generous campaign contributions. But the council and city administrators also benefited directly from growth. "Illegal activities" and "payoffs" were suspected although never proved. But collusion was patently obvi-

ous. Builders, local merchants, and politicians were, after all, part of the same class; they thought alike and they met frequently. Exchanging information or making deals involving land speculation or development was easy, even natural. (Trounstine and Christensen 1982, 97)

One method by which community power findings of *Movers and Shakers* are communicated to a larger audience is through the inclusion of a journalist in the research team. Trounstine and Christensen make a convincing case for the special skills journalists can bring to community power research. The journalists' contacts with important sources of information, their superior writing skills, and their ability to get the findings "out of the library and into the public forum" can contribute substantially to a higher public awareness of community power research. Another way in which Trounstine and Christensen hoped to spread the influence of community power research is by "demystifying" the methodology of community power and thereby making it more available to the average person. In *Movers and Shakers* they have provided a methodological primer on the reputational approach to community power that encourages local citizens to undertake the challenge of discovering the true patterns of leadership in their own community. (We agree with Trounstine and Christensen on this point, and such a primer is provided in the next chapter.)

Thus, *Movers and Shakers* continues the legacy of *Community Power Structure* by more accurately informing citizens about local leadership so that a power structure more responsive to the needs of all the community can be created.

While *Movers and Shakers* focused on a lay audience, another case study led to an important new path for *academic* community research. It is a path leading away from the uncovering of local elites in order to promote community activism, moving instead to a more theoretical and consensual understanding of local politics. Ironically, this new path began in Atlanta.

A Case Study of Atlanta and the Emergence of Regime Politics

Clarence Stone's study of economic growth in Atlanta, *Regime Politics: Governing Atlanta, 1946–1988*, proposed a new understanding of community power that fell somewhere between the elitist and pluralist positions but tilted toward pluralism. Stone (1989, xi) claimed to have "reformulated the problem of community power in a manner intended to break the impasse between the elites and the pluralists," focusing on "social production" rather than "social control." Discovering who has control over local citizens is not the key to understanding community power. Rather, who can work with others to assemble resources and set policy is the key question, and the answer is the urban regime. Thus, Stone's (1989,1) focus was on the regime, "the informal arrangements that surround and compliment the formal workings of governmental authority." The somewhat abstract concept of a regime becomes personified when the analysis turns to the governing coalition, "the core group at the center of the workings of the regime," and how they cooperate.

Stone argues that since no single group can govern a city, coalitions form that typically include the business elite (lots of money, few votes) and the middle class (lots of votes, little money). In Atlanta, this meant the white business elite co-opting and joining the black middle class in a ruling regime that enhanced the power of both groups. Left out are the lower-class blacks, and Stone concludes that the coalition's drive for economic growth in Atlanta did little to help the poor.

Today, Stone's case study of Atlanta might not seem all that different in its conclusions than Hunter's of over three decades earlier. We find local government playing a role, but it is a role circumscribed by business interests and their desire for economic growth. We now find blacks with power, but it is power representing the interests of the growth machine. However, the subsequent works responding to and extending Stone's analysis were largely of an incremental, theoretical vein—quite different from the ideological and methodological battles that followed Hunter—and these subsequent works largely emphasized consensus and the role of government. Why the response would be so different this time is difficult to explain. Perhaps there is less controversy and a more consensual view of politics because Stone is a political scientist, as are most of those responding to Stone. In any case, the dominant understanding of community power is now the more pluralistic urban regime.

So, exactly what is an urban regime? It is a long-term, mutually beneficial arrangement that always includes business and government, is geared toward encouraging economic growth, and sometimes pursues other tasks as well. Note in the following quotation how this focus on growth is also a significant part of Elkin's (1987, 81) case study of Dallas, that Stone cites Elkin as key to his own conception of an urban regime: "Whatever the differences among types of political economies, however, all show efforts to create and maintain growth coalitions. The motivations of public officials may vary, but the results are much the same" (*ibid.*).

Here we see, both in Stone's study of Atlanta and Elkin's similar study of Dallas, the influence of Molotch's "Growth Machine" as well as what appears to be a certain inevitability about urban regimes. All American cities[4] are governed by regimes, and all regimes include business leaders and pursue economic growth.[5] Today the unbridled pursuit of growth can be seen as inherently exploitative, as Feagin (1988) maintains in his case study of Houston, or it can be more progressive, as Molotch et al. (2000) finds in Santa Barbara, but the idea that local elites work together to promote growth remains.

Although they both share the underlying premise of a business-dominated coalition seeking economic growth, applications of and references to *urban regime theory* have outpaced the growth machine model (Lauria 1997a), perhaps because the more conservative regime theory is more susceptible to emphasizing the role of government and reducing the role of business—two characteristics that might appeal to political scientists.[6] The more radical extensions of the growth machine can now be found in *Regulation Theory* (Boyer 1990), part of an ongoing attempt by Marxists to explain the continued existence of capitalism. Like most Marxist approaches, however, most of the focus of Regulation Theory is on the nation-state rather than the community (Lauria 1997b).[7] Thus, the most likely and productive direction in studying community politics is through the regime, with a new growing emphasis on how regimes might differ, despite the common roles of business and government and the common pursuit of economic growth. The differentiation among regimes emerges from different community cultures.

Community Cultures

The idea of business-influenced local regimes pursuing economic growth achieved broad acceptance because it seemed to accurately describe the nature of political power in most communities. However, if the nature of local power does not vary (i.e., if they are all coalitions seeking growth), then how do we account for all the variation in development, politics, and values in local communities?

Molotch was among the first to tackle this question by comparing two adjacent California communities, Santa Barbara and Ventura. In geography and demography "one might consider these two cities to be virtually interchangeable." Politically, "like other American cities, growth machine entrepreneurs are exceedingly active" (Molotch et al. 2000, xx). Yet, Santa Barbara grew into a cool, hip, knowledge-based economy characterized by a New Urbanist style of development while Ventura became a blue collar, oil-based economy characterized by "the qualities that preoccupy critics of US urban places" (*ibid.*). How did two geographically, politically similar communities become so different? Molotch's answer: largely by a historical accident that set in motion the development of two distinct community cultures.

Oil was discovered in and near Ventura before it was found in Santa Barbara, so Ventura became an early center of oil production, storage, and distribution. Santa Barbara, on the other hand, had already developed a beach-centered tourism that encouraged the support for local amenities and natural aesthetics that would be threatened by the oil industry. Thus, the oil industry was embraced in Ventura as an engine of economic development but resisted in Santa Barbara as a potential threat to economic development, even after the discovery of oil there. This crucial, though largely accidental, distinction played out over the next 125 years in ways that produced very different community cultures. Those cultural differences created a social structure that tends to lock in certain future paths of development, with Santa Barbara continuing to exhibit more progressive response to local challenges than Ventura.

In the case of Ventura and Santa Barbara, community politics may in part account for *how* the differences emerged (i.e., growth was pursued differently by the two growth machines), but they were not part of the *why*, which was due to the timing of discovering oil. In this study by Molotch, we reach a conclusion similar to the comparative community power studies. Community politics does not seem to account for many community differences.

Still, the idea that communities have distinctive cultures that can help us understand both communities and local politics continues to drive research. A recent effort using a variation of Hunter's and Clark's reputational approach is the most prominent and promising. Reese and Rosenfeld (2008, 355) have led a study of ten communities in search of *civic culture* as "a means for understanding how municipal policy makers weigh the interests of different groups, govern the local community, frame local issues, engage in decision making, and ultimately select and implement public policies." At this point, the major finding is that different communities possess different political cultures which, in turn, yield different community outcomes.

For example, two southern cities are examined. Charlotte is blessed with a progressive, active culture and an efficient, professional government. Louisville is burdened with a stifled, passive culture and a government with little professionalization or progressive planning—suggesting comparisons with Molotch's study of Santa Barbara and Ventura. However, two differences between this comparative civic culture project and the earlier work of

Table 12-2   Taxonomy of Civic Culture in Two of Reese and Rosenfeld's Case Cities

Overall Culture	Charlotte: Progressive Southern City Market/ Active	Stifled Politics Market/ Passive
Power system	Development regime, low participation level; government-solicited input; strong corporate elites; strong government; stable coalitions	Development regime; mayor, chamber, big corporations, university and media dominate; business the most powerful; strong incumbency; stable coalitions; citizens less organized
Value system	Paternalistic; protestant work ethic; image conscious; cooperates/ compromises to maintain political balance; preserves status quo	Past images valued; historic downtown; revival of past glory; avoidance of obvious political conflict; polite conservatism
Decision-making system	High level of professionalism; proactive planning/ evaluation; TQM	Decisions made expediently/reactively; low level of professionalism; weak in planning/evaluation

Source: Adapted from table 4 in Laura A. Reese and Raymond Rosenfeld (2008), "Comparative Civic Culture," *Journal of Urban Affairs* 30: 355–374.

Molotch imply more potential for civic culture over the historical approach as an emerging paradigm. First, while Molotch goes back over one hundred years to find the reasons for the cultural differences, this project takes the local culture as a given. Vogel's team of researchers (Savitch, Tsukamoto, and Vogel 2008) initiated its study of Louisville by examining a series of failed economic development efforts that began in the 1970s. The reason that Louisville's efforts failed when Charlotte's succeeded is due to their different civic cultures. The reasons the civic cultures differ are not considered to any significant degree. Historical investigations into first causes could be conducted in the future, but it would not necessarily comport with the forward-looking goal of identifying "[w]hat sorts of events are likely to effect change in local civic culture" (Reese and Rosenfeld 2008, 356).

The idea that culture matters suggests a second reason to expect continued research on community cultures. This progressive, optimistic idea that as we learn more about civic culture we can enact policies to transform it (Reese and Ye 2011) to improve communities runs counter to the historical determinism of Molotch's study. Once historical events "nudged" Santa Barbara in one way and Ventura in another, attempts by "change agents" to steer the community in another direction were likely to fail.[8] While historians may resonate with Molotch's approach, the idea that local culture can be both an independent and dependent variable probably has more appeal to social scientists.

From Community Power to Community Culture

So, in over half a century of research into local politics, we began in Atlanta, with findings of business elite dominance similar to the classic case study of Middletown. Response from case studies refuting the business elite model in New Haven and beyond initiated a methodological and political debate leading to large-sample comparative studies. Results from those studies were disappointing, and Molotch's growth machine thesis gained immediate traction as the key goal to understanding the essence of community politics. The growth machine eventually morphed into a slightly more conservative emphasis on local governmental regimes, which in time expanded to include all of community culture, not just politics. Interestingly, and perhaps even ironically, this new, broad interest in community culture is not all that different than many of the classic holistic community studies of the mid-twentieth century, such as Middletown.

NOTES

[1] We are told very little about this aspect of Hunter's methodology. In an appendix to *Community Power Structure* (1953, 258), he describes similar informants as persons "who had lived in the community for some years and who had a knowledge of community affairs."

[2] There was, during this time, a widely accepted belief that political scientists typically studied local power with decisional approaches and discovered pluralism while sociologists were

likely to employ reputational approaches to uncover elitism. However, subsequent analyses (Clark, Kornblum, Bloom, and Tobias 1968; Nelson 1974) have shown there is very little relationship among discipline, method, and findings.

[3] An availability sample of seventeen communities exists that uses a reputational approach. See Grimes et al. (1976) as well as the Clark community sample for comparison and analysis of this sample.

[4] In less capitalistic societies with less mobile businesses and in countries with less decision-making vested in localities, this may not be the case (DiGaetano and Lawless 1999).

[5] While some communities have enacted growth controls, the controls typically benefit current property owners (Katz and Rosen 1987) or they are opposed by business interests, are weakened, and become ineffectual (Baldassare and Protash 1982; Donovan, Neiman, and Brumbaugh 1994). Clavel (1986) claimed that the era of growth-based coalitions came to an end in the 1970s, leading to more progressive coalitions. He provided case studies of progressive regimes in Hartford, Cleveland, Berkeley, Santa Monica, and Burlington, but Molotch's business-oriented view remains more accepted.

[6] See Domhoff (2006) for a critique of Stone's regime theory and a defense of Molotch's more conflict-oriented growth machine.

[7] Many analysts include growth machine, regime, and sometimes even regulation theory under the general category of "New Urban Politics" (Cox 1993; Hall and Hubbard 1996), but urban regime theory appears to be the most common term and approach.

[8] It is possible to do historical community research that demonstrates the significance of change agents. Gendron and Domhoff's (2009) study of Santa Cruz shows considerable influence being wielded by progressives, but such studies (and, probably, such communities) are rare.

chapter thirteen

Measuring Local Power

Hunter initiated the study of community power because he believed that improvements in the local quality of life are more likely when the structure of community power is clearly understood. If he is correct, it behooves those interested in improving a community's quality of life to invest some time and energy in mapping out the patterns of local power. Following is a general methodological guide for determining who governs in the community. The measurement techniques will work equally well for uncovering a community-wide distribution of power or for focusing on power patterns within a single area of community affairs. For academic and journalistic goals of general description and explanation, a broad study of power throughout the entire community (or at least for several individual community issues in a particular area) is the common approach. However, for the more pragmatic concerns of community development and change, a narrower focus on one or two specific community issues is usually more appropriate. In either case, this application of community power measurement techniques is presented in a step-by-step process that allows considerable modification for different needs and issues.

Step One: Community Overview

One important similarity between *Community Power Structure* and *Who Governs?* is that both include substantial amounts of background material on the community. In fact, the first step in most reputational and decisional techniques is a thorough background analysis of the entire community.

A major lesson from classic holistic studies and the more recent developments in community culture is that the separate structures and institutions within the community do not exist in a vacuum. This means that community power is interrelated with the class structure, economic structure, and religious and educational institutions; in short, a community's power structure is interwoven with all the other parts of the community. It is impossible to reach an understanding of a community's power structure without first possessing a considerable amount of general knowledge about that community.

How does one gather such information? Assuming that a temporal investment in several years or at least several months (as is common in holistic community studies) is impractical, a few weeks online and in the local library can suffice. Past issues of local newspapers and local magazines or newsletters are valuable data sources, as are published histories of the community. More sophisticated research might include analysis of census data (growth patterns, race and age composition, residential segregation, workforce participation and composition), results of previous elections, financial contributors to the campaigns, and master plans for the city. The list of data sources is virtually endless, but the amount of time is not. Sometimes, shortcuts are available. If the community has a college or university, there may be a local urban or community research center that has produced community overviews with much of the needed background information. Urban planning and community development departments in the city government often have statistical profiles of the community. Planners within the school district, county, or other community-wide entities are other possible resources.

There is a temptation to devote relatively little time to this initial step or perhaps even to skip it entirely and move on to the "real" study of community power.[1] However, the subsequent steps of interviewing and drawing up lists of potential leaders depend upon a thorough understanding of the whole community. So, how does one know when enough background information has been gathered? There is no precise rule, but before proceeding to the second step the following questions should be answered:

1. What are the important environmental factors affecting the community (e.g., regional characteristics, transportation arteries, nearby communities)?

2. What is the demographic structure of the community (e.g., population size, workforce composition, age and race proportions, residential and business land-use patterns)?

3. What are the most important, or at least the most visible, issues before the community? Which groups or individuals are on which side?

4. What are the major values of the community? Are most concerns related to economic growth and a favorable business climate? Do moral or religious issues arise with any regularity? Is there an inherent desire to preserve the status quo, or is there progressive support for change?[2]

5. What are the dynamics of questions 1 through 4? How have the issues they represent changed over time?

When these questions are answered, it can be assumed that the community background information is sufficient to move on to the second step.

Step Two: Choosing the Positional Informants

After an overview of the community has been developed, the next step is to select those people who can provide the initial responses necessary to learn about the structure of community power. Since these informants will supply crucial information about who will be interviewed next and why, we want individuals who are likely to possess knowledge about power in the community and how it is wielded in local issues. An effective and widely used technique is to select people who, because of their official positions in the community, are likely to be especially knowledgeable. For example, the authors of this book were a part of a community study that interviewed as the first set of community informants:

1. The editor of the largest daily newspaper
2. The president of the largest bank
3. The superintendent of the largest school district
4. The director of the chamber of commerce
5. The director of the local NAACP chapter
6. The director of the local LULAC chapter
7. The pastor of the largest predominantly Anglo church
8. The pastor of the largest predominantly black church
9. The pastor of the largest predominantly Hispanic church
10. The mayor of the central city
11. The city manager of the central city
12. All minority members of the city council of the central city

This list was designed for a broad view of a particular community (Waco, Texas); more specific focuses in other communities will necessitate different lists. However, regardless of the focus or community, the selection procedure for the initial informants considers *positions* rather than *individuals*. By selecting positions, the research can be replicated even if many of the original informants are no longer in the community. Specific individuals will come and go in a community, but the positions will remain.

The key question is, of course, which positions should be selected? The above list was constructed to represent a wide range of knowledgeable positions. Based on background analysis of the community, it was modified to include religious leaders and exclude union leaders. Other communities will require other modifications, just as some issues may provide a focus on one set of positions rather than another. The characteristics of the community as well as the characteristics of the issue(s) guide the choice of positions.

Step Three: Interviewing the Positional Informants

At this stage of the initial interviews, as well as at the second stage of interviews discussed in step five later in the chapter, we are attempting to converse with people who often consider themselves very important and very busy. The most efficient means of securing an interview with local elites depends on the resources of the researcher. If he or she represents an important local organization or if influential people are associated with the research effort, then a third-party letter or call of introduction can ease the entree. If that is not possible, then a letter or call from the researcher asking for a confidential interview about key issues in the community may suffice. Mention that the interview will take only about thirty minutes and again stress its confidentiality.

As the interview begins, briefly explain your reason for talking to the individual (i.e., the person occupies a key community position) and mention again that the source of the observations recorded (by hand, not machine)[3] will remain confidential. Then ask the informant:

1. "In your opinion, which five individuals in this community are the most influential in _____?" (either choose a general issue—e.g., education, health care, economic growth—or you might simply ask for the entire community—e.g., Waco).

2. "Now, would you please rank those individuals, one through five, in terms of their influence in _____?" (again, either a general issue or the whole community). Be prepared at this point to answer questions from the informant such as "Influential in what way?" or "What do you mean by _____?" (issue) with a direct response that introduces as little bias as possible. In other words, develop a standard definition of influence (e.g., the ability to lead others or to get things done) and issues that can be used in subsequent interviews. When possible, allow the informants to use their own definitions; but if you are asked for a clarification, provide explanations that will move informant responses toward the information you desire.

After the ranking, a good follow-up is asking open-ended questions about the issue, the individuals named, and the ranking. The goal here is to gather additional background information about the people and processes involved in the topic of interest. After recording the responses to the open-ended questions, the interview can move on to other issue areas. At this point, questions 1 and 2 and the open-ended follow-up questions are repeated for each issue.

If only a few issues are considered, the interview is likely to be relatively brief with time available to go over the lists again for revisions. If this is done for one positional informant, however, it should be done for all.

Step Four: Choosing the Reputational Leaders

There are several ways to combine the information gathered in the first interviews. One straightforward method is to list everyone mentioned for a particular issue and their given ranks. Then use a point system, giving 5 points for a first-place rank, 4 points for second, and so on. Thus, if an individual were named by three different informants for a particular issue and ranked first once (1 × 5 = 5) and third twice (2 × 3 = 6), the total points given to that person would be eleven (5 + 6 = 11). Next, prepare a frequency distribution that rates the individuals mentioned by point total, and choose a cutoff point at (with luck) a natural break in the distribution. For example, in table 13-1 a numerical break occurs between Susan Silver and John April, and the ten top reputational leaders are selected for the second round of interviewing.[4]

Table 13-1   Hypothetical Ranking of Reputational Leaders from Responses of Positional Informants in Issue One

Aggregate Rank	Name	Total Points
1	Charles Tolbert*	38
2	Preston Dyer*	36
3	Paulette Edwards*	30
4	Lawrence Felice*	28
5	Mike Mansfield*	27
6	Nancy Evans*	24
7	Cynthia Burns*	23
8	Tom Meyers*	18
8	Troy Abell*	18
10	Susan Silver*	16
11	John April	4
11	Ross Staton	4
13	Harold Osborne	3
14	Jean Frank	2
15	Tillman Rodabough	1
15	John Fox	1
15	Kjell Enge	1
15	Larry Lyon	1

*selected for second round of interviews

Step Five: Interviewing the Reputational Leaders

If these reputational leaders are issue specific (i.e., if you asked about specific issues in the positional informant interviews rather than about the entire community), they are only asked about those issues that resulted in their being added to the list. Thus, for many reputational leaders there will be only one issue covered in the questioning. For some, two or more issues will be covered if those persons were mentioned as influential in more than one area. As was the case with the interviews with the positional informants, ask questions 1 and 2 to produce a ranking of leaders. And again, they are followed with open-ended questions designed to learn more about the issue(s) and the leaders.

Step Six: Choosing the "Top" Leaders

After this second series of interviews, issue-specific leadership lists are again prepared in the same way as they were for the responses from the positional informants (i.e., establish cutoff points and choose top-ranking reputational leaders for each issue). Table 13-2 is an example of responses from the same issue as in table 13-1. Because this second list is based on the responses of individuals who are perceived as leaders by knowledgeable informants in key local positions, it is assumed that it is more valid than the list of leaders produced by the first set of interviews. Thus, the top-ranked individuals from the second set of interviews are seen as the most powerful individuals for that particular issue area.

Table 13-2   Hypothetical Ranking of Top Reputational Leaders from Responses of Reputational Leaders in Issue One

Aggregate Rank	Name	Total Points
1	Troy Abell*	43
2	Charles Tolbert*	36
3	Mike Mansfield*	27
3	Robert Miller*	27
5	Susan Silver*	21
6	Harold Osborne *	18
7	Nancy Evans	5
8	Ross Staton	4
9	John April	3
10	Paulette Edwards	2
10	Cynthia Burns	2
10	Lawrence Felice	2
13	Jean Frank	1
13	Kjell Enge	1
13	Tom Meyers	1

*selected as top-ranked reputational leaders

Step Seven: Analyzing the Top Leadership

At this point, any individual or group who has gathered all the background material and conducted the forty or so interviews associated with steps three and five should possess considerable insight into the power structure of a community. However, much more information about local leadership can be gained from a systematic comparison of the questionnaire responses.

Decentralization

Figure 13-1 illustrates some of the comparisons that can be made. If a total of four separate issues were examined, we can see, for example, that power in issue three (with twelve top-ranked leaders) is considerably more decentralized than the other areas examined. Additionally, comparing the top leadership lists of issue areas one and three shows substantial overlap between the leaders since four of the six top-ranked leaders named for issue area one are also named for issue three. In effect, we can trace two patterns of decentralization: intra-issue (the number of leaders per issue) and inter-issue (the number of leaders with influence in more than one issue).

Figure 13-1   Examples of Comparisons between Leadership Lists to Determine Decentralization

	Issue 1	Issue 2	Issue 3	Issue 4	
Total number of individuals named	18	12	23	21	(10 positional informants interviewed)
Reputational leaders	10	8	10	12	(30 reputational leaders interviewed)
Total number of individuals named	15	10	20	15	
Top-ranked leaders	6	4	12	8	

Overlap of leaders between issue areas (decentralization)

Visibility and Legitimacy

Further comparisons of the leadership lists can provide information on additional dimensions of community power. One dimension is the *visibility* of the leaders. Comparing the lists in tables 13-1 and 13-2 reveals three types of leaders. Notice that in table 13-1, six persons were named as powerful in the first round of reputational interviews but were not listed among the top leadership in table 13-2 (Preston Dyer, Paulette Edwards, Lawrence Felice, Nancy Evans, Cynthia Burns, and Tom Myers). These six individuals may be perceived as symbolic leaders—leaders whose power is more apparent than real. Four persons are listed as powerful in both lists (Charles Tolbert, Mike Mansfield, Troy Abell, and Susan Silver). These four individuals may be perceived as visible leaders—leaders whose power is both apparent and real. Finally, two leaders who were not in the first group were named as powerful in the second series of interviews (Harold Osborne, Robert Miller). The influence of these two leaders is concealed from the view of many in the community. Thus, it is possible to distinguish three types of leaders by comparing the two sets of interviews: symbolic, visible, and concealed leaders (Bonjean 1963).

Still another dimension of community power may be discerned from this technique. The *legitimacy* of the leadership structure is determined by examining the elite's organizational positions in the community. For example, if the four top leaders in the issue area of education are a school superintendent, a college dean, a PTA president, and a school board member, they would all be classified as legitimate leaders for this issue area. On the other hand, if they did not hold such positions but rather had no more official authority in the area than anyone else in the community, the leadership structure would rank low in legitimacy.

Organizational Structure

Knowledge of the organizational affiliations of local elites is necessary to determine the legitimacy of their power. However, once these affiliations are determined, it becomes possible to learn about the organizational structure of community power. Through the use of sociometric or network analysis, you can trace the patterns of interconnections among key local organizations. The techniques for constructing these organizational maps of community influence were pioneered by Hunter (1953) and continued in increasingly sophisticated community power research efforts (Galaskiewicz 1985).

By charting the organizational affiliations of local elites one may find, for example, one or two organizations that include in their membership a significant portion of the community's leaders. In such a case, that organization would be seen either as a base for power in the community or as a meeting place for the powerful. In the best chicken-or-egg tradition, the correct interpretation depends on whether people are powerful because of the organizations to which they belong, or whether organizations are powerful because of the people who belong to them. In either case, knowledge of such organizational memberships remains useful. For example, in table 13-3 we see the considerable influence of the chamber of commerce. However, in this type of analysis it is important to consider the size of the organization. If the chamber of commerce has two hundred members and the local philanthropic foun-

Table 13-3   Hypothetical Distribution of Top Leaders by Organizational Membership

Organizations with more than one member	Number of members named as top leaders
Chamber of commerce	8
Rotary Club	6
Community philanthropic foundation	6
United Way	5
First National Bank	2
Prominent state university	2

dation has only ten, then the foundation's inclusion of six top leaders may be more significant than the chamber's eight.

Mapping the membership patterns of the community's leaders can also uncover various forms of organizational interlock. The same group of powerful people may belong to the same organizations. In such a case, one might assume that these organizations will pursue similar goals and represent similar interests in the community even though their formal structures and goals appear quite different. In figure 13-2 we might expect the chamber of com-

Figure 13.2   Organizational Interlock among Top Local Leaders

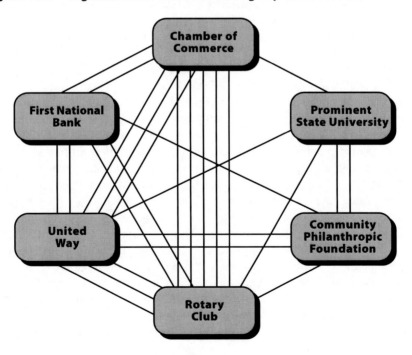

merce, the United Way, and the Rotary Club to take similar positions on local issues because of the considerable overlap in membership by top leaders.

Step Eight: Applying the Analysis toward Community Change and Development

The ability to classify local leaders by various dimensions of power is of more than academic interest. Remember that the original goal of community power research was a pragmatic one: to better understand community power in order to work more efficiently for community change and a higher quality of life. Clearly, community change strategies should vary by the degree to which power is decentralized, legitimate, or visible in the community. Producing community development models without some understanding of the structure and dynamics of community power is futile. However, two important qualifiers about applying community power research should be introduced at this point.

First, it is easy to become too impressed with the findings. After hundreds of hours and dozens of interviews, it is natural for the researcher(s) to feel that something very important has been discovered. The findings are important, but the influence of the local leadership should not be overestimated. The impact of the mass society severely limits the ability of community leaders to affect community events. If the major businesses and industries are owned by organizations headquartered thousands of miles away, then the economic impact of local decisions is lessened. Similarly, if the state and national governments have more rules and money for urban development than the municipal government, then the political impact of local decisions is likewise lessened. And, of course, the local power structure is not independent of local history (Molotch et al. 2000) or culture (Reese and Rosenfeld 2008). This is not to say that the community is a helpless pawn, completely manipulated by historical, extracommunity or nonpolitical forces, but it is necessary to acknowledge the limitations of agency when incorporating community power characteristics into community development strategies.

Second, while there is a long line of community power research contending that those who hold local power (especially if it is a centralized, concealed power) are exploitative, consistently making decisions that improve their own lives while lowering the quality of life for the rest of the community (Hunter 1953; Hayes 1972; Molotch 1976; Domhoff 1978; Feagin 1988), it does not follow that all communities and all leaders fit this mold. Although it is possible that an elite power structure is typically detrimental to a community, research that does exist on the relationship between community power and the quality of community life is mixed, with some research indicating that power structures with certain elite characteristics may be beneficial in some instances (Clark 1976, 1983; Clavel 1986; Clark and Goetz 1994).

In sum, local leaders may not always be unscrupulous capitalists working behind the scenes to enrich themselves at the expense of others. Additionally, increased knowledge of the local power structure will not necessarily bring about a more just and efficacious community. Still, as we have argued in chapter 8, it is difficult to conceive of substantial community development occurring without a systematic understanding of local decision making.

Community power research, then, is a necessary antecedent to meaningful community development, but it is not sufficient by itself. Rather, knowledge of community power should be supplemented with an understanding of other community phenomena. For example, if we discover that a hidden, centralized local elite is in opposition to increasing the number of low-cost housing units, that is an important piece of information; but without knowledge of the current number, quality, and location of low-cost housing units, the chance for a successful campaign to make low-cost housing more available is remote. Similarly, if we learn that the local leadership, as represented by the municipal government and various civic affairs groups, is strongly in favor of community growth, it is still important to discover the sentiments of the entire community as well as environmental characteristics that may inhibit or encourage growth. We are saying, then, that a holistic community research effort which considers multiple sources and types of information is best suited for guiding efforts at local change. The ways in which community power research, community polls, local indicators, and other types of community information can be combined to provide a holistic view of the community is the subject of the following chapter.

NOTES

[1] This temptation is especially strong for those who have lived in the community to be studied for a number of years. While such firsthand knowledge of the community certainly can be of value, it is not a substitute for this step. Holistic studies from *Middletown* to *Small Town in a Mass Society* have shown the subjective bias residents can have in viewing their own community.

[2] Questions of community values are clearly subjective and difficult to answer. Nevertheless, we have known ever since the *Middletown* studies that unless local values are understood, the local actions they support cannot be understood. The "community culture" studies in the previous chapter are based on this assumption.

[3] The use of an audio recording device is likely to cost more in lost respondent candor than can be gained through the more accurate recording of detailed responses.

[4] If any of the top reputational leaders were interviewed as a positional informant (a common occurrence), then they may not need to be questioned in the second round of interviews since the questions to be asked are identical.

chapter fourteen

Field Research
Holistic Studies and Methods

hello

This methods chapter is quite different from the four that precede it. The methods discussed here stand as methodological and epistemological counterpoints to formal approaches to measuring community power, to RDD and web-based surveys, and especially to objective community indicators. By way of contrast and introduction, consider the following comment from Robert Park, the University of Chicago sociologist who, in chapter 1, gave us the definition of community used in this text.

> You have been told to go grubbing in the library, thereby accumulating a mass of notes and a liberal coating of grime. You have been told to choose routine records based on trivial schedules prepared by tired bureaucrats and filled out by reluctant clerks. This is called "getting your hands dirty in real research." Those who thus counsel you are wise and honorable; the reasons they offer are of great value. But one thing more is needful: first-hand observation. Go and sit in the lounges of the luxury hotels and on the doorsteps of the flophouses; sit on the Gold Coast settees and on the slum shakedowns; sit in Orchestra Hall and in the Star and Garter Burlesk. In short, gentlemen, go get the seats of your pants dirty in *real* research. (quoted in Lindner 1996, 81*ff.*)

You may also recall that in chapter 1, holistic studies based primarily on the qualitative methods advocated by Park were introduced as prime examples of the community's preeminence as an object of sociological inquiry. The Lynds' description of life in Middletown, Park and his associates' analyses of Chicago, and Warner's Yankee City series all became classics that remain as widely cited examples of sociological research. In this penultimate chapter we look back at some of the major findings from these classic studies, determine what it was about their holistic methodology that made them classics, and update our review with some recent examples. Finally, since the holistic studies' forte is describing the various characteristics of communities, we set the stage for our final chapter—deciding which community characteristics lead to a high quality of life.

The Classic Community Studies

Holistic descriptions of community life have a history that traces back at least as far as the nineteenth century and Charles Booth's monumental studies of London (London School of Economics, 1886–1903). No other body of community research is as widely read or cited as these attempts to describe all the interrelated parts of local life.[1] Yet, from the hundreds of holistic community books and articles published since Booth, the three sets of community studies mentioned in the introduction above are generally acknowledged as the most important, as the "classic" community studies. We briefly overview each, looking at who did the research, how the community was studied, and what some of the major findings were.

The Middletown Studies

The husband-and-wife team of Robert and Helen Lynd did not set out to do a holistic community study in Middletown (Muncie, Indiana). Rather, their more focused initial goal was a study of religious worship[2] in a community "having many features common to a wide group of communities" (Lynd and Lynd 1929, 3). They soon discovered, however, that in order to study religion they needed to study all the other local phenomena related to religion as well. Thus, during the eighteen months of 1924–25 when they lived in Middletown, their concern was with all of the "interwoven trends that are the life of a small American city" (*ibid.*).

Middletown.   The product of the Lynds' field research in Muncie was one of the best-written, most interesting, best-selling books sociology has ever produced: *Middletown: A Study in Contemporary American Culture*. This book, along with the remarkably similar fictional works of Sinclair Lewis (*Main Street* [1920] and *Babbitt* [1922]), created the dominant images of small-town America during the 1920s and 1930s.

The goal of the Lynds (1929, 3) was description: "Neither fieldwork nor report has attempted to prove any thesis: the aim has been, rather, to *record* observed phenomena." In this regard, they succeeded almost too well. Ruth Glass (1966, 148) calls such works "the poor sociologist's substitute for a novel." Bell and Newby (1972, 13) note that "the highly descriptive nature of many community studies leads to the danger of their being dismissed as pieces of documentary social history, contributing little to our knowledge of social processes." And Stein (1960, 47) warns us that it is "too easy to read both *Middletown* volumes as if they were purely descriptive reports" so that the "mass of absorbing details lulls the reader into an aesthetic rather than a scientific frame of mind."

Certainly, the amazingly detailed description of life in Muncie is a striking characteristic of the *Middletown* volumes. In the first book, for example, we are treated to nine pages simply describing and explaining how the residents dress:

Were the sole use of clothing that of protection of the body, the urgent
local discussion of the "morality" of women's clothing would probably
never have arisen. Today, men's clothing still covers the body decorously
from chin to soles of the feet. Among women and girls, however, skirts
have shortened from the ground to the knee and the lower limbs have
been emphasized by sheer silk stockings; more of the arms and neck are
habitually exposed; while the increasing abandonment of petticoats and
corsets reveals more of the natural contours of the body. . . . All of which
reveals the fact that the moral function of clothing, while it has persisted
without variation among the males, has undergone marked modification
among the females. As one high school boy confidently remarked, "The
most important contribution of our generation is the one-piece bathing
suit for women. . . ." Even among the men, including working-class men,
it is apparently less common today than in the nineties to renounce any
effort at appearing well dressed by speaking scornfully of dudes. . . . The
early sophistication of the young includes the custom of wearing expensive clothing; as in other social rituals, entrance to high school appears to
be the dividing line. The cotton stockings and high black shoes of 1890
are no longer tolerated. The wife of a working man with a total family
income of $1,638, said as a matter of course, "No girl can wear cotton
stockings to high school. Even in winter my children wear silk stockings
with lisle or imitations underneath. . . ." Only a minority of the junior
and senior boys attending big dances wear tuxedos, but the obligatory
nature of special evening dress for the girls is much more marked. . . . All
of which helps to explain the observed trend in the preparation of clothing
in Middletown. The providing of clothing for individual members of the
family is traditionally an activity of the home, but since the nineties it has
tended to be less a hand-skill activity of the wife in the home and more a
part of the husband's money-earning. (Lynd and Lynd 1929, 156–65)

The Lynds document this movement away from home sewing with statistical data measuring how many bolts of fabric have been sold in local
department stores, the amount of time Muncie women devote to sewing and
mending; how the amount of time varies by class; and even whether most of
the sewing is for themselves, daughters, sons, or husbands. (It is, by the way,
for their daughters.)

In short, *Middletown* is page after page of verbal and statistical description, with largely value-neutral interpretation, in the best anthropological tradition. For example, while today's social analysts often point to the need of
American women to dress in provocative styles as an example of sex-based
exploitation, the Lynds (1929, 63) simply observe that "girls fight with
clothes in competition for a mate as truly as Indians of the Northwest coast
fight with potlatch for social prestige."

Middletown in Transition.   Value-laden interpretations become more
common in *Middletown in Transition*, however. When the Lynds returned to
Muncie in 1935, they wished to learn how the residents had reacted to the
Great Depression. Generally, they reacted surprisingly well. The business

leaders saw the Depression as a temporary inconvenience and Roosevelt's New Deal as unnecessary government intrusion. The working class, even with high levels of unemployment, appeared remarkably patient, waiting for the return of prosperity. This lack of class consciousness, this "apathy" among the workers that the Lynds discovered, was so upsetting that their disappointment colored the analysis:

> . . . the sprawled inertness of Middletown working-class opinion—as over against the more vocal and coherent opinion of the business class—may conceivably take shape slowly in a self-conscious sharpening of class lines. But neither class morale, sources of information, nor personal leadership for such a development is apparent at present among Middletown's working class. Much depends upon whether "good times" return in as beguiling a form as they were in the 1920s. If they do, the deeper pattern of political loyalty to the old symbols, plus the willingness of these individual working-class atoms to dance to any tune that will give them an automobile and "show them a good time," will transform their momentary position in the political limelight under the New Deal and in the election of 1936 into only a vaguely remembered benchmark. For today, as in 1924, the Middletown voter is not a political self-starter, and Elihu Root's advice, widely heralded in Middletown at the time of the 1924 election, still applies: "All you have got to do is to wake them up, have someone take the head of the crowd and march them. Tell them where to go, whether Democrats or Republicans, I do not care . . . and the organizers . . . will welcome them and set them to work." (Lynd and Lynd 1937, 367)

The Lynds' values are most clearly on display, however, in their description of the X family. This powerful business family is never mentioned in *Middletown,* but in *Middletown in Transition* they dominate Muncie. While the Lynds explain that the Depression so strengthened the position of the X family that they could not be overlooked in the second book,[3] others suggest it may have been the authors' exposure to Marx's writing between the two volumes (e.g., Bell and Newby 1972, 90). Whatever the reason, the ability of the business class (exemplified by the X family) to define the values of Muncie is the dominating theme of *Middletown in Transition.* They quote one citizen: "The big point about this town" is that "the Xs dominate the whole town, *are* the town in fact." On the same page, they conclude that "Middletown has, therefore, at present what amounts to a reigning royal family" and ominously conclude that

> if one views the Middletown pattern as simply concentrating and personalizing the type of control which control of capital gives to the business group in our culture, the Middletown situation may be viewed as epitomizing the American business-class control system. It may even foreshadow a pattern which may become increasingly prevalent in the future as the American propertied class strives to preserve its controls. (Lynd and Lynd 1937, 77)

As we shall see, the Lynds were better in their fieldwork than in their social forecasting. In terms of the X family, Muncie today has changed considerably from the Lynds' last visit. Though the jars that made the Xs immune to the Depression still say "Ball" on the side, they are not manufactured in Muncie and ownership is in a Colorado-based conglomerate. Few of the X family are still in Muncie, and those that remain are not active in local affairs.

Middletown III.   Still, the X family notwithstanding, it would be incorrect to assume that modern Muncie is that different from the way it was in the 1920s and 1930s. When Theodore Caplow and his associates returned to restudy Muncie in 1976, they found a community remarkably similar to the one described by the Lynds fifty years earlier. The Middletown III project replicated the Lynds' research and produced two books, *Middletown Families* (Caplow, Bahr, Chadwick, Hill, and Williamson 1982), *All Faithful People* (Caplow, Bahr, and Chadwick 1983), and numerous articles. The general theme of these publications has been the continuity of lifestyles in Muncie. They maintain that a "Middletown Rip van Winkle, awakening in the 1970s from a 50-year-long sleep, would have noticed innumerable changes but would not have had any trouble finding his way around town. . . . Robert Lynd is gone, but we, walking the same streets half a century later, feel the same continuity while noting the changes" (Caplow et al. 1982, 3–4).

The changes that have occurred are almost all externally induced. Middletowners are described as grudgingly accepting the adjustments forced upon them by the larger postindustrial society. Thus, Caplow and his associates are not surprised to find that the residents have not changed all that much since their grandparents were studied by the Lynds:

> Change, for Middletown, is something flowing irresistibly from the outside world. Continuity is furnished locally. The outside world continuously proposes new ways of living and thinking. The local community steadfastly resists most of these suggestions and modifies those it adopts into conformity with its own customs. . . . The decision to live in Middletown, a voluntary one for most of its adult residents, is a vote for custom and against innovation, and it is not surprising that a population recruited in that way should be able to resist innovation with considerable success. (Caplow et al. 1982, 5)

One of the most intriguing findings from the Middletown III project concerns the effect of class position on lifestyles. Caplow and Bruce Chadwick (1979) used census data to measure occupational inequality between 1920 and 1970. They found that Muncie experienced an overall increase in both occupational prestige and in inequality—a trend similar to that for the entire US workforce during that period. Yet, when they replicated the Lynds' community surveys and compared the responses by social class, a very different pattern emerged. By reconstructing the Lynds' detailed lifestyle descriptions, they found that the pronounced differences between the "business" and "working" classes in Muncie have virtually disappeared. For many lifestyle variations—housework (broken down by time spent washing and ironing, sewing and mending, baking), the availability of paid help, educational aspirations, desired traits for their children, time spent with children, the quality of housing, marital satisfaction, unemployment, women working outside the home, and even the time waking up—there has been a dramatic narrowing of differences between the classes. In fact, the class differences in lifestyles have narrowed to a degree that Caplow and Chadwick conclude that it is no longer the significant dividing line it was in the Lynds' day.

This Middletown III stratification research is interesting at two levels. First, it shows that the classic studies' almost obsessive reporting of detail is not altogether trivial or idiosyncratic. In this case, when replicated fifty years later, it tells us something very important about lifestyles that was missed with census data: namely, that social class differences *in how we live* are not nearly as pronounced as they once were. Second, this project illustrates an inherent strength in community research and an inherent flaw in much national research. When the society is the unit of analysis, as it is in most modern stratification research, it is difficult to capture the detailed description inherent in community research. National data often miss the important stuff of which lives are made. Thus, Roland Warren and Larry Lyon (1983, 84) argued that the Middletown III[4] replication illustrates a continuing importance for holistic community studies—an importance that extends beyond the role envisioned in Maurice Stein's *Eclipse of the Community:*

> [s]omething very important has occurred in Middletown—an equalization of lifestyles between classes—that may well have also occurred throughout the United States. National data, however, do not have the intensive, descriptive quality of community studies necessary to find out. It may be, then, that we can extend Stein's conclusion about the role of holistic community studies. Communities "do provide a meeting ground . . . which the depersonalizing forces of mass society can diminish but never destroy." But beyond that, communities may provide a research site that allows the discovery of mass society characteristics that are not readily observable at the national level.

And finally, in support of Warren and Lyon's position, though the Lynds chose Middletown in part because it possessed only "a small Negro and foreign born population" (Lynd and Lynd 1929, 8) recent research in Muncie has found that racial divides have also lessened, though to a lesser degree than class (Bahr, Pearson, Elder, and Hicks 2007).

The Chicago Studies

The studies of Chicago by Robert Park and his associates were discussed in chapter 3. Here, rather than focusing on the ecological approach developed through these studies, we will look more generally at the views of Chicago they provided.

Disorder versus order. For Park and many of his colleagues who grew up in small communities, Chicago must have presented an extreme contrast.

Chicago was huge (with a population of approximately three million), diverse (e.g., extreme wealth and poverty, ethnic neighborhoods), disorganized (e.g., youth gangs, crime) and growing (adding about one-half million per decade). Thus, it is not surprising that the Chicago studies emphasize change (urban growth models, invasion–succession processes) while all three Middletown studies emphasize the continuity in Muncie. Also, since Chicago was so large and diverse, most of their analysis is not holistic in the strictest sense (i.e., focusing on *all* of Chicago). The primary unit of analysis was the natural areas of Chicago—studies of subcommunities such as Clifford Shaw's *Delinquency Areas* (1929), Frederick Thrasher's *The Gang* (1927), Harvey Zorbaugh's *The Gold Coast and Slum* (1929), and Louis Wirth's *The Ghetto* (1928). Still, the studies are holistic in that they seek to describe everything within the natural area and to explain how the natural areas were related to the rest of the city.

In many of these studies, the overriding theme (besides the ecological emphasis on spatial patterning) was social control. Much like Durkheim's questions about how organization and integration might be maintained in a modern industrial society, Park and his associates were concerned with how order could be maintained in the face of the disorganization brought by rapid urbanization. And for the Chicago sociologists, the key to learning how social control is maintained was to be found in the natural areas. Maurice Stein (1960, 20), in his review of Park's work, concludes that his "starting point was existing social disorganization in the city of Chicago and his main structural units the various subcommunities in which this disorganization appeared as well as the agencies of 'secondary control' which tried to keep it from getting out of hand."

Natural areas.   Zorbaugh's *The Gold Coast and Slum* (1929) may be used as an example. Here we find intensive description of two contrasting natural areas: (1) the Gold Coast along Lake Michigan, where many of the wealthiest residents live "in imposing stone mansions, with their green lawns and wrought-iron-grilled doorways" (*ibid.*, 7); and (2) the slums of "Little Sicily," "Little Italy," and "Little Hell," where "the criminal, the radical, the bohemian, the migratory worker, the immigrant, the unsuccessful, the queer, and the unadjusted" live (*ibid.*, 11).

The physical setting of the Gold Coast is described in detail, as well as the lifestyles of the rich who live there. The various cliques of wealthy families are mapped, and the informal rules for being added to the Social Register are described in terms of a "social game." Moving away from the lake, the transient "world of furnished rooms" is described next. Then comes the radical bohemia of "Towertown," and finally the slums where "one alien group after another has claimed this area. The Irish, the Germans, the Swedish, the Sicilians have occupied it in turn. Now, it is being invaded by a migration of the Negro from the south" (*ibid.*, 127). Each invasion, of course, leads to disorganization and the need to reestablish some modicum of social control.

The commonality between these contrasting natural areas was the attempts to deal with social disorganization. The "social game" and the Social Register helped establish order among the rich, just as "old world" norms and values maintained control in ethnic neighborhoods. Thus, the Chicago studies, Zorbaugh's *The Gold Coast and Slum* in particular, can be seen as an attempt to document the process that concerned both Durkheim and Park—how the solidarity and control that are inherently maintained during *gemeinschaft*-like times might be maintained during the current *gesellschaft*-like times. The descriptive studies of natural areas in Chicago document the precarious, fragile state of a *gemeinschaft*-based organic solidarity.

The Yankee City Studies

The five volumes[5] comprising W. Lloyd Warner's analysis of the New England town of Newburyport are the third of the classic community studies considered here. It is the most widely criticized of the classic studies, and most of the criticisms are well founded. Yet in spite of its faults, Warner's Yankee City series has had a substantial impact on American sociology. In this section we look at both the shortcomings and significance of Yankee City.

The Yankee City research was connected initially with Elton Mayo's famous productivity studies at the Western Electric Plant (e.g., the Hawthorne effect). Warner's role was to study the home environment of the Western Electric workers, but he rejected all the cities (subcommunities of Chicago) where the workers lived as being too diverse and disorganized and hence not well-suited for the anthropological field methods he had practiced with the Australian aborigines. So, after what he claims was an exhaustive search for a community that represents all of America, Warner chose Newburyport—small, organized, and "near-enough to Cambridge so that [we] could go back and forth without difficulty or loss of time" (Warner and Lunt 1941, 43). Of course, in deliberately selecting a small, organized community, he was also selecting a community not at all representative of much of America, and by choosing a community conveniently located near Cambridge, one must doubt how thorough the selection process actually was. In any event, Newburyport was Warner's representative for all US communities.

The first volume of the Yankee City series presents Warner's most important find: the stratification system of Newburyport.[6] In a sense, when social class was discovered in America, it was discovered in Yankee City by W. Lloyd Warner. Warner empirically demonstrated that the residents of Yankee City (1) can readily rank other members of the community even though they may disavow the existence of any local class system; (2) separate themselves into six distinct classes (in Warner's terms, upper-upper, lower-upper, upper-middle, lower-middle, upper-lower, and lower-lower); (3) do not view economic considerations as the sole indicator of class position; and (4) have much of their life determined (where they live, whom they may marry, organizations they belong to, the type of job, the amount of education) by their class position. Such findings may seem obvious today, but in the 1940s these were new and rather radical discoveries in a discipline that had conspicuously ignored stratification research.

The second major contribution from the Yankee City series appears in the fourth volume, *The Social System of the Modern Factory* (1947). While much of the volume traces ethnic mobility patterns, Warner's methodology was flawed here and his conclusions probably incorrect. However, this volume also includes insightful analysis of a strike in Newburyport that Stein uses to illustrate the bureaucratization trend in *The Eclipse of Community* (1960). Warner answers four questions about the strike:

1. In a community where there had been very few strikes and no successful ones, why did the workers in all of the factories of the largest industry of the community strike, win all their demands and, after a severe struggle, soundly defeat management?

2. In a community where unions had previously tried and failed to gain more than a weak foothold and where there had never been a strong union, why was a union successful in separating the workers from management?

3. Why was the union successful in maintaining the organization despite the intense and prolonged efforts of management to prevent unionization and to halt the continuation of the shoe union?

4. Why did Yankee City change from a nonunion to a union town? (Warner and Low 1947, 6–7).

At first glance, the answers to all four of these questions would seem to hinge on the Depression, but Warner shows that the economic problems of the 1930s are not sufficient to explain the changes in Newburyport:

> Plainly, labor had won its first strike in Yankee City, and, even more plainly, an industrial union had invaded the city for the first time and had become the recognized champion of the workers. When searching for the answers to why such significant, new changes could occur in Yankee City, the evidence is clear that economic factors are of prime importance. But before we are content to accept them as the only answers to our problems, let us once more remind ourselves (1) that there had been severe depressions and low wages before and the union had failed to organize the workers, and (2) that the last and most powerful strike which preceded the present one occurred not in a depression but during a boom period when wages where high and economic conditions were excellent. Other factors are necessary and must be found if we are to understand the strike and have a full explanation of why it occurred and took the course that it did. (Warner and Low 1947, 53)

A full explanation included a change in factory ownership. The local owners were replaced by "a vast, complex system owned, managed and dominated by New York City" (Warner and Low 1947, 64). Now, the "big-city outsiders" who made the policy decisions were beyond the influence of local workers. And in response, the local workers joined extracommunity unions, aligning themselves with workers in similar factories throughout the region. The result, then, was a situation in which events in the larger mass society began dominating the local community—thus Stein's conclusion about *The Eclipse of Community.*

The final volume, *The Living and the Dead,* considers the symbolism of Yankee City, how fictionalized history and political myths integrate the community. While the first four volumes emphasize description (one table in volume II, for example, is 86 pages long), this final volume is more an exercise in theory and interpretation. The first 100 pages are devoted to one "Biggy Muldoon":

> Our present story is concerned with the good and evil fortunes of Biggy Muldoon. It tells why all of Yankee City, where he was elected mayor, and millions of people throughout the United States became emotionally involved in his political and private life. It attempts to explain how the joy, anger, and sorrow they experienced in his spectacular triumphs and bitter defeats helped to develop and expand, yet control and limit, his career. Many of the crucial factors operating in his political life have always been powerful in the political and social life of America. If we can learn the meaning of his career we may gain deeper insight into some of the more important aspects of American politics. (Warner 1959, 9)

And we are told later that Biggy's political career is similar to those of Al Smith, Huey Long, Fiorello La Guardia, William Jennings Bryan, Andrew Jackson, Abraham Lincoln, and Franklin Roosevelt. Such comparisons of a small-town mayor with national leaders are not surprising, however, since Warner always felt his community studies could be translated to the national scene.[7]

Warner's concern with stratification continues, but in this final volume, perhaps in response to criticisms of the earlier volumes, class is not treated statistically. Rather, he returns to the ethnographic methods he used as an anthropologist in Australia to describe how Biggy's class position made him a hero of the "common man" and an enemy to the "better class" of Yankee City:

> Biggy Muldoon, the "Yankee City Bad Boy," is a big-shouldered, two-fisted, red-haired Irishman. He was born down by the river on the wrong side of the tracks, the only child of Irish-Catholic immigrant parents. Once a street-fighter, a brawler, and an all-round tough guy, he was arrested by the police for shooting dice, profane and abusive language, fighting, and other rough behavior distasteful to the pious and respectable. (Warner 1959, 9)

Biggy's skillful use of symbols (e.g., remodeling a mansion into a gas station) to crystallize class antagonisms were the key to his rapid rise, but his antagonistic relationship with the upper class eventually led to his downfall. "Biggy's continual attacks on political authority and on the status system forced people toward either open revolt against the system—too frightening for most of them to sustain—or annoyance, embarrassment, and finally confusion and weariness" (Warner 1959, 95). We learn, from Biggy, how symbols may be manipulated to induce change, but we also learn how the values on which the symbols are based define limits which eventually reduce the potential for change.

Thus, Warner ends his series on Newburyport in a very different way than his earlier volumes. Here we find less of the eclectic data collector-index builder and more of an ethnographer-novelist-political theorist-philosopher. This final volume has been ignored by most social scientists, which is probably a worse fate than being attacked (as the earlier volumes were). Still, Warner's flawed efforts continue to be cited in books on community, social change, and stratification. His works remain influential, as do the efforts in Muncie and Chicago. Our question now is *why*? Why are these studies classics? What makes them special?

Why Are the Classics Classic?

The qualities that make one study, one book, one play, one painting, one anything more important and enduring than another are continually debated. And while it is impossible to state precisely why the studies of Muncie, Chicago, and Newburyport have become community sociology's best-known products, examining some of their common characteristics should provide clues as to why these studies have achieved such an influential status.

Writing Style

Perhaps the most obvious trait shared by the classics is a remarkably lively, lucid writing style. They are so well written, in fact, that they sometimes seem more like classic works of fiction than fact. Bell and Newby (1972) compare Lloyd Warner's writings on Yankee City and Jonesville to Sinclair Lewis's Gopher Prairie and Zenith City in *Babbit* and *Martin Arrowsmith*. Warner himself felt obligated to disclaim a purported connection with his description of Biggy Muldoon and O'Connor's fictional mayor in *The Last Hurrah* (1956). Stein (1960) compares the Lynds' Middletown books with Lewis's *Babbit* and *Main Street* and compares many of the Chicago classics to the novels of Theodore Dreiser. Other near-classics, like Davis, Gardner, and Gardner's *Deep South* and especially John Dollard's *Class and Caste in a Southern Town,* can be seen as the sociological counterpart of William Faulkner's novels.

The ability of these classic works to describe communities without a preponderance of the jargon common in most sociological reports is unusual and no doubt accounts for much of their popularity in sales with the general public. It may also explain why so many noncommunity social scientists have read these works, and why, since their absence of jargon places them out of the mainstream, they are no longer cited in most of the major community research efforts.

One reason these classics are so well written, so free of technical jargon, is that they were often written by nonsociologists. Warner, of course, was trained as an anthropologist, and Robert Lynd did not receive a sociology

degree until after his Middletown research. That cannot be the whole explanation, however, since many community studies (e.g., the Chicago studies)
were authored by sociologists.

Another possible reason for the ease with which they are read is the subject matter—the whole community. When the focus is as broad as the holistic
studies, it is easier to be interesting. There is seldom extended, intensive, and
often tedious attention to one phenomenon. Rather, the authors move from
one local phenomenon to another and, in so doing, seldom reach the readers'
boredom threshold as often as other more tightly focused works. In any
event, these classics are well written, and that would seem to have something
to do with their achieving classic status.

A Holistic Approach

Another important common feature of these classics is the attempt to
describe all of the community. The community is not just the place where the
object of inquiry (a family, or school, or business) happens to be: *it is the object
of inquiry.* The Lynds initially may have been interested in religion, and stratification may have been especially important to Warner, but both the Middletown and Yankee City books show how the various local phenomena relate
to one another and to the greater whole. The Chicago studies, because of the
physical enormity of the subject, focus on subcommunities ("natural areas"),
but even here there is an explicit concern with the different parts of the natural area and how they relate to other parts of the city.

The Chicago studies' concern with how each subcommunity relates to
the larger community makes them perhaps less vulnerable to a common
charge leveled against holistic community studies: that by being so concerned
with describing all the different characteristics that influence local events,
important extralocal influences are ignored. Even the Chicago studies, however, paid little attention to national events affecting their community. While
Warner and, especially, the Lynds are less guilty of the omission than many
holistic researchers, it is impossible to study everything. Thus, even the best
holistic studies, in their attempts to broadly describe community life, often
give little attention to life outside the community.

The holistic studies are deliberately, necessarily broad. The goal is to
understand the community as a totality, and such a goal generally leads to
extensive description. It is not surprising, then, that another commonality in
these classic community studies is their abundance of descriptive detail.

Emphasis on Description

Description is often placed above analysis in the holistic community
studies. Remember the Lynds' (1929, 3) claim that "neither fieldwork nor
report has attempted to prove any thesis: The aim has been, rather to *record*
observed data, thereby raising questions and suggesting fresh points of departure in the study of group behavior." Such a "let the facts speak for them-

selves" approach is the rule for most of these studies. In fact, one might argue that when the Lynds strayed too far from this rule (e.g., predicting a national centralization of capital and power à la the X family) they were at their weakest. The same can be said for Warner when he ventured into the building of scales to measure social class, or the Chicago sociologists with their organic analogies. What these classic community studies do best is describe. Analysis was seldom their forte.[8]

Now it is often argued that such raw empiricism is atheoretical and hence ultimately sterile. Note, however, in the Lynds' quotation above, they imply that their descriptions can provide the basis for future analysis, and it has. As examples, Stein's *Eclipse of the Community* is an important theoretical work built upon the descriptions of local life provided by the classics, and the Lynds' seemingly trivial descriptions of how much time was devoted to household chores provided the basis for Middletown III's provocative analysis about changes in inequality.

Eclectic Methodology

For the holistic community studies, almost anything goes. That is, any method that can provide information is fair game. Bell and Newby (1972, 54) believe that "community study as a method has been so varied and eclectic, and so determined by the object of study, that some doubt must be cast on whether there is a single community study method." In the classic studies examined here, that is certainly the case. Surveys, analysis of available data, and especially field studies are part of the community methodology. In fact, all of the methods discussed in Part III of this text can be found in holistic studies. In this section we look briefly at how the methods discussed in the previous chapters—community surveys, measures of power, local indicators—are employed in holistic research and then consider in some detail the method most commonly associated with holistic community studies: field research.

Community surveys. Not all community sociologists believe surveys belong in holistic studies. In fact, some very influential ones have argued against surveys. Bell and Newby (1972, 61) maintained that "the survey is arguably of marginal relevance for studying the community." Vidich, Bensman, and Stein (1964, x) go even further in expressing their distaste for surveys, arguing that such "abstract" methods remove us so far from reality that "the analyst who uses the instruments is unable to present an image of social behavior as it appears in a 'natural setting'":

> The point may be emphasized by postulating what would result if all research were conducted by questionnaires, surveys, checklists, and the other modern technologies. These devices, which essentially allow the investigator to accumulate a relatively narrow dimension of experience from a large number of persons, produce a collective portrait of responses to an item. Theoretically a sufficient accumulation of such responses, when "recombined," should add up to a total portrait of reality. In actual

fact, however, the reality evoked is in response to the research instrument. (Vidich, Bensman, and Stein 1964, xi)

Such criticisms are indeed applicable to the *exclusive* reliance on surveys for local information, but when they are used in conjunction with other methods (as is always the case in a holistic approach), then the survey's weak points are offset by the strengths of the other methods. Certainly Warner's research was strengthened by surveys, and the Lynds' surveys provided the benchmarks necessary for the Middletown III project. In short, although the local survey is an important tool for holistic study, it is only one of many tools in the chest of community researchers.

Community indicators.   Since the term *community indicators* is a recent one, it is not used by the authors of the classic community studies. However, the use of available statistics to learn about community phenomena goes back far beyond the current local indicator movement. Warner's research team, for example, may well hold the all-time record for gathering social indicators. In his study of Yankee City lists, Warner claims to have gathered and used

> . . . directories, the records, rules, and histories of institutions, the regulations governing the community . . . membership lists of the several hundred associations . . . lists of pupils, voters, customers of stores, and city officials, . . . names of persons buried in the several cemeteries . . . lists of subscribers to all the Boston newspapers and the local newspaper . . . the city directory or the poll-tax book . . . census of the federal government . . . annual reports of the city government . . . records of school attendance . . . records of the books and reading club . . . records for individual attendance at the movies . . . plots of the plays . . . records of the parades. (Warner and Lunt 1941, 61–64)

The sources Warner used in his Yankee City study included much more than what he lists in the above quotation. To a lesser extent, the use of all available data is present in all the classic community studies. The rule for holistic studies is "if it's available, use it."

Field Research

Although holistic studies are eclectic in their methods, there is one method that is almost always employed—one method associated so closely with community research that it is the *sine qua non* for these studies. The first and most important generalization, from which much else follows, is that community sociologists have usually gone, sometimes for only a short while, to *live* in *their* community. Community sociologists are fieldworkers: They have shared *some* of the experience of *some* of the inhabitants of the locality in which they are interested (Bell and Newby 1972, 54–55).

Unlike the other methods in these chapters, exactly what one does in the field is difficult to specify. William F. Whyte, who was an exceptional field researcher for his *Street Corner Society* (1955), bemoaned the lack of instructional material for community field methods. Yet when he tried to explain his own field methodologies, he decided that "so much of analysis proceeds on the unconscious level, I am sure that we can never present a full account of it" (Whyte 1964, 4).

Fieldwork is an individualistic research method that requires unique adaptations by person and community. Training helps make a good field researcher, but insight and personality probably matter more. Whyte, for example, was studying to be a writer as an undergraduate at Swarthmore (being a good writer is a necessity for a field researcher who wants to be published) and had little instruction in field methods while he was a participant-observer in the *Street Corner Society*. Robert Lynd was trained for the ministry. Still, not everyone just stumbles into field research. Warner, an anthropologist, was trained formally in field methods. And while it may not be possible to develop a set of specific rules for effective field research, some general guidelines are available.

Definitions. To begin, what *exactly* is field research? The "exactly" makes this question a particularly difficult one. For example, Lofland et al. (2006, 5), in their primer on qualitative methods, argue that field research is similar to other techniques such as field studies, ethnography, "qualitative social research, qualitative methods, grounded theory and naturalism." And none of these slightly different terms appears able to lead us out of what they call a "terminological jungle where many labels compete." That is, no one can say precisely where naturalism becomes ethnography or where qualitative methods differ from field methods. And yet no label has been able to stand for all the variations. For qualitative analysis generally, such confusion over the appropriate term will probably continue. However, for holistic community studies, with their anthropological emphasis on living and participating in the community, it would seem that *field* research, *field*work, or *field* methods, is the preferred term. Thus, community field research is the direct descendant of anthropological field methods and implies the same types of participation and observation as anthropologists use to describe small, isolated, primitive villages.

Research roles. Since living in the community is a necessary part of field research, it is important to analyze the role played by community researchers. Do the researchers cover up their real role of researcher and pretend to be someone else, or should they simply announce to community residents that they are there to study them? There are, naturally, advantages and disadvantages with either strategy; but whether it is because of anthropological tradition (anthropologists could not easily pretend to be natives) or because of ethical considerations involved with deceiving the town's residents, the most commonly played role in community studies is that of researcher.

How researchers announce to the community that they are there to study is called an "entry" problem. Entry problems revolve around how access is gained into the community. In the typical anthropological tradition of the lone researcher, entry is gained through the sponsorship of a key informant. For example, until Whyte was adopted by "Doc," he could not make any progress towards acceptance in the *Street Corner Society* (1955). Liebow never could have written *Tally's Corner* (1967) without Tally's sponsorship. The informants who sponsored Whyte and Liebow provided the entree that allowed them to produce books of considerable insight, but they also introduce a certain bias in that the researchers are "captured" by the informant. If Whyte or Liebow had had different informants, they would have produced different books with different views of the neighborhood. This is not to say that their view is wrong, only that it is influenced strongly by the views of their informants.[9]

When the community is studied by a team of researchers, entry is usually not dependent upon the sponsorship of a key informant. And in most cases, when the researcher moves beyond the neighborhood to an entire community, the lone researcher gives way to the team approach. Robert and Helen Lynd were assisted by two additional researchers and a secretary. Caplow's team was considerably larger for the restudy, and Warner's project engaged a research staff of thirty, eighteen of whom were fieldworkers. For a truly holistic community study, teams are preferable because there is simply too much for one person to observe. A team can have observers in several places and can have informants from several strata. Of course, simply having a team of researchers will not, by itself, guarantee a less biased report. For example, although Warner was aware of six classes in Yankee City, his interviews were predominantly from the lower-upper class, a level with which he and his team members (mostly undergraduates from Harvard and Radcliffe) could identify.

Hypothesis testing. The question of whether the field researchers should have a theoretically based hypothesis to guide their descriptive efforts has usually been answered in the negative. Remember that the Lynds' goal was description rather than analysis, and most guides to field research agree that using hypotheses to guide the description is too inhibiting. Still, one often suspects that hidden hypotheses may be guiding the research. For example, the Middletown III project has been criticized for describing only those events that emphasize continuity and stability while ignoring other data that suggest radical change and discord (Cherlin 1982). Caplow and his associates did not explicitly set out to find a remarkably unchanged Muncie or a continuingly strong family, but such hypotheses may have developed unconsciously during the project and affected their data collection. In any event, fieldwork differs significantly from other methodologies in that it is more often a method for hypothesis generating than for hypothesis testing.

The role of the hypothesis is but one of the ways in which field methods differ from the other research methodologies available for community studies. It requires a distinctive kind of researcher whose personality and insight are more important than the possession of trainable skills.[10] It produces qualitative data that do not lend themselves to validation or comparison. Yet it also produces descriptions of behavior that seem much closer than other methods to the reality of human existence. This is what Vidich, Bensman, and Stein (1964, xi) refer to when they conclude that "as a consequence of the unwillingness of most community researchers to forsake direct observation and direct reporting of community life, we still have coherent images of the community and social life that are unattainable by other methodologies." Herbert Gans (1962, 350) draws a similar conclusion when he argues that the field research's "deficiencies in producing quantitative data are more than made up for by its ability to minimize the distance between the researcher and his object of study." So the distinctive advantages of field methods mean that it can make a unique contribution to a holistic community study, but its distinctive disadvantages also account for why other methods are typically used to supplement it.

More Recent Holistic Studies

The classic research in Middletown, Chicago, and Yankee City served as exemplars for the holistic community studies in this chapter, and they performed that role admirably. That is not to imply, however, that important holistic community research is not continuing in places besides Muncie. In this final section, we will look briefly at some of the more recent holistic studies of community. We will note that the focus narrows for these efforts, both methodologically and geographically. Methodologically ethnographic techniques predominate, crowding out surveys and community indicators. Geographically, the focus moves away from the entire community and focuses instead on one (typically disadvantaged) neighborhood.

Herbert Gans: The Urban Villagers and The Levittowners

Herbert Gans lived in what most of us would call a slum—the West End of Boston—in the late 1950s. His participation with and observation of the Italian Americans who lived there convinced him that the West End was not a slum, but rather an "urban village" in which *gemeinschaft*-like ties enabled poor people living in a rundown area of Boston to make the best of a bad situation. In fact, Gans concludes that, all things considered, the West Enders created a community with a reasonably good quality of life. Urban planners, with their surveys and census data, reached a different conclusion, however. They designated the entire neighborhood for urban renewal. By 1960, over 20,000 West-Enders had been "relocated" to make way for the high-rise office and apartment complexes.[11]

Much of *The Urban Villagers* (1962) can be read as a plea by Gans to urban planners—urging them to reassess their definitions of urban blight and slums. His book was a leader in a series of anti-urban renewal books (e.g., Jane Jacobs's *The Death and Life of Great American Cities,* 1961, and Scott Greer's *Urban Renewal and American Cities,* 1964). Perhaps even more important (since urban renewal was probably on the way out by the mid-1960s regardless), *The Urban Villagers* is a powerful testament both to what "objective" data cannot show about a community and to how community can exist in a place seemingly devoid of community by middle-class standards, a point echoed a few years later by Gerald Suttles in *The Social Order of the Slum* (1968).

Gans relied again on participant observation when he and his wife were among the first families to move into the new suburban community of Levittown in 1958. Levittown was a working-class suburb built "from scratch" by Levitt and Sons on the New Jersey side of Philadelphia. After moving away in 1960, Gans returned to Levittown two years later to complete additional fieldwork and interviews. *The Levittowners* (1967) is remembered today for two major findings. First, Gans (1967, 408) discovered that a new community "is not new at all, but only a new physical site on which people develop conventional institutions with traditional programs." The discussions of the "New Towns" movement in chapter 9 reached similar conclusions. Second, Gans found that moving to the suburbs does not change people into mass-produced, alienated status seekers.[12] When working-class families leave the central city for Levittown, "they do not develop new lifestyles or ambitions for themselves and their children," and to the degree they do change, "morale goes up, boredom and loneliness are reduced, family life becomes temporarily more cohesive, and social and organizational activities multiply" (Gans 1967, 409). In short, suburbs do not change people much, and what few changes may occur are largely for the good.[13]

William Kornblum: *Blue Collar Community*

Long before the songwriters Ray Price and Jim Croce, sociologists took a special interest in the South Side of Chicago. W. I. Thomas, for example, found his famous "Polish Peasants" there, but more recently, William Kornblum's *Blue Collar Community* (1974) has become an important addition to the holistic community literature and, as we will see in a few pages, *Slim's Table* is also located in South Chicago.[14]

Kornblum and his wife lived in a tenement flat in Irondale from 1968 to 1970, and Kornblum returned to the South-Side Chicago neighborhood again in 1972 to work with the steelworkers' union elections. Unions were a primary focus of Kornblum's work. He was especially interested in why there has never been a truly powerful, truly radical, working-class movement in the United States. From a Marxist perspective, this is a crucial question. And generally, Kornblum finds little of the alienation Marx predicted, finding rather a complicated pattern of "ordered segmentation" in which residential segregation, age, and sex segregation, and especially ethnic identity all combine to provide support for various subcommunities that block a broader working-class consciousness. In fact, some of his most important findings come from a comparison of differences in Polish, Mexican, and black steelmill workers. Blacks, for example, are discouraged from living in mill towns, so labor solidarity must rely on the union's grievance system to provide the identification with the union that comes more easily to the Polish workers living in the more ethnically and occupationally homogeneous neighborhoods near the steel mills.[15]

Ruth Horowitz: *Honor and the American Dream*

Horowitz provides our next example of community field research. Her *Honor and the American Dream* (1983) describes an inner-city Chicano community in Chicago, with special emphasis on teenage gangs. She lived in the 32nd Street neighborhood from 1972 to 1974 and returned to complete her project in 1977. Horowitz employs the concept of *Chicanismo* to explain the lifestyles on 32nd Street. "Chicanismo symbolizes the Mexican-American desire to be neither black nor Anglo, nor deprived but to be themselves: to encourage the traditions that they brought from Mexico and to demand the rights guaranteed them and the respect they deserve as hard-working residents of the United States" (Horowitz 1983, 219). The culture she finds in the Chicago neighborhood is not totally a response to poverty and racial discrimination. Horowitz argues that because of Chicanismo, even if full and equal opportunity were available for Chicanos, the occasional racial and ethnic portrayal of the United States as a melting pot (Glazer and Moynihan 1963) still would not and should not melt away their ethnic differences. Much of the concept of "honor," as exemplified by the extended family, norms of reciprocity, distinct sex roles, rigid moral codes, and respect will remain in the Chicano community. Thus, Horowitz finds that Chicano youths are torn between two conflicting sets of values: the conventional, middle-class American dream of success and the Chicanismo-based defense of honor.[16]

Streetwise and *Slim's Table*

We conclude with two of the most important and widely cited ethnographies of the last thirty years: Elijah Anderson's *Streetwise: Race, Class, and Change in an Urban Community* (1990) and Mitchell Duneier's *Slim's Table: Race, Respectability, and Masculinity* (1992). Both authors have produced subsequent well-received ethnographies,[17] but these two 1990s ethnographies are near-classics that are sometimes read as contrasting, almost contradicting views of black neighborhoods.

Streetwise: Race, Class, and Change in Urban Community reports fourteen years (1975–1989) of fieldwork in which Anderson immersed himself in two adjacent, fictitiously named Philadelphia neighborhoods—Northton, black and poor, and The Village, racially mixed but becoming increasingly white and affluent. Northton received the greater emphasis from Anderson, with particular focus on the generation gap between the "old heads" (men with jobs and family and matriarchal women active in the church) and the "young heads" (teens and young adults who reject traditional roles). While explainable by social isolation, racial oppression, out-migration, and declining labor markets, the behaviors of the young blacks Anderson chronicles are clearly dysfunctional: Addiction to crack cocaine, prostitution, begging, preteen sexual activity, theft, robbery, and violence began to characterize life on the streets of Northton. This behavior naturally elicits fear and mistrust from the white residents of the Village.

> When young black men appear, women (especially white women) sometimes clutch their pocketbooks. They may edge up against their companions or begin to walk stiffly and deliberately. On spotting black males from a distance, other pedestrians often cross the street or give them a wide berth as they pass. When black males deign to pay attention to passersby, they tend to do so directly, giving them a deliberate once-over; their eyes may linger longer than the others consider appropriate to the etiquette of "strangers in the streets." Thus the black males take in all the others and dismiss them as a lion might dismiss a mouse. Fellow pedestrians in turn avert their eyes from the black males, deferring to figures who are seen as unpredictable, menacing, and not to be provoked—predators. (Anderson 1990, 164)

An interesting but limited amelioration for these problems is for whites to become streetwise. Anderson argues that as Village residents learn the street "etiquette" and "wisdom" of Northton (e.g., walking with a dog and varying your route home reduce the chance of robbery), they become less afraid of blacks and more likely to interact with them. Thus, the necessity to become streetwise: "Street wisdom is a way of negotiating day-to-day actions and interactions with minimum risk and maximum mutual respect in a world full of uncertainty and danger. And it can help in building a stronger, more coherent community" (Anderson 1990, 253). As Anderson acknowledges, such wisdom will do little to solve the more basic economic problems facing Northton, but it does maximize the utility of what can be learned from the descriptive detail of an urban ethnography.

While Anderson's primary focus was on black youth, Duneier's study revolves around a middle-age black auto mechanic, Slim. (Again, pseudonyms are used and again, South Chicago is the area of interest.) Slim and the mostly black, mostly older men who hang out with him congregate at the Valois café. These men, akin to Anderson's "old heads," exemplify responsibility, masculinity, respect, and a well-developed work ethic. "They exhibit many of the attitudes one would expect from a group of working-class white men, especially in their views about American society and government, child rearing and discipline, about the welfare system, democracy, and authority" (Duneier 1992, 70–71). This ethnography of older working-class blacks could be seen as a valuable addition to Anderson's focus on younger blacks. Duneier, however, is not content to simply provide a positive view of working-class blacks and argues that "Anderson should have been far more wary of making a generalization about . . . young black men" and that his descriptions of ghetto youth are too easily misused.[18]

Anderson's richly documented account is obviously intended to represent only one ghetto type, and he makes clear that many middle- and upper-class whites exhibit these same characteristics, but there is nothing besides the reader's own stereotypes to suggest that this personality is even representative of the majority of respectable streetcorner men. . . . The collective ethnographic portrait of ghetto-specific masculinity is so one-sided that one would think any positive characteristics men in the ghetto have derive from mainstream modes of behavior. . . . The existing definition of ghetto-specific masculinity is far too narrowly focused. (Duneier 1992, 146–148)

While any misuse of his ethnography is not Anderson's fault, Duneier claims that a fundamental flaw with *Streetwise* is its reliance on William Wilson's (1987) influential theory of middle-class blacks migrating out of the ghetto and leaving those blacks left behind without role models. Duneier uses DuBois's early classic *Philadelphia Negro* (1899) to argue that middle- and lower-class blacks were seldom in residential proximity. It is the lack of economic opportunity rather than the lack of role models that accounts for the antisocial behavior. Duneier's claims that some ethnographies are biased in their descriptions, misused to support stereotypes, and based on faulty theories could be made almost as readily about more objective community research methods (e.g., the survey question is biased; certain types of crime are underreported). However, given the inherent accessibility of ethnographies to a larger audience, the impact of this type of community research is magnified. Thus, quarrels about methods and findings are also magnified. Still, conflicting findings between *Streetwise* and *Slim's Table* are rare, and the differences between implications seem a bit more apparent than real.

Summary

A common thread runs through these most recent examples of holistic community studies and separates them from the classic studies of Warner and the Lynds. No longer do we find the isolated, self-sufficient Middletown or Yankee City that is supposed to be America in microcosm. Instead, we find studies of special, distinct urban neighborhoods—neighborhoods studied because they are different from other urban neighborhoods or, in Levittown's case, a suburb studied because it is a different kind of suburb (working class). Gone are the eclectic data gatherers like the Lynds and Warners who employed virtually every available research methodology. Replacing them are ethnographers who never use surveys and seldom rely on any statistical data.

The reasons for this change in site selection reflect a more sophisticated view of the inaccurate stereotyping that comes from overgeneralizing about cities, communities, or neighborhoods. All communities are not alike. More specifically, urban neighborhoods differ, just as various types of suburbs do, and even isolated small cities can possess significant differences. In sum, we know now that while a community cannot be studied in order to generalize to all of America, in a sense, "all of America" does not exist. America remains sufficiently diverse to justify studying many types of neighborhoods and communities, though it does appear that predominantly poor, predominantly black neighborhoods are especially attractive to urban ethnographers.

Why these neighborhoods should be studied primarily through ethnographic methods is another question, and the answer is not so clear. Certainly the fact that census-type data are especially available for larger areas plays a role (i.e., statistical measures are more detailed and reliable for larger places, leaving smaller places like neighborhoods for the ethnographers), but it may also reflect a growing bifurcation in community research. These ethnographies seem to follow the University of Chicago school of community research suggested by Park, practicing a type of urban anthropology. The more methodologically eclectic holistic studies are now emerging in the area of community politics—the type illustrated by the community culture research discussed previously in chapter 12. The broad, historical accounts of Stone's Atlanta or Molotch's Santa Barbara and Ventura overlap with political science and economics, and they are qualitatively distinct from the Philadelphia and Chicago neighborhood studies by Anderson and Duneier that overlap more with anthropology and psychology than sociology.

NOTES

[1] Although holistic community studies are often difficult to distinguish from the neighborhood ethnographies that were mentioned in chapter 3 as a descent of sociocultural ecology, among the more notable of both genres are: W. E. B. Du Bois, *The Philadelphia Negro* (1899); John Dollard, *Caste and Class in a Southern Town* (1937); St. Clair Drake and Horace Cayton, *Black Metropolis*; James West, *Plainville U.S.A.* (1945); William Foote Whyte, *Street Corner Society* (1955); John Seeley, R. A. Sim, and E. W. Loosley, *Crestwood Heights* (1956); Arthur Vidich and Joseph Bensman, *Small Town in Mass Society* (1958); Bennett Berger, *Working Class Suburb* (1960); Art Gallaher, *Plainville Fifteen Years Later* (1961); Herbert Gans, *The Urban Villagers* (1962) and *The Levittowners* (1967); Elliot Liebow, *Tally's Corner* (1967); Gerald Suttles, *The Social Order of the Slum* (1968); Ulf Hannerz, *Soulside* (1969); Carol Stack, *All Our Kin* (1974); Elijah Anderson, *Streetwise* (1990); Mitchell Duneier, *Slim's Table* (1992); Steven Gregory, *Black Corona* (1998); Elijah Anderson, *Code of the Street* (1999); and Mitchell Duneier, *Sidewalk* (1999).

[2] Robert Lynd was a Presbyterian minister in the early 1920s, but his often "radical" interpretation of the scriptures (e.g., the rich should help the poor) helped to move his orientation and vocation more toward social activism/sociology (Lindt 1979; Lynd 1979).

[3] Ironically, while the Depression weakened most of Muncie's industries, the X's glass plant enjoyed increased demand for their canning jars.

[4] And to a degree, the less cited Middletown IV efforts, for which the most prominent product has been a PBS documentary, *The Measured Century.*

[5] W. Lloyd Warner and Paul S. Lunt, *The Social Life of a Modern Community* (1941) and *The Status System of a Modern Community* (1942); Warner and Leo Srole, *The Social Systems of American Ethnic Groups* (1945); Warner and J. O. Low, *The Social System of the Modern Factory* (1947); Warner, *The Living and the Dead* (1959). Sometimes the Yankee City series is referred to as a six-volume set including Warner's abridged summary (Warner 1963).

[6] Warner's use (or misuse) of "class" and "status" added considerably to the continuing confusion and controversy over when to use which term. C. Wright Mills's (1942) review of the first

Yankee City volume was one of the first (but hardly the last) critics of Warner's analysis. Mills was especially concerned with Warner's use of class in a noneconomic (and therefore in a non-Marxist) way. For other notable criticisms of Warner's treatment of local stratification, see Pfautz and Duncan (1950), Lipset and Bendix (1951), Kornhauser (1959).

[7] In his Jonesville study, for example, Warner et al. (1949, xv) tells us that "Jonesville is in all Americans and all Americans are in Jonesville, for he that dwelleth in America dwelleth in Jonesville, and Jonesville in him." (And yes, Warner actually wrote such prose.)

[8] Notable exceptions include Wirth's *The Ghetto,* Dollard's *Caste and Class in a Southern Town,* and Seeley, Sim, and Loosley's *Crestwood Heights.* Each provides sophisticated insight and analysis that the authors of this book believe is superior to the *analysis* of the classics discussed in this chapter.

[9] Whyte and Liebow's key informants were dominant members in the neighborhoods into which the researchers wanted entry. Doc and Tally's high status obviously eased Whyte and Liebow's acceptance, but the favored position of their informants may have also contributed to the sympathetic descriptions of the residents in *Street Corner Society* and *Tally's Corner.* In contrast, Vidich and Bensman (1958) argue that alienated or marginal community members are better informants because they are more detached from the community and hence more objective. Not surprisingly, Vidich and Bensman's *Small Town in Mass Society* (1958) has a more critical, almost mocking description of the small-town residents.

[10] As an example, perhaps the best field researcher ever (or at least the most widely cited) was Erving Goffman—the author of *The Presentation of Self in Everyday Life* (1959), *Asylums* (1961), "On Cooling the Mark Out" (1962), *Stigma* (1963), and *Gender Advertisement* (1977)—but his attempt to explain the theory and methods of his field research, *Frame Analysis* (1974), has not been as cited as widely as his research.

[11] Gans maintains that very few of the West Enders were actually relocated by the government. While urban renewal forced them to leave, only 10% found government housing. The rest were housed independently in the private housing market.

[12] This stereotype of the suburban lifestyle is often and incorrectly attributed to William H. Whyte's *The Organization Man* (1956). See Berger's *Working Class Suburb* (1960) for a detailed analysis of the "myth of suburbia."

[13] Both of Gans's works include methodological appendices. A comparison of the two shows interesting differences in how field techniques differ by field characteristics.

[14] Interestingly, the author of *Slim's Table,* Mitchell Duneier (1992, 50) argues that South Chicago may have been studied so much that it inappropriately represents our view of urban ghettos.

[15] Kornblum also concludes his book with a methodological appendix. Of special interest is his description of becoming a steel-mill worker. Unlike Gans and most other field researchers, Kornblum worked with the people he studied.

[16] An interesting methodological note in this study concerns the techniques Horowitz, a young Jewish woman, uses to participate in the activities of young Chicano males, especially the activities of violent gangs. While being fluent in Spanish was a necessity, she mentions "my lack of care with appearance, which both males and females continually remarked upon," (9) as one of her most important ways of mixing in. See also Horowitz (1983).

[17] For Anderson, *Code of the Street* (1999) and for Duneier, *Sidewalk* (1999).

[18] Not only Anderson's *Streetwise* but also Ulf Hannerz's *Soulside* receives a significant amount of similar criticism.

chapter fifteen

The Quality of Life and the Quality of Communities

The good community, the better community, the very best possible community—all have been elusive and value-laden goals for centuries. We will begin this chapter with two famous descriptions of the ideal community—one from Plato, the other from John the Evangelist. Plato, in *The Laws,* wrote rationally and extensively about what the best possible community would be like—centrally located, no more than 5,000 households, distributed among 5,040 plots, and grouped into twelve districts around an acropolis. Each household would be equal in both the quality of the land and number of children ("excess" children were to be transferred when infanticide and abortion proved insufficient). In Plato's community a prescribed optimum number of farmers, soldiers, artists, and priests would live together, all under the leadership of philosopher-kings.

Plato's prescription for a rationally designed city was not the only vision of the perfect living environment, which is described much differently by John in his Revelation to the seven Asian churches. Here, the emphasis is less upon secular rationality and more on sacred spirituality:

> And I, John, saw the Holy City, the new Jerusalem, coming down from God out of heaven. It was a glorious sight, beautiful as a bride at her wedding. . . . It was filled with the glory of God, and flashed and glowed like a precious gem, crystal clear like jasper. Its walls were broad and high, with twelve gates guarded by twelve angels. . . . The twelve gates were made of pearls—each gate from a single pearl! And the main street was pure, transparent gold, like glass. . . . Nothing evil will be permitted in it—no one immoral or dishonest—but only those whose names are written in the Lamb's Book of Life. . . . The throne of God and of the Lamb will be there, and his servants will worship him. And they shall see his face; and his name shall be written on their foreheads. And there will be no night there—no need for lamps or sun—for the Lord God will be their light; and they shall reign forever and ever. (Revelation 21–22, *The Living Bible*)

John's and Plato's visions have little in common because both make very different assumptions about the causes of and solutions to problems in the communities of their day. Plato reasoned that if rational citizens followed his rational laws, a more efficient, more perfect community would necessarily result. John, however, believed that only Christ's return could bring the perfect community. Many other views of what a good living environment should be like have been voiced since Plato and John, and about all they have in common is their diversity. The search for a better community is a value-laden quest, and different people can have very different values. Thus, it is impossible to imagine a community that is right for everyone. Even John's New Jerusalem is designed only for "those whose names are written in the Lamb's Book of Life."

Still, the fact that one cannot please everyone should not dissuade us from striving for improvement. Rather, it means only that there are limits to our ability to improve our human condition. The community, however, presents an excellent focus for our attempts at improvement.

Why Focus on the Community?

The quality of our lives depends on the quality of several things besides the community: our society, our jobs, our families, and ourselves. And while all of these factors are undeniably important, there is some reason to believe that the community contributes more to the quality of our lives than many of these other areas. But more important to establishing the potential for the community as a focus for improving life quality is *the potential for meaningful change and improvement that exists at the community level.* Compare, for example, attempts to improve the quality of life at the community level with the more micro attempts based on providing psychological counseling or the more macro attempts based on implementing societal change.

The Limitations of Micro Approaches to the Quality of Life

From a micro perspective, we can help people deal more efficiently with myriad personal problems (unemployment or job dissatisfaction, parenting difficulties, alienation, sexual dysfunction, marital conflict) through individual counseling. And many psychiatrists, psychologists, social workers, and other trained counselors do just that. The ratio of trained counselors to troubled people is so very small, however, that we must be pessimistic about the ability of micro-level counseling to substantially change the life quality for very many people. In most cases, counselors will assist only those who have the most overt problems or those with the time and money necessary to secure the counseling. In either case, counseling is a "Band-Aid" approach to general quality-of-life problems—a very important Band-Aid, and, on an individual basis, a relatively effective one—but the inability of counseling to impact large numbers of people has led to attempts at *community* mental health in psychiatry and psychology and *community* organizing in social work.

Limitations of Macro Approaches

Macro approaches to the quality of life, by definition, will affect a large number of people. If we choose the society for our level of analysis and change, then we can potentially improve the life quality of all poor Americans, all American women, all black Americans, all American teenagers, all the working parents in the United States, or, more broadly still, simply all *Americans*. For example, most of our social welfare legislation attempts to improve the quality of life of various categories of Americans. And, broader still, attempts to stimulate the economy or protect the natural environment are attempts to improve the quality of life for all Americans.

Most sociologists lean toward the macro approach. From Durkheim's "social facts" to C. Wright Mills's "sociological imagination," sociology's most distinctive contribution has been expanding our understanding of social phenomena beyond the individual level. Indeed, those sociologists who are the most "macro" in their work are our "grand" masters who produce "grand" theories of entire societies. Yet, when it is time to put these theories to work and produce pragmatic guides for improving the quality of life in a society, the macro approach often has little to offer. When the source of the problem is in the basic structure of society (as it almost always is with a macro approach), then it is often argued that until truly fundamental social change occurs, truly fundamental improvement in the quality of life cannot occur. Marxist applications to American social problems often take this tack (see chapter 5), but until the revolution, what can we do to make things better?

Admittedly, not all societal-level approaches are so "all-or-nothing" in their attempts to improve the quality of life. Incremental approaches are common, producing limited changes in our society. For example, minimum-wage laws increase the wages of the working poor, and civil rights legislation has given minorities more opportunities for housing, education, and jobs.[1] And yet, many people who are resistant to fundamental social change are also disenchanted with these piecemeal government programs as well. They perceive limits in the government's ability to improve our lives. Politicians successfully run for office by being against traditional government solutions to social problems, and many Americans appear to be increasingly skeptical of the government's ability to make things better. Government solutions are often seen as too complex, too costly, and too remote from the problem.

The community, then, whether it is a neighborhood, a city, or a county, can be a *mid-range alternative*. Like the individualistic micro approach, it is close to the problem and manageable in design and implementation. Like the societal macro approach, it is potentially substantial in its effects, impacting entire neighborhoods or communities. Thus, a case can be made that the community matters very much in attempts to improve the quality of life. And if communities do matter, then what should good communities be like?

What Constitutes a Good Community?

While it is true, as our opening selections from Plato and John illustrate, that different people can have very different views of what constitutes a good community, this should not keep us from striving to make clear what a good community would be like. The problem of different definitions of a good community must be considered, but let's back away from that dilemma until we examine what *most* people would include as necessary for a good community.

The Bare Necessities

The basis for a high quality of life would almost have to include six community components: (1) public safety, (2) a strong economy, (3) health care, (4) educational opportunities, (5) a clean, healthy natural environment, and (6) an optimum population size. These community characteristics are so basic that they are almost beyond debate. There will be disagreement over how best to supply health care, what constitutes educational opportunities, or how much should be spent to protect the environment, but few will argue that hospitals or schools or breathable air are not needed.

The basic components are not only necessary, they are measurable as well. A look back at chapter 11 shows that they are included in the general groupings for local indicators of the quality of life, so to a degree we can assess the contributions communities make to life quality for these six components. This does not mean that we know exactly how to strengthen the local economy or precisely how many police are needed to help maintain public security, but it does mean we can determine which communities offer the greatest opportunity for achieving high levels of these necessary components, as well as how our own community compares with others.

The only objective component not included in all the local indicators research mentioned in chapter 10 is population size, so we will consider it briefly here. Ever since Louis Wirth's classic analysis (discussed in chapter 2), we have appreciated the influence of population size on lifestyle. More recently, research has focused on how it affects the quality of life. Larger populations apparently do, as Wirth argued, lead to greater impersonality and less community attachment (Mayhew and Levinger 1976; Wilson 1985).

In addition, large cities usually have the highest crime rates. Moreover, people living in large cities are likely to have more negative attitudes toward their city than those living in smaller ones. In fact, smaller population levels apparently allow at least equal and typically higher levels of life quality in all of the other five "bare necessities" except one—a strong local economy. *Large cities are very good places to find jobs and make money* (Alonso 1975), *but if you can afford it, smaller cities are generally better places to live.* After reviewing most of the research on population size and the quality of life, Spates and Macionis (1982, 529) conclude that "it would seem reasonable, on the basis of the data we have encountered, that the population of a good city might hover somewhere between the 50,000–100,000 mark." That seems like a reasonable conclusion, but it does remind us again that what is an excellent place to live for one person may not be best for someone else (in this case, for someone in need of a high-paying job or the public services found in large cities).

A high-level quality of life is not guaranteed by these six community characteristics.[2] We could live in a community of about a hundred thousand that is secure, prosperous, and clean, with fine schools and hospitals, and still not be satisfied.[3] For example, according to Abraham Maslow's well-known hierarchy of needs (1970), as soon as our basic needs for survival and security are met they are replaced by higher-level needs for belonging and self-actualization. As we turn now to a consideration of these higher-level needs it is important to remember Maslow's argument that when the lower-level needs are met, the need to fill the higher-level needs then becomes just as strong. These more subjective, higher-level community needs are more than just the whims of an affluent society. If Maslow is correct, they are just as important as the more basic needs we just discussed.

The Subjective Components

The good community has at least six more subjective, more debatable components. When the "bare necessities" are available, as they are to a substantial degree in most American communities, then a high quality of life becomes more dependent on: (1) individual liberty, (2) categorical equality, (3) communal fraternity, (4) representative, responsive government, (5) local identification, and (6) resident heterogeneity. Since factors such as these are more difficult to define, to measure, and to agree upon, we will consider each in some detail.

Individual freedom.   Freedom is a basic American value (Williams 1970) that flourishes in our large cities. There is a German proverb—*Stadtluft macht frei*—that roughly translates "breathing city air makes one free." Large cities do allow us more freedom since we do not know one another, do not care very much about one another, and, therefore do not try to control one another. All of the classic typologists (Tönnies, Simmel et al.) have noted the individual freedom that comes with the impersonality of the large city.

The problem comes with deciding how much freedom is too much freedom. Certainly we do not want people to be free to exploit, to steal, or to terrorize, but how can we restrict these actions while at the same time preserving individual freedom? For example, we often praise large cities such as New York and San Francisco for their tolerance of various lifestyles (Becker and Horowitz 1971; Florida 2003); yet this very tolerance, this encouragement of personal expression and freedom, can restrict a more basic need—security. Note how criminologist James Wilson (1983, 78–79) famously argues that tolerance for deviant behavior is the first step toward community crime:

> I suggest that untended behavior also leads to the breakdown of community controls. A stable neighborhood of families who care for their

homes, mind each other's children, and confidently frown on unwanted intruders can change in a few years, or even a few months, to an inhospitable and frightening jungle. A piece of property is abandoned, weeds grow up, a window is smashed. Adults stop scolding rowdy children; the children, emboldened, become more rowdy. Families move out, unmarried adults move in. Teenagers gather in front of the grocery; in time, an inebriate slumps to the sidewalk and is allowed to sleep it off. Pedestrians are approached by panhandlers. . . . Such an area is vulnerable to criminal invasion. Though it is not inevitable, it is more likely that here, rather than in places where people are confident they can regulate public behavior by informal controls, drugs will change hands, prostitutes will solicit, and cars will be stripped. Drunks will be robbed by boys who do it as a lark, and the prostitutes' customers will be robbed by men who do it purposefully and perhaps violently. Muggings will occur.

Similarly, Zorbaugh (see chapter 3), in his classic *The Gold Coast and Slum* (1929), describes the "world of furnished rooms" as free from the prying eyes of neighbors. Yet this was also a world of extremely high crime, suggesting, unfortunately, that security and freedom are mutually exclusive. Since we can maximize one only at the expense of the other, and since we value both security and freedom, there is often an uneasy compromise in our communities between those who would restrict liberty to increase security (e.g., more police, "tougher" laws) and those who would run the risk of less security to ensure personal freedoms (due process and civil rights). Again, as with population size, we are faced with the dilemma of different people making different choices about what constitutes a good community.

Categorical equality. Broad, collective equality has never had much appeal in America. The idea of equal *opportunity* for everyone is about as close as we come. However, equality between categories of people, especially between races and sexes, has much broader support. The idea that desirable housing should not be restricted to whites only or that men and women should receive equal pay for equal work has an established body of legal support and a growing base of popular support.

Still, there is disagreement in this area. Should individuals be allowed to sell their homes to whomever they wish, even if it means black buyers will not be considered? When we find that blacks and women receive less income than white males, what do we do? Focus on improving educational opportunities, on strengthening blacks' families, on redefining sex roles, on more vigorous affirmative action programs, or on comparable pay for sex-segregated jobs? The value-laden implications of each proposal are significant, and the controversy surrounding each proposal is considerable.

Again, we find a value conflict. Whereas before, it was between liberty and security, this time it is between liberty and equality. We can make a community more equal, but it will require reducing the liberty of the homeowner to sell the home or of the employer to determine the wages of the employee. And again we will find people with different views on how equal a community should be.

Communal fraternity.   Here we have the very essence of the *gemein-schaft*-like community. Baker Brownell, in *The Human Community* (1950, 198), wrote that "[a] community is a group of people who know each other well." In a "good" community, we are to know one another, like one another, help one another. Roland Warren (1970, 15) believes the basis for a good community is "a regard for the whole and a compassion for the individual, a way in which we can treat others as brothers, a sense of caring and being cared about." I suspect there is little disagreement over this characteristic. The question here is how such a characteristic is possible in a modern, often *gesell-schaft*-like America. Harvey Cox (1965, 41), in his treatise on religion in a secular society, notes the decline in our truly knowing people:

> During my boyhood, my parents never referred to "the milkman," "the insurance agent," "the junk collector." These people were respectively, Paul Weaver, Joe Villanova, and Roxy Barozano. All of our family's market transactions took place within a web of wider and more inclusive friendship and kinship ties with the same people. They were never anonymous. In fact, the occasional salesman or repairman whom we did not know was always viewed with dark suspicion until we could make sure where he came from, who his parents were, and whether his family was any good.

After moving to the *Secular City,* Cox (*ibid.*) is no longer in Brownell's *Human Community* where everyone knows everyone:

> Now, as an urbanite, my transactions are of a very different sort. If I need to have the transmission on my car repaired, buy a television antenna, or cash a check, I find myself in functional relationships with mechanics, salesmen, and bank clerks whom I see in no other capacity. These contacts are in no sense "mean, nasty, or brutish," though they tend to be short . . . unifaceted and "segmental." I meet these people in no other context. To me they remain essentially just as anonymous as I do to them.

Cox's description of these segmental, functional, anonymous personal relationships is not necessarily a description of a social problem. Cox claims to be satisfied with them, and anonymity does bring a measure of freedom. Look back to our discussion of individual liberty. There is a trade-off here. How much freedom are we willing to surrender in return for more communal fraternity? Different people will, of course, be willing to make different trades.

Representative, responsive government.   Most of us desire to be governed by leaders who represent the community's best interests. Further, we want our leaders to respond quickly and efficiently when our community needs action. What, exactly, would such a representative, responsive government be like? In order to be representative, our leaders need to be democratically elected, much like Robert Dahl's mayor of New Haven (see chapter 12). Of course, Floyd Hunter's Atlanta also had a popularly elected mayor, but he had little real power. Atlanta was run by unelected business leaders who were bound together by a desire to create an Atlanta that increased the profitability of their businesses. Certainly Hunter's research as well as many of the community power studies that followed all desired to "expose" covert elites and thereby help make local government more democratic. However, it is not clear how one goes about establishing a more democratic local government, nor is it clear what happens when local governments become more democratic.

Democratic, pluralistic, representative local government is not necessarily the most responsive local government. The research of Robert Crain, Elihu Katz, and Donald Rosenthal (1969) into the fluoridation controversies and much of Terry Clark's (1971) analysis of the NORC 51 community sample suggest that leaders can become so responsive to various groups in the community as to be paralyzed into inaction. That is, leaders can become *too responsive* to conflicting demands and thereby become unable to respond effectively to local needs. And to further complicate matters, some researchers question Hunter's assumption that, in pursuing private gain, business leaders reduce public gain. Clark and Ferguson (1983) find that communities with significant input into decision making from business leaders are in better financial condition than those with most of the input coming from the mayor and labor unions. And while research by Lyon, Felice, Perryman, and Parker (1981) supports Molotch's (1976) contention that power in the hands of local business leaders leads to local growth, they did not find support for his contention that growth benefits local business at the expense of other residents. Rather, they find that when a community grows, property values increase, per capita local expenditures decline, and net revenues grow. The point here is that we are a long way from being able to say what is necessary for an efficient, responsive local government, and it may be that we will find democratic governments are not always the most efficient and responsive governments.

Identification and commitment.   A good community should matter to the people who live there. Residents should define themselves in terms of the community, should care about the community, and should be willing to sacrifice to improve the community. The philosopher Lawrence Haworth (1963, 87) argues that this is the difference between a community and a mere city when he writes that "If a city is to become a community, then, the inhabitants must identify the settlement itself as the focal point of their individual lives." In chapter 7 we examined how difficult it is to maintain the physical community as the basis for psychological community. Yet we also saw that for many people, the local community continues to be a place that matters, a place where friends live, a place where money is invested, where children are educated, and so on. Not all Americans are, in Robert Merton's terms, cosmopolitans; some are localites, and many of us are bits of both. So again, is it possible to devise a community that fits the needs of different people—in this case, those people who see their local community as merely the location of their sleeping quarters as well as those who see it as the geographic focus for much of what matters in their lives?

Heterogeneity. It is time now to face up to perhaps the thorniest issue facing the concept of a good community: *How different should community residents be?* and *How different can community residents be allowed to be?* Roland Warren (1970, 20) notes that "it has simply been accepted as a value that it is better for people to live in communities which are more or less a cross-section of the population than to live in economically or racially or ethnically segregated communities." Continuing efforts to enhance diversity and representativeness in our cities, schools, and workplaces all reflect this value. Yet considerable research shows that heterogeneous communities possess less community (Putnam 2000). Economists Dora Costa and Matthew Kahn (2003, 104) review years of research and conclude that "all of these studies have the same punch line: Heterogeneity reduces civic engagement. In more diverse communities, people participate less as measured by how they allocate their time, their money, their voting, and their willingness to take risks to help others." More recent reviews find similar results (Twigg, Taylor, and Mohan 2010).

We can see another dilemma here. Some people will want to live in heterogeneous communities; others will want to surround themselves with people like themselves. Some view conflict as sometimes necessary, often even invigorating and stimulating. Others will avoid conflict at all cost.

The idea that a heterogeneous community (consisting of diverse people with different ideas of what constitutes a high-level quality of life) will have a hard time being a good community for all of its residents brings us back to the problem we encountered at the beginning of this section on subjective characteristics, a problem that reappeared in our examination of *every* subjective characteristic. Since different people have different ideas about what constitutes the good life, how is the good community possible? The truth is, I believe, that *the* good community *is not* possible; good *communities*, however, are both possible and desirable.

Good Communities

While it is impossible to design *the* community that will maximize the quality of life for everyone, *a* community that will maximize life quality for certain kinds of people is possible. And since there are many kinds of people, our discussion must be directed toward good communities. Roland Warren (1970, 21), who devoted more time and better thoughts to the issue of the good community than have most of us, concludes finally that "there is no such thing as *the* good community. There are *many* good communities, all according to the specific combination of preferences which may be held . . . [on issues where] . . . there is simply no way to demonstrate that one viewpoint is more valid or more moral than another." And that is, it seems, the key to insuring the highest quality of life for us all. The state, of course, will continue to influence the basic necessities of life quality mentioned earlier (safety, economic security, health care, environment, education), but for these

[handwritten: ∪ ffll state provides]

more subjective components of life quality, the community—or more precisely, communities—is the key. Even if the state could provide us with the subjective elements, communities would still be the preferable source. Robert Nisbet's ideas on the primacy of the community are worth quoting at length at this point:

> It may well be asked: why should we seek communities at all? Is it not sufficient, in an age of the welfare state, that we should live simply and solely in terms of the great regulations, laws, and associations which this state provides? It is often said that today, for the first time in human history, the state has become a benevolent and protective association which is able to meet both the social and the physical demands of people formerly met by a plurality of smaller communities. To this we must say, firmly, however, that the state which possesses the power to do things *for* people has also the power to do things *to* them. Freedom cannot be maintained in a monolithic society. Pluralism and diversity of experience are the essence of true freedom. Therefore even if the state were able to meet the basic problems of stability and security through its own efforts, we should have to reject it as the solution simply because of our concern for the problem of freedom.
>
> However, it is to be noted that the state does not even serve the security need. No large-scale association can really meet the psychic demand of individuals because, by its very nature, it is too large, too complex, too bureaucratized, and altogether too aloof from the residual meanings by which human beings live. The state can enlist popular enthusiasm, can conduct crusades, can mobilize in behalf of great "causes," such as wars, but as a regular and normal means of meeting human needs for recognition, fellowship, security, and membership, it is inadequate. The tragedy is that where the state is most successful in meeting the needs for recognition and security, it is most tyrannical and despotic, as the histories of Communist Russia and Nazi Germany have made clear. The only proper alternatives to large-scale, mechanical political society are communities small in scale but solid in structure. They and they alone can be the beginning of social reconstruction because they respond, at the grass roots, to fundamental human desires: living together, working together, experiencing together, being together. Such communities can grow naturally and organically from the most elementary aspirations, they remain continuously flexible, and, by their very nature, they do not insist upon imposing and rigid organizations. (Nisbet 1960, 82–83)

Communities are seldom viewed in this light—as guardians of individual liberty. Typically, communities are viewed in their *gemeinschaft*-like nature of inhibiting free thought and action—requiring conformity to the dictates of local values. And this more common view is largely an accurate one. Although some communities will tolerate more individuality than others (Brint 2001), most will discourage those actions that run counter to the community's norms. But Nisbet's point, we believe, is that if we have a multitude of communities, each reflecting different values, and if the state supports the basic needs and guarantees the right to move from one community to another, then a pluralistic society becomes possible—a heterogeneous society made of many, often more homogeneous, communities. In this way, then, communities become an important focus for improving the quality of life in urban America.

NOTES

[1] These examples are all from the federal government's realm, and this is not coincidental. Certainly, since Franklin Roosevelt's New Deal, the government has been the primary instigator *of purposive* social change. Other contributors to social change (e.g., industrialization, urbanization) may have an even greater impact, but they invariably produce *crescive* social change (Warren 1978).

[2] In fact, the *perception* of one's life quality depends so much on its quality relative to other people in the community that the correlation between these community characteristics and an individual's response to life-quality questions usually varies between weak and nonexistent (Campbell 1981; Andrews 1981).

[3] Plato, in *The Republic* (Book 11), has Socrates tell us that "we must no longer provide them only with the necessities we mentioned at first, houses and clothes and shoes, but we must call in painting and embroidery; we must acquire gold and ivory and all such things. . . . That healthy community is no longer adequate, but it must be swollen in bulk and filled with a multitude of things which are no longer necessities, as, for example, all kinds of hunters and artists."

Bibliography

Abbott, Andrew. 1997. "Of Time and Space: The Contemporary Relevance of the Chicago School." *Social Forces* 75(4): 1149–1182.

Abell, Peter. 2000. "Putting Social Theory Right?" *Sociological Theory* 18(3): 518–523.

Abu-Lughod, Janet L. 1991. *Changing Cities: Urban Sociology.* New York: Harper Collins.

———. 1999. *New York, Chicago, Los Angeles: America's Global Cities.* Minneapolis: University of Minnesota Press.

Agger, Robert E., Daniel Goldrich, and Bert Swanson. 1964. *The Rulers and the Ruled: Political Power and Impotence in American Communities.* New York: John Wiley & Sons.

Ahlbrandt, Roger. 1984. *Neighborhoods, People and Community.* New York: Plenum.

Aiken, Michael. 1970. "The Distribution of Community Power." In *The Structure of Community Power*, edited by Michael Aiken and Paul E. Mott. New York: Random House.

Alba, Richard D., and John R. Logan. 1993. "Minority Proximity to Whites in Suburbs: An Individual-Level Analysis of Segregation." *American Journal of Sociology* 98(6): 1388–1427.

Alba, Richard D., John R. Logan, and Kyle Crowder. 1997. "White Ethnic Neighborhoods and Assimilation: The Greater New York Region, 1980–1990." *Social Forces* 75(3): 883–909.

Alba, Richard D., John R. Logan, and Brian J. Stults. 2000. "The Changing Neighborhood Contexts of the Immigrant Metropolis." *Social Forces* 79(2): 587–621.

Alba, Richard D., John R. Logan, Brian J. Stults, Gilbert Marzan, and Wenquan Zhang. 1999. "Immigrant Groups in the Suburbs: A Reexamination of Suburbanization and Spatial Assimilation." *American Sociological Review* 64: 446–460.

Alihan, Milla. 1938. *Social Ecology: A Critical Analysis.* New York: Columbia University Press.

Alinsky, Saul D. 1946. *Reveille for Radicals.* Chicago: University of Chicago Press.

———. 1971. *Rules for Radicals.* New York: Random House.

Alonso, William. 1965. *Location and Land Use: Toward a General Theory of Land Rent.* Cambridge, MA: Harvard University Press.

———. 1970. "What Are New Towns For?" *Urban Studies* 7: 37–45.

———. 1975. "The Economics of Urban Size." Pp. 434–451 in *Regional Policy*, edited by John Friedman and William Alonso. Cambridge, MA: MIT Press.

Altman, I. 1975. *The Environment and Social Behavior.* Monterey, CA: Brooks/Cole.

Anderson, Elijah. 1990. *Streetwise: Race, Class and Change in an Urban Community.* Chicago: The University of Chicago Press.

————. 1999. *Code of the Street: Decency, Violence, and the Moral Life of the Inner City.* New York: W.W. Norton.

Anderson, Nels. 1923. *The Hobo.* Chicago: The University of Chicago Press.

Anderson, Theodore R., and Janice A. Egelend. 1961. "Spatial Aspects of Social Area Analysis." *American Sociological Review* 26: 392–399.

Andrews, Frank. 1981. "Subjective Social Indicators, Objective Social Indicators, and Social Accounting Systems." In *Social Accounting Systems,* edited by F. Thomas Juster and Kenneth Land. New York: Academic Press.

Ardrey, Robert. 1966. *The Territorial Imperative.* New York: Atheneum.

Aronson, Ronald. 1995. *After Marxism.* New York: Guilford Press.

Austin, D. M., and Y. Baba. 1990. "Social Determinants of Neighborhood Attachment." *Sociological Spectrum* 10: 59–78.

Bachrach, Peter, and Morton S. Baratz. 1970. *Power and Poverty: Theory and Practice.* New York: Oxford University Press.

Bagley, Christopher. 1989. "Urban Crowding and the Murder Rate in Bombay, India." *Perceptual and Motor Skills* 69 (Aug.): 1241–1242.

Bahr, Howard, Mindy Pearson, Leif Elder, and Louis Hicks. 2007. "Erasure, Convergence, and the Great Divide: Trends in Racial Disparity in Middletown." *City & Community* 6(2): 95–117.

Bailey, James, ed. 1973. *New Towns in America.* New York: John Wiley & Sons.

Bailey, Roy, and Mike Brake. 1975. *Radical Social Work.* New York: Pantheon.

Baldassare, Mark. 1992. "Suburban Communities." *Annual Review of Sociology* 18: 475–494.

————, ed. 1994. *The Los Angeles Riots.* Boulder: Westview Press.

Baldassare, Mark, and William Protash. 1982. "Growth Controls, Population Growth, and Community Satisfaction." *American Sociological Review* 47(3): 339–346.

Bardo, John W., and John J. Hartman. 1982. *Urban Sociology.* Itasca, IL: F. E. Peacock.

Barnes, Barry. 2001. "The Macro/Micro Problem and the Problem of Structure and Agency." Pp. 339–352 in *Handbook of Social Theory,* edited by George Ritzer and Barry Smart. London: Sage.

Baum, Andrew, and Paul B. Paulus. 1991. "Crowding." Pp. 533–70 in *Handbook of Environmental Psychology,* Vol. 1, edited by D. Stokols and I. Altman. Malabar, FL: Krieger.

Baumgartner, M. 1988. *The Moral Order of a Suburb.* New York: Oxford University Press.

Bausch, K. 2001. *The Emerging Consensus in Social Systems Theory.* New York: Plenum.

Beatty, P. 2004. "Pretesting Questionnaires: Paradigms of Cognitive Interviewing Practice, and Their Implications for Developing Standards of Best Practice." In *Questionnaire Evaluation Standards, Quest 2003,* edited by P. Prufer, M. Rexroth, and F. J. Fowler, Jr. Mannheim, Germany: ZUMA—Nachrichten Spezial Band 9.

Beauregard, Robert. 2003. "City of Superlatives." *City & Community* 2(3): 183–199.

Becker, Howard P. 1940. "Constructive Typology in the Social Sciences." *American Journal of Sociology* 5: 40–55.

————. 1956. *Man in Reciprocity.* New York: Praeger.

————. 1957. "Current Sacred-Secular Theory and Its Development." In *Modern Sociological Theory in Continuity and Change,* edited by Howard Becker and Alvin Boskoff. New York: Dryden.

Becker, Howard S., and Irving Louis Horowitz. 1971. "The Culture of Civility." Pp. 4–19 in *Culture and Civility in San Francisco,* edited by Howard S. Becker. New Brunswick, NJ: Trans-Action.

Becker, Richard, Lorraine Denby, Robert McGill, and Allan R. Wilks. 1987. "Analysis of Data from the Places Rated Almanac." *The American Statistician* 41(3): 169–186.

Beeton, Sue. 2006. *Community Development through Tourism*. Collingwood, Victoria (Australia): Landlinks Press.

Beggs, John J., Valerie A. Haines, and Jeanne S. Hurlbert. 1996. "Revisiting the Rural-Urban Contrast: Personal Networks in Nonmetropolitan and Metropolitan Settings." *Rural Sociology* 61(2): 306–325.

Bell, Colin, and Howard Newby. 1972. *Community Studies: An Introduction to the Sociology of Local Community*. New York: Praeger.

Bell, Daniel. 1969. "The Idea of a Social Report." *The Public Interest* 15 (spring).

Bell, Wendell. 1953. "The Social Areas of the San Francisco Bay Region." *American Sociological Review* 18: 29–47.

———. 1955. *Social Area Analysis*. Stanford, CA: Stanford University Press.

———. 1959. "Social Areas: Typology of Urban Neighborhoods." In *Community Structure and Analysis*, edited by M. Sussman. New York: Thomas Crowell.

Bellah, Robert. 1992. *The Good Society*. New York: Vintage Books.

Bellah, Robert, Richard Madsen, William M. Sullivan, Ann Swidler, and Steven M. Tipton. 1996. *Habits of the Heart: Individualism and Commitment in American Life*. Berkeley: University of California Press.

Berger, Bennett M. 1960. *Working Class Suburb*. Berkeley: University of California Press.

Bernard, Jessie. 1973. *The Sociology of Community*. Glenview, IL: Scott Foresman.

Berner, Erhard, and Benedict Phillips. 2005. "Left to Their Own Devices? Community Self-Help between Alternative Development and Neo-Liberalism." *Community Development Journal* 40(1): 17–29.

Berry, Brian, and Philip H. Rees. 1969. "The Factorial Ecology of Calcutta." *American Journal of Sociology* 74(5): 447–491.

Berry, Brian, and John Kasarda. 1977. *Contemporary Urban Ecology*. New York: Macmillan.

Bestor, Theodore. 1989. *Japanese Urban Life*. Palo Alto, CA: Stanford University Press.

Betancur, John J. 1996. "The Settlement Experience of Latinos in Chicago: Segregation, Speculation, and the Ecology Model." *Social Forces* 74(4): 1299–1324.

Block, Fred. 1981. "The Fiscal Crisis of the Capitalist State." In *Annual Review of Sociology*, edited by Ralph Turner and James Short. Palo Alto, CA: Annual Reviews Inc.

Boase, Jeffrey, and Barry Wellman. 2006. "Personal Relationships: On and Off the Internet." Pp. 709–733 in *The Cambridge Handbook of Personal Relationships*, edited by Anita L. Vangelisti and Daniel Perlman. Cambridge, UK: Cambridge University Press.

Bobo, Kimberly, Jackie Kendall, and Steve Max. 2001. *Organizing for Social Change: Midwest Academy Manual for Activists*. Santa Ana, CA: Seven Locks Press.

Bonjean, Charles. 1963. "Community Leadership: A Case Study and Conceptual Refinement." *American Journal of Sociology* 68: 672–681.

Bonjean, Charles. 1966. "Mass, Class, and the Industrial Community." *American Journal of Sociology* 72: 149–162.

Bonnes, Mirilia, Marino Bonaiuto, and Anna Paola. 1991. "Crowding and Residential Satisfaction in the Urban Environment: A Contextual Approach." *Environment and Behavior* 23 (Sept.): 531–552.

Botes, Lucius, and Dingie van Rensburg. 2000. "Community Participation in Development: Nine Plagues and Twelve Commandments." *Community Development Journal* 35(1): 41–58.

Boyer, Ernest. 1990. *Scholarship Reconsidered: Priorities for the Professoriate.* Princeton, NJ: The Carnegie Foundation for the Advancement of Teaching.

Boyer, Richard, and David Savageau. 1985. *Rand McNally Places Rated Almanac: Your Guide to Finding the Best Places to Live in America.* New York: Rand McNally.

Bressi, Todd W. 2002. *The Seaside Debates: A Critique of the New Urbanism.* New York: Rizzoli.

Brint, Steven. 2001. "Gemeinschaft Revisited: A Critique and Reconstruction of the Community Concept." *Sociological Theory* 19(1): 1–23.

Brooks, Richard O. 1974. *New Towns and Communal Values: A Case Study of Columbia, Maryland.* New York: Praeger.

Brownell, Baker. 1950. *The Human Community: Its Philosophy and Practice for a Time of Crisis.* New York: Harper and Brothers.

Bryant, Barbara K. 1975. "Respondent Selection in a Time of Changing Household Composition." *Journal of Marketing Research* 12: 129–135.

Bullard, Robert D., Glann S. Johnson, and Angel O. Torres, eds. 2000. *Sprawl City: Race, Politics, and Planning in Atlanta.* Washington, DC: Island Press.

Burby, Raymond J., III, and Shirley F. Weiss. 1975. *New Communities, U.S.A.* Washington, DC: Subcommittee on Housing of the Committee on Banking, Currency and Housing, House of Representatives.

Burgess, Ernest. 1925. "The Growth of the City." In *The City,* edited by Robert Park, Ernest Burgess, and Roderick D. McKenzie. Chicago: The University of Chicago Press.

Burgess, M. Elaine. 1962. *Negro Leadership in a Southern City.* Chapel Hill: University of North Carolina Press.

Byler, D. 2009. "Online Social Networks and Their Relationship to Social Capital and Political Attitudes." B.A Thesis, Government Department, Faculty of Arts and Sciences, The College of William and Mary.

Calhoun, J. B. 1961. "Phenomena Associated with Population Density." *Proceedings of the National Academy of Sciences* 47: 429–449.

———. 1962. "Population Density and Social Pathology." *Scientific American* 206: 139–148.

Callahan, Steve, Neil Mayer, Kris Palmer, and Larry Ferlazzo. 1999. "Rowing the Boat with Two Oars." Paper presented as part of the On-Line Conference on Community Organizing and Development. April 1999. Retrieved from http://comm-org.utoledo.edu/papers99/callahan.htm.

Campbell, Angus. 1981. *The Sense of Well-Being in America.* New York: McGraw-Hill.

Campbell, Angus, Philip E. Converse, and Willard L. Rodgers. 1976. *The Quality of American Life: Perceptions, Evaluations, and Satisfactions.* New York: Russell Sage Foundation.

Campbell, Karen, and Barrett Lee. 1992. "Sources of Personal Neighbor Networks: Social Integration, Need, or Time?" *Social Forces* 70(4): 1077–1100.

Caplow, Theodore, and Bruce Chadwick. 1979. "Inequality and Life Styles in Middletown, 1920–1978." *Social Science Quarterly* 60: 367–386.

Caplow, Theodore, Howard Bahr, and Bruce Chadwick. 1983. *All Faithful People: Change and Continuity in Middletown's Religion.* Minneapolis: University of Minnesota Press.

Caplow, Theodore, Howard Bahr, Bruce Chadwick, Reuben Hill, and Margaret Williamson. 1982. *Middletown Families: Fifty Years of Change and Continuity.* Minneapolis: University of Minnesota Press.

Castells, Manuel. 1977. *The Urban Question.* Translated by Alan Sheridan. London: Edward Arnold.

———. 1983. *The City and the Grassroots: A Cross-Cultural Theory of Urban Social Movements.* Berkeley: University of California Press.

———. 1991. *The Informational City: Information Technology, Economic Restructuring and the Urban-Regional Process.* Oxford, UK: Blackwell.

———. 1996. *The Rise of the Network Society.* Malden, MA: Blackwell.

———. 1997. *The Power of Identity.* Malden, MA: Blackwell.

———. 1998. *End of Millennium.* Malden, MA: Blackwell.

———. 2000a. *End of Millennium (The Information Age: Economy, Society. and Culture, Vol. III),* 2nd ed. Cambridge, MA; Oxford, UK: Blackwell.

———. 2000b. *The Rise of the Network Society (The Information Age: Economy, Society, and Culture, Vol. I),* 2nd ed. Cambridge, MA; Oxford, UK: Blackwell.

———. 2000c. "Toward a Sociology of the Network Society." *Contemporary Sociology* 29(5): 693–699.

———. 2004. *The Power of Identity (The Information Age: Economy, Society and Culture, Vol. II),* 2nd ed. Cambridge, MA; Oxford, UK: Blackwell.

———, ed. 2005. *The Network Society: A Cross-Cultural Perspective.* Northampton, MA: Edward Elgar.

———. 2009. *Communication Power.* New York: Oxford University Press.

Chadee, Derek, Liz Austen, and Jason Ditton. 2007. "The Relationship between Likelihood and Fear of Criminal Victimization: Evaluating Risk Sensitivity as a Mediating Concept." *The British Journal of Criminology* 47(1): 133–153.

Chaskin, Robert J. 1997. "Perspectives on Neighborhood and Community: A Review of the Literature." *Social Service Review* (Dec.): 521–545.

Chaskin, Robert J., and Ali Abunimah. 1999. "A View from the City: Local Government Perspectives on Neighborhood-Based Governance in Community-Building Initiatives." *Journal of Urban Affairs* 21(1): 57–78.

Chaskin, Robert J., Mark L. Joseph, and Selma Chipenda-Dansokho. 1998. "Implementing Comprehensive Community Development: Possibilities and Limitations." Pp. 17–28 in *Community Building: Renewal, Well-Being, and Shared Responsibility,* edited by Patricia L. Ewalt, Edith M. Freeman, and Dennis L. Poole. Washington, DC: NASW Press.

Cherlin, Andrew. 1982. "Middletown III: The Story Continues." *Contemporary Sociology* 11(6): 617–619.

Christaller, Walter. 1933. *Die Zentralen Orte in Suddeutschland* [Central Places in Southern Germany]. Jena, Germany: Gustav Fisher Verlag.

Christenson, James A. 1989. "Themes of Community Development." Pp. 26–47 in *Community Development in Perspective,* edited by James A. Christenson and Jerry W. Robinson, Jr. Ames: Iowa State University Press.

Christenson, James A., Kim Fendley, and Jerry W. Robinson, Jr. 1989. "Community Development." Pp. 3–25 in *Community Development in Perspective,* edited by James A. Christenson and Jerry W. Robinson, Jr. Ames: Iowa State University Press.

Christian, Leah, Michael Dimock, and Scott Keeter. 2009. "Accurately Locating Where Wireless Respondents Live Requires More Than a Phone Number." Paper presented at the annual meeting of the American Association for Public Opinion Research, May 14–17, Hollywood, Florida.

Christian, L., S. Keeter, K. Purcell, and A. Smith. 2010. "Assessing Cell Phone Non-coverage Bias across Different Topics and Subgroups." Paper presented at the

65th annual conference of the American Association of Public Opinion Research, Chicago.

Clark, Colin. 1951. "Urban Population Densities." *Journal of the Royal Statistical Society,* Series A, 114: 490–496.

Clark, Terry N. 1968. "Community Structure, Decision-Making, Budget Expenditures, and Urban Renewal in 51 American Communities." *American Sociological Review* 33: 576–593.

———. 1971. "Community Structure and Decision-Making, Budget Expenditures, and Urban Renewal in 51 American Communities." In *Community Politics,* edited by Charles M. Bonjean, Terry Clark, and Robert Lineberry. New York: Free Press.

———. 1976. "How Many More New Yorks?" *New York Affairs* 3(4). Reprinted in *New Perspectives on the American Community* (1983), edited by Roland Warren and Larry Lyon. Homewood, IL: Dorsey Press.

———. 2000. "Old and New Paradigms for Urban Research: Globalization and the Fiscal Austerity and Urban Innovation Project." *Urban Affairs Review* 36(1): 3–45.

Clark, Terry N., and Loma C. Ferguson. 1983. *City Money: Political Processes, Fiscal Strain, and Retrenchment.* New York: Columbia University Press.

Clark, Terry N., and Ernest Goetz. 1994. "The Antigrowth Machine: Can City Governments Control, Limit or Manage Growth?" Pp. 105–145 in *Urban Innovations: Creative Strategies for Turbulent Times,* edited by Terry N. Clarke. Thousand Oaks, CA: Sage.

Clark, Terry N., William Kornblum, Harold Bloom, and Susan Tobias. 1968. "Discipline, Method, Community Structure and Decision Making." *The American Sociologist* 3: 214–217.

Clavel, Pierre. 1986. *The Progressive City.* New Brunswick, NJ: Rutgers University Press.

Cloward, A., and Richard Elman. 1966. "Advocacy in the Ghetto." *Trans-Action* 4(2): 27–35.

Cobb, Clifford. 2000. *Measurement Tools and the Quality of Life.* San Francisco: Redefining Progress.

Cochrane, J. D. 1999. *Market Dynamics II: Healthcare Systems.* Integrated Healthcare Report August, 1–13.

Coit, Katharine. 1978. "Local Action, Not Citizen Participation." In *Marxism and the Metropolis,* edited by William K. Tabb and Larry Sawers. New York: Oxford University Press.

Coleman, James S. 1957. *Community Conflict.* New York: Free Press.

———. 1988. "Free Riders and Zealots: The Role of Social Networks." *Sociological Theory* 6(1): 52–57.

———. 1990a. *Foundation of Social Theory.* Cambridge, MA: Harvard University Press.

———. 1990b. "Social Institutions and Social Theory." *American Sociological Review* 55(3): 333–339.

———. 1993. "The Rational Reconstruction of Society." *American Sociological Review* 58(1): 1–15.

Cooley, Charles H. 1902. *Human Nature and the Social Order.* New York: Scribner.

Coser, Lewis. 1956. *The Functions of Social Conflict.* New York: Free Press.

Costa, Dora L., and Matthew E. Kahn. 2003. "Civic Engagement and Community Heterogeneity: An Economist's Perspective." *Perspectives on Politics* 1(1): 103–111.

Cottrell, W. F. 1951. "Death by Dieselization: A Case Study in the Reaction to Technological Change." *American Sociological Review* 16: 358–365.

Cox, Harvey. 1965. *The Secular City.* Toronto: Macmillan.

Cox, K. 1993. "The Local and the Global in the New Urban Politics: A Critical View." *Environment and Planning D: Society and Space* 11(4): 433–448.

Crain, Robert L., Elihu Katz, and Donald B. Rosenthal. 1969. *The Politics of Community Conflict.* New York: Bobbs-Merrill.

Crenshaw, Edward M., Matthew Christenson, and Doyle Ray Oakey. 2000. "Demographic Transition in Ecological Focus." *American Sociological Review* 65: 371–391.

Cressey, Paul Goalby. 1932. *The Taxi Dance Hall.* Chicago: The University of Chicago Press.

Cummins, Robert A. 1996. "The Domains of Life Satisfaction: An Attempt to Order Chaos." *Social Indicators Research* 38(3): 303–328.

Curtis, James E., and John W. Petras. 1970. "Community Power, Power Studies and the Sociology of Knowledge." *Human Organization* 29: 204–218.

D'Antonio, William V., Howard J. Ehrlich, and Eugene C. Erickson. 1962. "Further Notes on the Study of Community Power." *American Sociological Review* 27: 848–853.

Dahl, Robert A. 1961. *Who Governs?* New Haven, CT: Yale University Press.

———. 1998. *On Democracy.* New Haven, CT: Yale University Press.

Dasgupta, Samir. 2004. *The Changing Face of Globalization.* New Delhi, India: Sage.

Davis, Allison, Burleigh B. Gardner, and Mary R. Gardner. 1941. *Deep South: A Social Anthropological Study of Caste and Class.* Chicago: The University of Chicago Press.

Dear, Michael J. 2000. *The Postmodern Urban Condition.* Oxford, UK: Blackwell.

Dewey, Richard. 1960. "The Rural-Urban Continuum." *American Journal of Sociology* 66: 60–66.

Diers, Jim. 2004. *Neighbor Power: Building Community the Seattle Way.* Seattle: University of Washington Press.

DiGaetano, A,. and P. Lawless. 1999. "Urban Governance and Industrial Decline: Governing Structures and Policy Agendas in Birmingham and Sheffield, England, and Detroit, Michigan, 1980–1997." *Urban Affairs Review* 34: 546–577.

Dillman, Don. 2000. *Mail and Internet Surveys: The Tailored Design Method.* New York: John Wiley and Sons.

Dillman, Don, Jolene D. Smyth, and Leah Melani Christian. 2009. *Internet, Mail, and Mixed-Mode Surveys: The Tailored Design Method,* 3rd ed. New York: John Wiley and Sons.

Dillman, D. A., and Smyth, J. D. 2007. "Design Effects in the Transition to Web-Based Surveys." *American Journal of Preventive Medicine 32*(5), Supp. 1: S90–S96.

Dollard, John. 1937. *Caste and Class in a Southern Town.* New Haven, CT: Yale University Press.

Domhoff, G. William. 1978. *Who Really Rules.* Santa Monica, CA: Goodyear.

———. 2006. *Who Rules America? Power, Politics, and Social Change.* 5th ed. New York: McGraw-Hill.

Donath, Judith S. 1999. "Identity and Deception in the Virtual Community." Pp. 29–59 in *Communities in Cyberspace,* edited by M.A. Smith and P. Kollock. New York: Routledge.

Donovan, T., M. Neiman, and S. Brumbaugh. 1994. "The Dimensions of Local Growth Strategies." *Research in Community Sociology* 4: 153–169.

Doreian, Patrick. 1981. "Estimating Linear Models with Spatially Distributed Data." *Sociological Methodology* 12: 359–388.

———. 1986. "Measuring Relative Standing in Small Groups and Bounded Social Networks." *Social Psychology Quarterly* 49(3): 247–259.

———. 2001. "Causality in Social Network Analysis." *Sociological Methods and Research* 30(1): 81–114.

Drake, St. Clair, and Horace Clayton. 1945. *Black Metropolis: A Study of Negro Life in a Northern City.* New York: Harcourt Brace Jovanovich.

Dressel, Paula L., and Harold L. Nix. 1982. "The Rural-Urban Typology: Its Utility for Community Research and Development." *Community Development Society Journal* 13(2): 91–99.

Driskell, Robyn, Elizabeth Embry, and Larry Lyon. 2008. "Faith and Politics: The Influence of Religious Beliefs on Political Participation." *Social Science Quarterly* 82(2): 294–314.

Driskell, Robyn, and Larry Lyon. 2002. "Are Virtual Communities True Communities? Examining the Environments and Elements of Community." *City and Community* 1(4): 373–390.

Driskell, Robyn, Larry Lyon, and Elizabeth Embry. 2008. "Civic Engagement and Religious Activities: Examining the Influence of Religious Tradition, Participation, and Beliefs." *Sociological Spectrum* 28: 578–601.

Duany, Andres, and Elizabeth Plater-Zyberk. 1995. "Neighborhoods and Suburbs." *Design Quarterly* 164: 10–23.

DuBois, W. E. B. 1899. *The Philadelphia Negro.* Philadelphia: The University of Pennsylvania.

Duncan, Beverly, and Stanley Lieberson. 1970. *Metropolis and Region in Transition.* New York: Sage.

Duncan, Otis Dudley. 1959. "Human Ecology and Population Studies." In *The Study of Population*, edited by Philip M. Hauser and Otis Dudley Duncan. Chicago: The University of Chicago Press.

———. 1969. *Towards Social Reporting: Next Steps.* New York: Sage.

Duncan, Otis Dudley, and Beverly Duncan. 1955. "Residential Distribution and Occupational Stratification." *The American Journal of Sociology* 60: 493–503.

———. 1957. *The Negro Population of Chicago.* Chicago: The University of Chicago Press.

Duncan, Otis Dudley, W. R. Scott, Stanley Lieberson, Beverly Duncan, and Hailliman H. Winsborough. 1960. *Metropolis and Region.* Baltimore, MD: Johns Hopkins University Press.

Duneier, Mitchell. 1992. *Slim's Table: Race, Respectability, and Masculinity.* Chicago: The University of Chicago Press.

———. 1999. *Sidewalk.* New York: Farrar, Straus, and Giroux.

Durkheim, Émile. 1893, 1964. *The Division of Labor in Society.* New York: Free Press.

———. 1897, 1952. *Suicide.* London: Routledge & Kegan Paul.

Dutton, John A. 2000. *New American Urbanism: Re-Forming the Suburban Metropolis.* Milan: Skira.

Dye, Thomas R. 1970. "Community Power Studies." In *Political Science Annual*, Vol. 2, edited by James A. Robinson. New York: Bobbs-Merrill.

Edmonston, Barry, and Thomas M. Guterbock. 1984. "Is Suburbanization Slowing Down? Recent Trends in Population Deconcentration in U.S. Metropolitan Areas." *Social Forces* 62(4): 905–925.

Edwards, Allan, and Dorothy Jones. 1976. *Community and Community Development.* The Hague: Mouton and Co.

Effrat, Andrew. 1972. "Power to the Paradigms." *Sociological Inquiry* 42: 3–33.

Egan, Timothy. 2002. "A Development Fuels a Debate on Urbanism." *The New York Times.* June 14.

Eichler, Mike. 2007. *Consensus Organizing: Building Communities of Mutual Self-Interest.* Thousand Oaks, CA: Sage.

Elkin, Stephen L. 1987. *City and Regime in the American Republic.* Chicago: The University of Chicago Press.

Ellin, N. 1996. *Postmodern Urbanism.* Oxford, UK: Blackwell.

Engels, Friedrich. 1845, 1958. *The Condition of the Working Class.* Translated by W. O. Henderson and W. H. Chaloner. New York: Macmillan.

———. 1969. *The Condition of the Working Class in England in 1844.* St. Albans, UK: Panther Books.

Epley, Donald R., and Mohan Menon. 2008. "A Method of Assembling Cross-Sectional Indicators into a Community Quality of Life." *Social Indicators Research* 88(2): 281–296.

Epstein, David G. 1974. *Brasilia, Plan and Reality.* Berkeley: University of California Press.

Etzioni, Amitai. 1996a. *The Golden Rule: Community and Morality in a Democratic Society.* New York: Basic Books.

———. 1996b. "The Responsive Community: A Communitarian Perspective." *American Sociological Review* 61(1): 1–11.

Etzioni, Amitai, and Oren Etzioni. 2001. "Can Virtual Communities Be Real?" Pp. 77–101 in *The Monochrome Society,* edited by Amitai Etzioni. Princeton, NJ: Princeton University Press.

Evans, Gary W., Eunju Rhee, Camille Forbes, Karen Mata Allen, and Stephen J. Lepore. 2000. "The Meaning and Efficacy of Social Withdrawal as a Strategy for Coping with Chronic Residential Crowding." *Journal of Environmental Psychology* 20(4): 335–342.

Fabiani, Donna, and Terry F. Buss. 2008. *Reengineering Community Development for the 21st Century: Transformational Trends in Governance and Democracy.* Armonk, NY: M. E. Sharpe.

Falk, William, and Shanyang Zhao. 1990a. "Paradigms, Theories and Methods in Contemporary Rural Sociology: A Partial Replication." *Rural Sociology* 54: 587–600.

———. 1990b. "Paradigms, Theories and Methods Revisited: We Respond to Our Critics." *Rural Sociology* 55: 112–122.

Farley, R. 1976. "Components of Suburban Population Growth." In *The Changing Face of the Suburbs,* edited by B. Schwartz. Chicago: The University of Chicago Press.

Faust, Katherine, and Stanley Wasserman. 1993. "Correlation and Association Models for Studying Measurements on Ordinal Relations." *Sociological Methodology* 23: 177–215.

Feagin, Joe R. 1988. *Free Enterprise City.* New Brunswick, NJ: Rutgers University Press.

Fear, Frank, Larry Gamm, and Frederick Fisher. 1989. "The Technical Assistance Approach." Pp. 69–88 in *Community Development in Perspective,* edited by James A. Christenson and Jerry W. Robinson, Jr. Ames: Iowa State University Press.

Ferguson, Ronald F., and William T. Dickens. 1999. "Introduction." Pp. 1–32 in *Urban Problems and Community Development,* edited by Ronald F. Ferguson and William T. Dickens. Washington, DC: Brookings Institution Press.

Feuer, Lewis S., ed. 1959. *Marx and Engels: Basic Writing on Politics and Philosophy.* Garden City, NY: Doubleday Anchor Books.

Firey, Walter. 1945. "Sentiment and Symbolism as Ecological Variables." *American Sociological Review* 10: 295–302.

———. 1947. *Land Use in Central Boston.* Cambridge, MA: Harvard University Press.

Firey, Walter, and Gideon Sjoberg. 1982. "Issues in Sociocultural Ecology." In *Urban Patterns,* edited by George A. Theodorson. University Park: Pennsylvania State University Press.

Fischer, Claude. 1973. "On Urban Alienation and Anomie: Powerlessness and Social Isolation." *American Sociological Review* 38: 311–326.

———. 1975. "Toward a Subcultural Theory of Urbanism." *American Journal of Sociology* 80: 1319–1341.

———. 1982. *To Dwell Among Friends: Personal Networks in Town and City.* Chicago: The University of Chicago Press.

———. 1992. *America Calling: A Social History of the Telephone to 1940.* Berkeley, CA: University of California Press.

———. 1995. "The Subcultural Theory of Urbanism: A Twentieth-Year Assessment." *American Journal of Sociology* 101: 543–577.

———. 1997. "Technology and Community: Historical Complexities." *Sociological Inquiry* 67(1): 113–118.

Fischer, Claude, Mark Baldassare, and Richard Ofshe. 1975. "Crowding Studies and Urban Life: A Critical Review." *Journal of the American Institute of Planners* 41: 406–418.

Flanagan, William G. 2002. *Urban Sociology: Images and Structure*, 4th ed. Boston: Allyn & Bacon.

Flax, Michael. 1978. *Survey of Urban Indicator Data 1970–1977.* Washington, DC: The Urban Institute.

Florida, Richard. 2003. "Cities and the Creative Class." *City and Community* 2(1): 3–19.

Foot, David H. S. 1981. *Operational Urban Models.* New York: Methuen.

Forrest, Ray, Adrienne La Grange, and Yip Ngai-Ming. 2002. "Neighborhood in a High Rise, High Density City: Some Observations on Contemporary Hong Kong." Pp. 215–240 in *The Editorial Board of The Sociological Review.* Oxford, UK: Blackwell.

Fox, S. 2005. "Digital Divisions: There Are Clear Differences among Those with Broadband Connections, Dial-up Connections, and No Connections at All to the Internet." Washington, DC: Pew Research Center: 1–17. Retrieved at http://www.pewinternet.org/Reports/2005/Digital-Divisions.aspx.

Frantz, Douglas, and Catherine Collins. 1999. *Celebration, U.S.A.: Living in Disney's Brave New Town.* New York: Henry Holt.

Freedman, J. L. 1975. *Crowding and Behavior.* San Francisco: W. H. Freeman.

Freeman, Linton C. 2004. *The Development of Social Network Analysis.* Vancouver, BC: Empirical Press.

Freeman, Linton, and Robert Winch. 1957. "Societal Complexity: An Empirical Test of a Typology of Societies." *American Journal of Sociology* 62(5).

Freilich, Morris. 1963. "Toward an Operational Definition of Community." *Rural Sociology* 28: 117–127.

Freudenburg, William R. 1986. "The Density of Acquaintanceship: An Overlooked Variable in Community Research?" *American Journal of Sociology* 92: 27–63.

Frey, William H. 2003. "Melting Pot Suburbs: A Study of Suburban Diversity." Pp. 155–180 in *Redefining Urban and Suburban America: Evidence from Census 2000*, edited by Bruce Katz and Robert E. Lang. Washington, DC: Brookings Institution Press.

Friedland, Roger, Donald Palmer, and Magnus Stenbeck. 1990. "The Geography of Corporate Production: Urban, Industrial, and Organizational Systems." *Sociological Forum* 5(3): 335–359.

Friedland, Roger, Frances Fox Piven, and Robert R. Alford. 1984. "Political Conflict, Urban Structure, and the Fiscal Crisis." Pp. 273–297 in *Marxism and the Metropolis: New Perspectives in Urban Political Economy*, 2nd ed., edited by William K. Tabb and Larry Sawers. New York: Oxford University Press.

Friedland, Roger, and A. F. Robertson, eds. 1990. *Beyond the Marketplace: Rethinking Economy and Society.* New York: Aldine de Gruyter.

Friedrichs, Robert. 1970. *A Sociology of Sociology.* New York: Free Press.

Frug, Gerald. 1999. *City Making: Building Community without Building Walls.* Princeton, NJ: Princeton University Press.

Fuchs, Christian. 2007. "Transnational Space and the 'Network Society." *21st Century Society: Journal of the Academy of Social Sciences* 2(1): 49–78.

Galaskiewicz, Joseph. 1979. *Exchange Networks and Community Politics.* Beverly Hills, CA: Sage.

———. 1985. *Social Organization of an Urban Grants Economy.* Orlando, FL: Academic Press.

Galaskiewicz, Joseph, and Stanley Wasserman. 1993. "Social Network Analysis: Concepts, Methodology, and Directions for the 1990s." *Sociological Methods and Research* 22: 3–22.

Gallaher, Art, Jr. 1961. *Plainville Fifteen Years Later.* New York: Columbia University Press.

Galle, Omer R., Walter R. Gove, and J. Miller McPherson. 1972. "Population Density and Pathology." *Science* 176: 23–30.

Gamson, William A. 1966. "Rancorous Conflict in Community Politics." *American Sociological Review* 31: 71–81.

———. 1991. "Commitment and Agency in Social Movements." *Sociological Forum* 6(1): 27–50.

———. 1992. *Talking Politics.* Cambridge, UK: Cambridge University Press.

Gans, Herbert J. 1962. *The Urban Villagers.* New York: Free Press.

———. 1967. *The Levittowners.* New York: Columbia University Press.

Garkovich, Lorraine, and Jerome M. Stam. 1980. "Research on Selected Issues in Community Development." In *Community Development in America,* edited by James Christenson and Terry Robinson. Ames: Iowa State University Press.

Garreau, Joel. 1992. *Edge City: Life on the New Frontier.* New York: Anchor Books.

Gendron, Richard, and G. William Domhoff. 2009. *The Leftmost City: Power and Progressive Politics in Santa Cruz.* Boulder, CO: Westview.

Giddens, Anthony. 1991. *Modernity and Self-Identity: Self and Society in the Late Modern Age.* Stanford, CA: Stanford University Press.

Gilchrist, Alison. 2004. *The Well-Connected Community: A Networking Approach to Community Development.* Bristol, UK: The Policy Press.

Glasgow, Douglas. 1972. "Black Power through Community Control." *Social Work* 17(3): 59–65.

Glass, Ruth. 1966. *Conflict in Society.* London: Churchill.

Glazer, Nathan, and Daniel Moynihan. 1963. *Beyond the Melting Pot.* Cambridge, MA: MIT Press.

Glenn, Norval D. 1967. "Massification versus Differentiation." *Social Forces* 46: 172–180.

Goffman, Erving. 1959. *The Presentation of Self in Everyday Life.* Garden City, NY: Doubleday.

———. 1961. *Asylums.* Garden City, NY: Doubleday.

———. 1962. "On the Cooling the Mark Out." In *Human Behavior and Social Processes,* edited by Arnold M. Rose. Boston: Houghton Mifflin.

———. 1963. *Stigma.* Englewood Cliffs, NJ: Prentice-Hall.

———. 1974. *Frame Analysis: An Essay on the Organization of Experience.* Cambridge: Harvard University Press.

———. 1977. *Gender Advertising.* New York: Harper & Row.

Gold, Harry. 2002. *Urban Life and Society.* Upper Saddle River, NJ: Prentice-Hall.

Goldsmith, Harold F., David J. Jackson, and J. Philip Shambaugh. 1982. "A Social Area Analysis Approach." In *Population Estimates: Methods for Small Area Analysis,* edited by Everett S. Lee and Harold F. Goldsmith. Beverly Hills, CA: Sage.

Gosling, Samuel D., Simine Vazire, Sanjay Srivastava, and Oliver P. John. 2004. "Should We Trust Web-Based Studies? A Comparative Analysis of Six Preconceptions about Internet Questionnaires." *American Psychologist* 59(2): 93–104.

Gottdiener, Mark, and Ray Hutchison. 2006. *The New Urban Sociology,* 3rd ed. Boulder, CO: Westview.

Goudy, W. J. 1990. "Community Attachment in a Rural Region." *Rural Sociology* 55: 178–198.

Gove, Walter R., M. Hughes, and O. R. Galle. 1979. "Overcrowding in the Home: An Empirical Investigation of Its Possible Pathological Consequences." *American Sociological Review* 44: 59–80.

Graesser, Arthur C., Zhiqiang Cai, Max M. Louwerse, and Frances Daniel. 2006. "Question Understanding Aid (QUAID): A Web Facility that Tests Question Comprehensibility." *Public Opinion Quarterly* 70(1): 3–22.

Green, Gary Paul, and Anna Haines. 2008. *Asset Building and Community Development,* 2nd ed. Thousand Oaks, CA: Sage.

Green, H. W. 1931. *Characteristics of Cleveland's Social Planning Areas.* Cleveland, OH: Welfare Federation of Cleveland.

Greer, Scott. 1962. *The Emerging City.* New York: Free Press.

———. 1964. *Urban Renewal and American Cities: the Dilemma of Democratic Intervention.* New York: Bobbs-Merrill.

Gregory, Steven. 1998. *Black Corona: Race and the Politics of Place in an Urban Community.* Princeton, NJ: Princeton University Press.

Greisman, Harvey C. 1986. "The Paradigm That Failed." Pp. 273–291 in *Structures of Knowing,* edited by R.C. Monk. Lanham, MD: University Press of America.

Grimes, Michael D., Charles M. Bonjean, J. Larry Lyon, and Robert Lineberry. 1976. "Community Structure and Leadership Arrangements." *American Sociological Review* 14(4): 706–725.

Grogan-Kaylor, Andrew M., Michael Wooley, Carol Mowbray, Thomas M. Reischl, Megan Guster, Rebecca Karb, Peter Macfarlane, Larry Gant, and Katherine Alaimo. 2006. "Predictors of Neighborhood Satisfaction." *Journal of Community Practice* 14(4): 27–50.

Gross, Bertram M. 1966. "The State of the Nation: Social Systems Accounting." In *Social Indicators,* edited by R. Bauer. Cambridge, MA/ London, UK: MIT Press.

Grossberg, Lawrence, and Cary Nelson, eds. 1988. *Marxism and the Interpretation of Culture.* Urbana: University of Illinois Press.

Groves, Robert. 1990. "Theories and Methods of Telephone Surveys." *Annual Review of Sociology* 16: 221–240.

Groves, Robert L., and Robert M. Kahn. 1979. *Surveys by Telephone: A National Comparison with Personal Interviews.* New York: Academic Press.

Guba, Egon G., and Yvonna S. Lincoln. 1994. "Competing Paradigms in Qualitative Research." Pp. 105–117 in *Handbook of Qualitative Research,* edited by Norman K. Denzin and Yvonna S. Lincoln. Thousand Oaks, CA: Sage.

Guest, Avery M., Barrett A. Lee, and Lynn Staeheli. 1982. "Changing Locality Identification in the Metropolis." *American Sociological Review* 47(4): 543–549.

Gurin, Arnold. 1966. "Current Issues in Community Organization Practice and Education." Brandeis University Reprint Series No. 21, p. 30. Florence Heller Graduate School for Advanced Studies in Social Welfare.

Hagen, Dan E., and Charlotte M. Collier. 1982. "Respondent Selection Procedures for Telephone Surveys: Must They Be Intrusive?" Paper presented at the Conference of the American Association for Public Opinion Research, Baltimore, MD.

Hall, Edward Twitchell. 1966. *The Hidden Dimension.* Garden City, NY: Doubleday.

Hall, Tim, and Phil Hubbard. 1996. "Geography and the Entrepreneurial City: Futures, Strategies, Perspectives." *Area* 28(2): 258–259.

Hamilton, Richard F. 2001. *Mass Society, Pluralism, and Bureaucracy.* Westport, CT: Praeger.

Hampton, Keith, and Barry Wellman. 2001. "Long Distance Community in the Network Society." *American Behavioral Scientist* 45(3): 476–495.

Hannerz, Ulf. 1969. *Soulside.* New York: Columbia University Press.

Hanson, Royce. 1978. "New Towns: Utopian Prospects—Hard Realities." In *Psychology of the Planned Community,* edited by Donald C. Klein. New York: Human Sciences Press.

Harris, Chauncey D., and Edward L. Ullman. 1945. "The Nature of Cities." *The Annals of the American Academy of Political Science* 242: 7–17.

Harvey, David. 1973. *Social Justice and the City.* Baltimore, MD: Johns Hopkins University Press.

———. 1978. "The Urban Process under Capitalism." *International Journal of Urban and Regional Research* 2: 101–131.

———. 1985a. *Consciousness and the Urban Experience.* Baltimore, MD: Johns Hopkins University Press.

———. 1985b. *The Urbanization of Capital.* Baltimore, MD: Johns Hopkins University Press.

———. 1988. *Social Justice and the City,* 2nd ed. Oxford, UK: Blackwell.

———. 1989. *The Urban Experience.* Baltimore, MD: Johns Hopkins University Press.

———. 2000. *Spaces of Hope.* Berkeley: University of California Press.

———. 2001. *Spaces of Capital: Toward a Critical Geography.* New York: Routledge.

———. 2003a. *The New Imperialism.* Oxford, UK: Oxford University Press.

———. 2003b. *Paris, Capital of Modernity.* New York: Routledge.

———. 2006. *The Limits to Capital.* London: Verso.

———. 2007. *A Brief History of Neoliberalism.* Oxford, UK: Oxford University Press.

———. 2008. "The Right to the City." *New Left Review* 53: 23–40.

———. 2009 [1973]. *Social Justice and The City,* rev. ed. Athens: University of Georgia Press.

———. 2010. *The Enigma of Capital: And the Crises of Capitalism.* Oxford, UK: Oxford University Press.

Hassard, John. 1995. *Sociology and Organization Theory: Positivism, Paradigms and Postmodernity.* Cambridge, UK: Cambridge University Press.

Haveman, Heather A. 2000. "The Future of Organizational Sociology: Forging Ties between Paradigms." *Contemporary Sociology* 29: 476–486.

Hawley, Amos. 1950. *Human Ecology.* New York: Ronald Press Hawley, Amos. 1971. *Urban Society: An Ecological Approach.* New York: Ronald Press.

———. 1968. "Human Ecology: A Theory of Community Structure." *International Encyclopedia of the Social Sciences.* New York: Macmillan/Free Press.

Hayes, Edward C. 1972. *Power Structure and Urban Policy: Who Rules in Oakland.* New York: McGraw-Hill.

Haworth, Lawrence. 1963. *The Good City.* Bloomington: Indiana University Press.

Heckscher, August, and Phyllis Robinson. 1977. *Open Spaces: The Life of American Cities.* New York: Harper & Row.

Hendrick, Rebecca. 2004. "Assessing and Measuring the Fiscal Health of Local Governments: Focus on Chicago Suburban Municipalities." *Urban Affairs Review* 40(1): 78–114.

Herman, Leon M. 1971. "Urbanization and New Housing Construction in the Soviet Union." *American Journal of Economics and Sociology* 30(2): 203–219.

Hillery, George A., Jr. 1955. "Definitions of Community: Areas of Agreement." *Rural Sociology* 20(2): 111–123.

———. 1963. "Villages, Cities, and Total Institutions." *American Sociological Review* 28: 779–791.

———. 1968. *Communal Organizations: A Study of Local Societies.* Chicago: The University of Chicago Press.

Hiltz, Starr Roxanne, and Murray Turoff. 1993. *The Network Nation: Human Communication via Computer,* rev ed. Cambridge, MA: MIT Press.

Hong, Traci, and Thomas Farley. 2008. "Urban Residents' Priorities for Neighborhood Features: A Survey of New Orleans Residents after Hurricane Katrina." *American Journal of Preventative Medicine* 34(4): 353–356.

Horowitz, Ruth. 1983. *Honor and the American Dream.* New Brunswick, NJ: Rutgers University Press.

Howard, Tharon W. 1997. *A Rhetoric of Electronic Communities.* Greenwich, CT: Ablex.

Howard, Ebenezer. 1898, 1965. *Garden Cities of To-Morrow.* Edited by F. J. Osborn. Cambridge, MA: MIT Press. Page references are to the 1965 edition.

Hoyt, Homer. 1939. *The Structure and Growth of Residential Neighborhoods in American Cities.* Washington, DC: Federal Housing Administration.

Hunter, Albert. 1974. *Symbolic Communities: The Persistence and Change of Chicago's Local Communities.* Chicago: The University of Chicago Press.

———. 1975. "The Loss of Community." *American Sociological Review* 40: 537–552.

Hunter, Floyd. 1953. *Community Power Structure.* Chapel Hill: University of North Carolina Press.

Iannacchione, V. G., J. M. Staab, & D. T. Redden. 2003. "Evaluating the Use of Residential Mailing Addresses in a Metropolitan Household Survey." *The Public Opinion Quarterly* 67(2): 202–210.

Inkeles, Alex, and David Smith. 1974. *Becoming Modern.* Cambridge, MA: Harvard University Press.

Jacobs, Jane. 1961. *The Death and Life of Great American Cities.* New York: Random House.

Janson, Carl-Gunnar. 1980. "Factorial Social Ecology: An Attempt at Summary and Evaluation." *Annual Review of Sociology* 6: 433–456.

Jones, Sydney, and Susannah Fox. 2009. "Generations Online in 2009." Pew Internet and American Life Project Report (Jan.). Retrieved from http://pewinternet.org/Reports/2009/Generations-Online-in-2009.aspx

Kamolnick, Paul. 2001. "Simmel's Legacy for Contemporary Value Theory: A Critical Assessment." *Sociological Theory* 19(1): 65–85.

Karp, David A., Gregory P. Stone, and William C. Yoels. 1991. *Being Urban: A Sociology of City Life,* 2nd ed. New York: Praeger.

Kasarda, John D., and Edward M. Crenshaw. 1991. "Third World Urbanization: Dimensions, Theories, and Determinants." *Annual Review of Sociology* 17: 467–501.

Kasarda, John D., and Morris Janowitz. 1974. "Community Attachment in Mass Society." *American Sociological Review* 39: 328–339.

Katz, Bruce, and Robert E. Lang. 2003. "Introduction." Pp. 1–12 in *Redefining Urban and Suburban America: Evidence from Census 2000*, edited by Bruce Katz and Robert E. Lang. Washington, DC: Brookings Institution Press.

Katz, James E., and R. E. Rice. 2002. "Project Syntopia: Social Consequences of Internet Use." *City & Society* 1(1): 166–179.

———. 2009. "Falling into the Net: Main Street America Playing Games and Making Friends Online." *Communications of the ACM* 52(9): 149–150.

Katz, James E., Ronald E. Rice, and Philip Aspden. 2001. "The Internet, 1995–2000: Access, Civic Involvement, and Social Interaction." *American Behavioral Scientist* 45(3): 405–419.

Katz, Lawrence, and Kenneth T. Rosen. 1987. "The Interjurisdictional Effects of Growth Controls on Housing Prices." *Journal of Law and Economics* 30: 149–160.

Kaufman, Harold. 1959. "Toward and Interactional Conception of Community." *Social Forces* 38: 17.

Kellner, Douglas. 1989. "Introduction: Jameson, Marxism, and Postmodernism." Pp. 1–42 in *Postmodernism, Jameson, Critique*, edited by Douglas Kellner. Washington, DC: Maisonneuve Press.

Kenny, Sue. 2002. "Tensions and Dilemmas in Community Development: New Discourses, New Trojans?" *Community Development Journal* 37(4): 284–299.

Kish, Leslie. 1949. "A Procedure for Objective Respondent Selection within the Household." *Journal of the American Statistical Association* 44: 380–387.

———. 1965. *Survey Sampling*. New York: John Wiley & Sons.

Kleniewski, Nancy. 1997. *Cities, Change and Conflict: A Political Economy of Urban Life*. Belmont, CA: Wadsworth.

Kleniewski, Nancy, and Alexander R. Thomas. 2010. *Cities, Change, and Conflict: A Political Economy of Urban Life*, 4th ed. Belmont, CA: Wadsworth.

Knoke, David. 1994. *Political Networks: The Structural Perspective*. Cambridge, UK: Cambridge University Press.

Kohlberg, Lawrence. 1984. *The Psychology of Moral Development: The Nature and Validity of Moral Stages*. San Francisco, CA: Harper and Row.

Kornblum, William. 1974. *Blue Collar Community*. Chicago: The University of Chicago Press.

Kornhauser, William. 1959. "Power and Participation in the Local Community." *Health Education Monographs*, No. 6. Oakland, CA: Society of Public Health Educators.

Kotkin, Joel. 2005. "The New Suburbanism: A Realist's Guide to the American Future." Costa Mesa, CA: The Planning Center. Retrieved from www.planningcenter.com.

Kotlowitz, Alex. 1991. *There Are No Children Here: The Story of Two Boys Growing Up in the Other America*. New York: Anchor Books.

Kraut, R. E., M. Patterson, V. Lundmark, S. Kiesler, T. Mukopadhyay, and W. Scherlis. 1998. "Internet Paradox: A Social Technology that Reduces Social Involvement and Psychological Well-being?" *American Psychologist* 53(9): 1017–1032.

Kraut, Robert, Sara Kiesler, Bonka Boneva, Jonathan Cummings, Vicki Helgeson, and Anne Crawford. 2002. "Internet Paradox Revisited." *Journal of Social Issues* 58(1): 49–74.

Kraut, Robert, M. Patterson, V. Lundmark, S. Kiesler, T. Mukopadhyay, and W. Scherlis. 1998. "Internet Paradox: A Social Technology That Reduces Social Involvement and Psychological Well-Being?" *The American Psychologist* 52(9): 1017–1032.

Kretzmann, John P., and John L. McKnight. 1993. *Building Communities from the Inside Out: A Path toward Finding and Mobilizing a Community's Assets*. Chicago: ACTA Publications.

Krosnick, J., and L. Fabrigar. 2003. *Designing Questionnaires to Measure Attitudes*. New York: Oxford University Press.

Kruger, Daniel J. 2008. "Verifying the Operational Definition of Neighborhood for the Psychosocial Impact of Structural Deterioration." *Journal of Community Psychology* 36(1): 53–60.

Kruger, Daniel J., Thomas M. Reischl, and Gilbert Gee. 2007. "Neighborhood Social Conditions Mediate the Association between Physical Deterioration and Mental Health." *American Journal of Community Psychology* 40(3-4): 261–271.

Kuhn, Thomas S. 1962. *The Structure of Scientific Revolutions*. Chicago: The University of Chicago Press.

Ladd, Everett C. 1999. *The Ladd Report*. New York: Free Press.

Land, Kenneth. 1983. "Conceptualization and Measurement in the Social Sciences." *Sociology and Social Research* 67(2): 224–225.

Lang, Robert. 2003. *Edgeless Cities: Exploring the Elusive Metropolis*. Washington, DC: Brookings Institution Press.

Laumann, Edward. 1973. *Bonds of Pluralism: The Form and Substance of Urban Social Networks*. New York: John Wiley & Sons.

Lauria, Mickey. 1997a. "Communicating in a Vacuum: Will Anyone Hear?" *Planning Theory* 17: 40–42.

———. 1997b. *Reconstructing Urban Regime Theory: Regulating Urban Politics in a Global Economy*. Thousand Oaks, CA: Sage.

Ledwith, Margaret, and Jo Campling. 2005. *Community Development: A Critical Approach*. Bristol, UK: The Policy Press.

Lefebvre, Henri. 1976. *The Survival of Capitalism*. London: Allison & Busby.

———. 1991. *The Production of Space*. Oxford, UK: Blackwell.

Lehrer, A., and R. Milgrom. 1996. "New (Sub)urbanism: Countersprawl or Repackaging the Product." *Capitalism, Nature, Socialism* 7(2): 49–64.

Lenski, Gerhard. 1963. *The Religious Factor*. Garden City, NY: Anchor.

Lepore, Stephen J., and Gary W. Evans. 1991. "Social Hassles and Psychological Health in the Context of Chronic Crowding." *Journal of Health and Social Behavior* 32 (Dec.): 357–367.

Lepore, Stephen J., Gary W. Evans, and M. N. Palsane. 1991. "Social Hassles and Psychological Health in the Context of Chronic Crowding." *Journal of Health and Social Behavior* 32 (Dec.): 357–367.

Levitt, S. D. 2004. "Understanding Why Crime Fell in the 1990s: Four Factors That Explain the Decline and Six That Do Not." *The Journal of Economic Perspectives* 18(1): 163–190.

Lewis, Oscar. 1951. *Life in a Mexican Village: Tepoztlan Restudied*. Urbana: University of Illinois Press.

Lewis, Sinclair. 1920. *Main Street*. New York: Harcourt, Brace.

———. 1922. *Babbitt*. New York: Harcourt, Brace.

———. 1925. *Arrowsmith*. New York: Harcourt, Brace.

Liebow, Elliot. 1967. *Tally's Corner*. Boston: Little Brown.

Lindner, Rolf. 1996. *The Reportage of Urban Culture—Robert Park and the Chicago School*. Cambridge, MA: Cambridge University Press.

Lindt, Gillian. 1979. "Robert S. Lynd: American Scholar-Activist." *Journal of the History of Sociology* 2: 1–13.

Lineberry, Robert L., and Edmund P. Fowler. 1967. "Reformism and Public Policies in American Cities." *American Political Science Review* 61: 701–716.

Link, M. W., M. P. Battaglia, M. R. Frankel, L. Osborn, and A. H. Mokdad. 2008. "A Comparison of Address-Based Sampling (ABS) Versus Random-Digit Dialing (RDD) for General Population Surveys." *Public Opinion Quarterly* 72(1): 6–27.

Lipset, Seymour Martin, and Reinhard Bendix. 1951. "Social Status and Social Structure." *British Journal of Sociology* 2: 150–168, 230–254.

Liska, Allen E. 1990. "The Significance of Aggregate Dependent Variables and Contextual Independent Variables for Linking Macro and Micro Theories." *Social Psychology Quarterly* 53(4): 292–301.

Littrell, Donald W., and Daryl Hobbs. 1989. "The Self-Help Approach." Pp. 48–68 in *Community Development in Perspective*, edited by James A. Christenson and Jerry W. Robinson, Jr. Ames: Iowa State University Press.

Littrell, Donald W., and Doris P. Littrell. 2006. *Practicing Community Development.* Columbia: University of Missouri–Columbia Extension Services, DM7616.

Liu, Ben-Chieh.1976. *Quality of Life Indicators in U.S. Metropolitan Areas: A Statistical Analysis.* New York: Praeger.

Lofland, John. 1971. *Analyzing Social Settings: A Guide to Qualitative Observation and Analysis.* Belmont, CA: Wadsworth.

Lofland, John, Lyn Lofland, David Snow, and Leon Anderson. 2006. *Analyzing Social Settings: A Guide to Qualitative Observation and Analysis*, 4th ed. Belmont, CA: Wadsworth.

Logan, John, and Harvey Molotch. 1987. *Urban Fortunes: The Political Economy of Place.* Los Angeles: University of California Press.

Logan, John R., Richard D. Alba, and Shu-Yin Leung. 1996. "Minority Access to White Suburbs: A Multiregional Comparison." *Social Forces* 74(3): 851–881.

Long, Norton E. 1958. "The Local Community as an Ecology of Games." *American Journal of Sociology* 64: 251–261.

Loomis, Charles. 1960. *Social Systems.* Princeton, NJ: D. Van Nostrand.

Lösch, August. 1954. *The Economics of Location*, 2nd ed., translated by W. H. Woglom with the assistance of W. F. Stolper. New Haven: Yale University Press.

Lowe, Jeffrey S. 2006. *Rebuilding Communities the Public Trust Way: Community Foundation Assistance to CDCs, 1980–2000.* Lanham, MD: Lexington Books/Rowman & Littlefield.

Lynd, Staughton. 1979. "Robert S. Lynd: The Elk Basin Experience." *Journal of the History of Sociology* 2: 14–22.

Lynd, Robert S., and Helen M. Lynd. 1929. *Middletown.* New York: Harcourt Brace Jovanovich.

———. 1937. *Middletown in Transition: A Study in Cultural Conflicts.* New York: Harcourt Brace Jovanovich.

Lyon, Larry. 1977a. "Community Power and Policy Outputs." In *New Perspectives on the American Community,* edited by Roland Warren. Chicago: Rand McNally.

———. 1977b. "A Re-Examination of the Reform Index and Community Power." *Journal of the Community Development Society* 8: 86–97.

Lyon, Larry, and Charles M. Bonjean. 1981. "Community Power and Policy Output: the Routines of Local Politics." *Urban Affairs Quarterly* 17(1): 3–21.

Lyon, Larry, Lawrence G. Felice, M. Ray Perryman, and E. Stephen Parker. 1981. "Community Power and Population Increase." *American Journal of Sociology* 86(6): 1387–1399. Reprinted in *New Perspectives on the American Community* (1983), edited by Roland Warren and Larry Lyon. Homewood, IL: Dorsey Press.

Macionis, John J., and Vincent N. Parrillo. 2010. *Cities and Urban Life*, 5th ed. Upper Saddle River, NJ: Pearson/Prentice-Hall.

MacDonald, A. P., Jr., and W. F. Throop. 1971. "Internal Locus of Control." *Psychological Reports,* Supplement I-V28.

MacLeod, Jay. 2009. *Ain't No Makin' It: Aspirations and Attainment in a Low-Income Neighborhood*, 3rd ed. Boulder, CO: Westview.

Marcuse, P. 2000. "The New Urbanism: The Dangers So Far." *DISP* 140: 4–6.

Marks, Mara A., Matt A. Barreto, and Nathan D. Woods. 2004. "Race and Racial Attitudes a Decade after the 1992 Los Angeles Riots." *Urban Affairs Review* 40(1): 3–18.

Martin, W. Allen. 2004. *The Urban Community.* Upper Saddle River, NJ: Pearson/Prentice-Hall.

Martindale, Don Albert. 1981. *The Nature and Types of Social Theory.* Boston: Houghton Mifflin.

Marx, Karl. 1867, 1967. *Capital.* New York: International Publishers.

Marx, Karl, and Friedrich Engels. 1846, 1970. *The German Ideology.* New York: International Publishers.

———. 1848, 1959. "Manifesto of the Communist Party." In *Marx and Engels: Basic Writings on Politics and Philosophy*, edited by Lewis S. Feuer. Garden City, NY: Doubleday Anchor Books.

Maslow, A. H. 1970. *Motivation and Personality,* 2nd ed. New York: Harper & Row.

Mathie, Alison, and Gord Cunningham. 2003. "From Clients to Citizens: Asset-Based Community Development as a Strategy for Community-Driven Development." *Development in Practice* 13(5): 474–486.

Mayhew, Bruce H. and Roger L. Levinger. 1976. "Size and Density of Interaction in Human Aggregates." *American Journal of Sociology* 82(1): 86–110.

McCann, Eugene J. 2004. " 'Best Places': Interurban Competition, Quality of Life and Popular Media Discourse." *Urban Studies* 41(10): 1909–1929.

McKinney, John C. 1966. *Constructive Typology and Social Theory.* New York: Appleton-Century-Crofts.

McKinney, John C., and Charles P. Loomis. 1958. "The Typological Tradition." In *Contemporary Sociology*, edited by Joseph S. Roucek. New York: The Philosophical Library.

McNeely, Joseph. 1999. "Community Building." *Journal of Community Psychology* 27(6): 741–750.

Michelson, William. 1977a. *Environmental Choice, Human Behavior, and Residential Satisfaction.* New York: Oxford University Press.

———. 1977b. "Planning and Amelioration of Urban Problems." In *Contemporary Topics in Urban Sociology,* edited by Kent P. Schwirian et al. Morristown, NJ: General Learning Press.

Milgram, Stanley. 1970. "The Experiences of Living in Cities." *Science* 167: 1461–1470.

Miller, Laura J. 1995. "Family Togetherness and the Suburban Ideal." *Sociological Forum* 10(3): 393–418.

Miller, Zane. 1992. "Pluralism, Chicago School Style: Louis Wirth, the Ghetto, the City, and 'Integration.' " *Journal of Urban History* 18 (May): 251–279.

Mills, C. Wright. 1942. "Review of the Social Life of a Modern Community." *American Sociological Review* 7: 263–271. Reprinted in Irving Horowitz, *People, Politics and Power* (1965). London: Oxford University Press.

———. 1959. *The Sociological Imagination.* New York: Oxford University Press.

Minar, David W., and Scott Greer, eds. 1969. *The Concept of Community.* Chicago: Aldine.

Miner, Horace. 1952. "The Folk-Urban Continuum." *American Sociological Review* 17: 537–549.

Mitchell, R. E. 1971. "Some Implications of High Density Housing." *American Sociological Review* 36: 18–29.

Molotch, Harvey. 1976. "The City as a Growth Machine." *American Journal of Sociology* 82: 309–332.

Molotch, Harvey, William Freudenburg, and Krista E. Paulsen. 2000. "History Repeats Itself, But How? City Character, Urban Tradition, and the Accomplishment of Place." *American Sociological Review* 65: 791–823.

Morin, Richard, and Jill Hanley. 2004. "Community Economic Development in a Context of Globalization and Metropolization: A Comparison of Four North American Cities." *International Journal of Urban and Regional Research* 28(2): 369–383.

Muro, Mark, and Christopher W. Hoene. 2009. "Fiscal Challenges Facing Cities: Implications for Recovery." Pp. 1–13 in *Recovery and the Local Fiscal Crisis.* Washington, DC: Brookings Institution, Metropolitan Policy Program.

Namboodiri, Krishnan. 1988. "Ecological Demography: Its Place in Sociology." *American Sociological Review* 53: 619–633.

Neal, Zachary. 2010. "From Central Places to Network Bases: A Transition in the U.S. Urban Hierarchy." *City & Community* 10: 49–74.

Nelson, Michael D. 1974. "The Validity of Secondary Analyses of Community Power Studies." *Social Forces* 52: 531–537.

Newman, Oscar. 1996. "Creating Defensible Space." Washington, DC: US Department of Housing and Urban Development, Office of Policy Development and Research.

Nie, Norman. 1999. "ZEITGEIST—Telecommuting and the Future of the Social Sphere." *American Demographics* 21(7): 50–80.

Nie, Norman, and Lutz Erbring. 2000. "Internet and Society: A Preliminary Report." Stanford Institute for the Quantitative Study of Society, Stanford University, published online in *IT&Society* 1(1) (summer) 2002: 275–283. Retrieved from http://www.vermario.com/wiki/lib/exe/fetch.php/internet_society_report.pdf

Nisbet, Robert. 1953, 1976. *The Quest for Community.* New York: Oxford University Press.

———. 1960. "Moral Values and Community." *International Review of Community Development* 5: 77–85.

———. 1966. *The Sociological Tradition.* New York: Basic Books.

Noll, H. 2004. "Heinz-Herbert Noll Social Indicators and Quality of Life Research: Background, Achievements and Current Trends." Pp. 151–181 in *Advances in Sociological Knowledge,* edited by N. Genov. Wiesbaden, Germany: Verlag.

O'Brien, David J. 1975. *Neighborhood Organization and Interest-Group Process.* Princeton, NJ: Princeton University Press.

O'Brien, David J., Andrew Raedeke, and Edward W. Hassinger. 1998. "The Social Networks of Leaders in More or Less Viable Communities Six Years Later: A Research Note." *Rural Sociology* 63(1): 109–127.

O'Connor, Edwin. 1956. *The Last Hurrah.* Boston: Little, Brown.

Ogburn, W. F. 1937. *Social Characteristics of Cities.* Chicago: International City Managers Association.

Oldenburg, Ray. 1999. *The Great Good Place: Cafes, Coffee Shops, Bookstores, Bars, Hair Salons and other Hangouts at the Heart of a Community.* New York: Marlowe.

———. 2001. *Celebrating the Third Place.* New York: Marlowe.

Oliver, J. Eric. 2001. *Democracy in Suburbia.* Princeton, NJ: Princeton University Press.

———. 2003. "Mental Life and the Metropolis in Suburban America: The Psychological Correlates of Metropolitan Place Characteristics." *Urban Affairs Review* 39(2): 228–253.

Oropesa, R. S. 1992. "Social Structure, Social Solidarity and Involvement in Neighborhood Improvement Associations." *Sociological Inquiry* 62(1): 108–117.

Osborn, Frederick J. 1969. *Green Belt Cities.* New York: Schocken.

Palen, John J. 1981. *The Urban World.* New York: McGraw-Hill.

———. 2005. "The Education of the Senior Military Decision-Maker." *Sociological Quarterly* 13(2): 147–160.

———. 2008. *The Urban World,* 8th ed. Boulder, CO: Paradigm.

Park, Robert E. 1936. "Human Ecology." *American Journal of Sociology* 17(1): 1–15.

———. 1952. *Human Communities.* New York: Free Press.

Parsons, Talcott. 1951. *The Social System.* Glencoe, IL: Free Press.

Parsons, Talcott, and Robert F. Bales. 1955. *Family, Socialization and Interaction Process.* Glencoe, IL: Free Press.

Parsons, Talcott, and Edward Shils, eds. 1951. *Toward a General Theory of Action.* Cambridge, MA: Harvard University Press.

Parsons, Talcott, and Neil J. Smelser. 1956. *Economy and Society.* Glencoe, IL: Free Press.

Payne, Geoffrey K. 1977. *Urban Housing in the Third World.* Boston: Routledge and Kegan Paul.

Perrow, Charles. 2000. "An Organizational Analysis of Organizational Theory." *Contemporary Sociology* 29(3): 469–476.

Peterman, William. 2000. *Neighborhood Planning and Community-Based Development: The Potential and Limits of Grassroots Action.* Thousand Oaks, CA: Sage.

Pew Internet and American Life Project. 2010. http://pewinternet.org./

Peytchev, Andy. 2009. "Survey Breakoff." *The Public Opinion Quarterly* 73(1): 74–97.

Pfautz, Harold, and O. D. Duncan. 1950. "Critical Evaluation of Warner's Work in Community Stratification." *American Sociological Review,* Vol. 15.

Phillips, Rhonda, and Robert H. Pittman. 2009. *An Introduction to Community Development.* New York: Routledge.

Pilisuk, Marc, JoAnn McAllister, and Jack Rothman. 1996. "Coming Together for Action: The Challenge of Contemporary Grassroots Community Organizing." *Journal of Social Issues* 52(1): 15–37.

Polsby, Nelson W. 1963. *Community Power and Political Theory.* New Haven, CT: Yale University Press.

Pool, Ithiel de Sola. 1983. *Forecasting the Telephone: A Retrospective Technology Assessment of the Telephone.* Norwood, NJ: Ablex.

Popkin, S., B. Katz, M. Cunningham, K. Brown, J. Gustafson, and M. Turner. 2004. "A Decade of HOPE IV: Research Findings and Policy Challenges." Washington, DC: The Urban Institute /Brookings Institution.

Poplin, Dennis E. 1979. *Communities: A Survey of Theories and Methods of Research.* New York: Macmillan.

Presthus, Robert. 1964. *Men at the Top: A Study in Community Power.* New York: Oxford University Press.

Presser, Stanley, Mick P. Couper, Judith T. Lessler, Elizabeth Martin, Jean Martin, Jennifer M. Rothgeb, and Eleanor Singer. 2004. "Methods for Testing and Evaluating Survey Questions." *The Public Opinion Quarterly* 68(1): 109–130.

Putnam, Robert D. 1995. "Bowling Alone: America's Declining Social Capital." *Journal of Democracy* 6(1): 65–78.

———. 2000. *Bowling Alone.* New York: Simon and Schuster.

Redfield, Robert. 1941. *The Folk Culture of Yucatan.* Chicago: University of Chicago Press.

———. 1947. "The Folk Society." *American Journal of Sociology* 52: 293–308.

Rees, Philip H. 1971. "Factorial Ecology: An Extended Definition, Survey, and Critique." *Economic Geography* 47: 220–233.

Reese, Laura A., and Raymond Rosenfeld. 2008. "Comparative Civic Culture." *Journal of Urban Affairs* 30: 355–374.

Reese, Laura A., and Minting Ye. 2011. "Policy versus Place Luck: Achieving Local Economic Prosperity." *Economic Development Quarterly* 4: 2–16.

Regoeczi, Wendy. 2002. "The Impact of Density: The Importance of Nonlinearity and Selection on Flight and Fight Responses." *Social Forces* 81(2): 505–530.

Reitzes, Donald C., and Dietrich C. Reitzes. 1992. "Saul D. Alinsky: An Applied Urban Symbolic Interactionist." *Symbolic Interaction* 15(1): 1–24.

Relph, Edward C. 1987. *The Modern Urban Landscape.* Baltimore, MD: Johns Hopkins University Press.

Rheingold, Howard. 1993. *The Virtual Community.* New York: Addison-Wesley.

Richmond, Anthony. 1969. "Migration in Industrial Societies." In *Migration*, edited by John A. Jackson. London: Cambridge University Press.

Riesman, David. 1953. *The Lonely Crowd.* New Haven, CT: Yale University Press.

Ritzer, George. 1975. *Sociology: A Multiple Paradigm Science.* Boston: Allyn & Bacon.

———. 1997. *Postmodern Social Theory.* New York: McGraw-Hill.

Ritzer, George, and Douglas J. Goodman. 2004. *Sociological Theory,* 6th ed. Boston: McGraw-Hill.

Robinson, Jerry W., and Gary Paul Green. 2010. *Introduction to Community Development: Theory, Practice, and Service-Learning.* Thousand Oaks, CA: Sage.

Robinson, Jerry W., Jr. 1989. "The Conflict Approach." Pp. 89–116 in *Community Development in Perspective*, edited by James A. Christenson and Jerry W. Robinson, Jr. Ames: Iowa State University Press.

Robinson, W. S. 1950. "Ecological Correlations and the Behaviour of Individuals." *American Sociological Review* 15: 351–357.

Rosenberg, M. 1989. *Society and the Adolescent Self-image,* rev. ed. Middeltown, CT: Wesleyan University Press.

Rossi, Peter H. 1955. *Why Families Move: A Study in the Social Psychology of Urban Residential Mobility.* New York: Free Press.

———. 1972. "Community Social Indicators." In *The Human Meaning of Social Change*, edited by Angus Campbell and Philip E. Converse. New York: Russell Sage Foundation.

Rossi, Peter H., and Robert L. Crain. 1968. "The NORC Permanent Community Sample." *Public Opinion Quarterly* 32: 261–272.

Rothman, Jack. 1996. "The Interweaving of Community Intervention Approaches." *Journal of Community Practice* 3(3/4): 69–99.

Rouse, James W. 1978. "Building a Sense of Place." In *Psychology of the Planned Community,* edited by Donald C. Klein. New York: Human Sciences Press.

Rousseau, François, and Lionel Standing. 1995. "Zero Effect of Crowding on Arousal and Performance: On 'Proving' the Null Hypothesis." *Perceptual and Motor Skills* 81 (Aug.): 72–74.

Ruben, Julius. 1961. "Canal or Railroad? Imitation and Innovation in the Response to the Erie Canal in Philadelphia, Baltimore, and Boston." *Transactions of the American Philosophical Society* 51, part 7.

Rubin, Israel. 1969. "Function and Structure of Community: Conceptual and Theoretical Analysis." *International Review of Community Development* 21-22: 111–19.

Ruhil, Anirudh V. S. 2003. "Structural Change and Fiscal Flows: A Framework for Analyzing the Effects of Urban Events." *Urban Affairs Review* 38(3): 396–416.

Saegert, S. 1978. "High Density Environments: Their Personal and Social Consequences." In *Human Response to Crowding,* edited by A. Baum and Y. Epstein. Hillsdale, NJ: Lawrence Erlbaum.

Sassen, Saskia. 1991. *The Global City.* Princeton, NJ: Princeton University Press.

———. 2001. *The Global City: New York, London, Tokyo,* 2nd ed. Princeton, NJ: Princeton University Press.

———. 2006. *Cities of a World Economy,* 3rd ed. Newbury Park, CA: Pine Forge Press/Sage.

Saunders, Peter. 1981. *Social Theory and the Urban Question.* New York: Holmes and Meier.

Savitch, H. V., Takashi Tsukamoto, and Ronald K. Vogel. 2008. "Civic Culture and Corporate Regime in Louisville." *Journal of Urban Affairs* 30(4): 437–460.

Schaeffer, Nora Cate, and Stanley Presser. 2003. "The Science of Asking Questions." *Annual Review of Sociology* 29: 65–88.

Schmitt, Robert C. 1963. "Implications of Density in Hong Kong." *Journal of the American Institute of Planners* 29: 210–217.

———. 1966. "Density, Health and Social Organization." *Journal of the American Institute of Planners* 32: 38–40.

Schwab, William. 1982. *Urban Sociology.* Reading, MA: Addison-Wesley.

Seder, J. P., and S. Oishi. "Racial Homogeneity in College Students' Facebook Friendship Network and Subjective Well-Being." *Journal of Research in Personality* 43: 438–443.

Seeley, John, R. A. Sim, and E. W. Loosley. 1956. *Crestwood Heights.* New York: Basic Books.

Seeman, Albert. 1938. "Communities in the Salt Lake Basin." *Economic Geography* 14: 306.

Seeman, Melvin, J. M. Bishop, and J. E. Grigsby. 1971. "Community and Control in a Metropolitan Setting." In *Race, Change, and Urban Society, Urban Affairs Annual Review,* Vol. 5, edited by P. Orleans and R. Ellis. Los Angeles: Russell Sage Foundation.

Shanklin, William M., and John K. Rayns, Jr. 1998. "Stoking the Small Business Engine." *Business Horizons* 41(1): 27–33.

Shaw, Clifford. 1929. *Delinquency Areas.* Chicago: The University of Chicago Press.

———. 1930. *The Jackroller, a Delinquent Boy's Own Story.* Chicago: The University of Chicago Press.

Shaw, Randy. 2001. *The Activist's Handbook,* 2nd ed. Berkeley: University of California Press.

Sheldon, Kennon M., Robert Cummins, and Shanmukh Kamble. 2010. "Life Balance and Well-Being: Testing a Novel Conceptual and Measurement Approach." *Journal of Personality* 78(4): 1093–1134.

Shevky, Eshref, and Wendell Bell. 1955. *Social Area Analysis.* Stanford, CA: Stanford University Press.

Shils, Edward Albert. 1972. *The Intellectuals and the Powers and Other Essays.* Chicago: The University of Chicago Press.

Shlay, Anne, and Peter Rossi. 1981. "Keeping Up the Neighborhood: Estimating Net Effects of Zoning." *American Sociological Review* 46: 703–719.

Simmel, Georg. 1950, 1936. "The Metropolis in Mental Life," translated and edited by K. H. Wolff, in *The Sociology of Georg Simmel.* New York: Free Press

———. 1983. "The Metropolis in Mental Life." In *New Perspectives on the American Community,* edited by Roland Warren and Larry Lyon. Homewood, IL: Dorsey Press.

Sjoberg, Gideon. 1965. *The Preindustrial City.* New York: Free Press.

Skocpol, Theda, and Morris P. Fiorina, eds. 1999. *Civic Engagement in American Democracy.* Washington, DC: Brookings Institution Press.

Skvoretz, John, and Katherine Faust. 1999. "Logit Models for Affiliation Networks." *Sociological Methodology* 29: 253–280.

Slovak, Jeffrey. 1985. "City Spending, Suburban Demands, and Fiscal Exploitation: A Replication and Extension." *Social Forces* 64: 168–190.

Small, Albion W., and George E. Vincent. 1894. *An Introduction to the Study of Society.* New York: American Book Company.

Smith, Janet. 2002. "HOPE IV and New Urbanism: Eliminating Low-Income Housing to Make Mixed-Income Communities." *Planners Network* 151: 22–25.

Soja, Edward W. 1996. *Thirdspace: Journeys to Los Angeles and the Real-and-Imagined Places.* Malden, MA: Blackwell.

———. 2000. *Postmetropolis: Critical Studies of Cities and Regions.* Malden, MA, and Oxford, UK: Blackwell.

———. 2003. *Postmodern Geographies: The Reassertion of Space in Critical Theory.* London: Verso.

Sommer, Robert. 1969. *Personal Space.* Englewood Cliffs, NJ: Prentice-Hall.

Sorokin, Pitirim A. 1963. Foreword. In Ferdinand Tönnies, *Community and Society,* translated and edited by Charles F. Loomis. New York: Harper Torchbooks.

Spates, James L., and John J. Macionis. 1982. *The Sociology of Cities.* New York: St. Martin's Press.

Stack, Carol B. 1974. *All Our Kin: Strategies for Survival in a Black Community.* New York: Harper & Row.

Stein, Maurice R. 1960. *The Eclipse of Community.* Princeton, NJ: Princeton University Press.

Stein, C. S. 1957. *Towards New Towns for America.* Cambridge, MA: MIT Press.

Stoecker, Randy. 1997. "The Community Development Corporation Model of Urban Redevelopment: A Critique and an Alternative." *Journal of Urban Affairs* 19: 1–23.

———. 2001. "Power or Programs? Two Paths to Community Development." Keynote speech at the International Community Development Conference, April, Rotorua, New Zealand. Retrieved at http://conserver.sa.utoledo.edu/drafts/twopathsba2.htm

———. 2009. "Community Organizing and Social Change." *Contexts* 8(1) (Feb.): 20–25.

Stone, Clarence N. 1989. *Regime Politics: Governing Atlanta, 1946–1988.* Lawrence: University Press of Kansas.

Stoutland, Sara E. 1999. "Levels of the Community Development System: A Framework for Research and Practice." *Urban Anthropology* 28(2): 165–191.

Strauss, Anselm. 1961. *Images of the American City.* New York: Free Press.

Strine, Tara, Daniel P. Chapman, Lina S. Balluz, David G. Moriarty, and Ali H. Mokdad. 2007. "The Associations between Life Satisfaction and Health-related Quality of Life, Chronic Illness, and Health Behaviors among U.S. Community-dwelling Adults." *Journal of Community Health* 33(1): 40–50.

Sudman, Seymour, and Norman Bradburn. 1982. *Asking Questions*. San Francisco: Jossey-Bass.

Suttles, Gerald D. 1968. *The Social Order of the Slum*. Chicago: The University of Chicago Press.

———. 1972. *The Social Construction of Communities*. Chicago: The University of Chicago Press.

Sutton, Willis, Jr., and Thomas Munson. 1976. "Definitions of Community: 1954 through 1973." Paper presented to the American Sociological Association, New York, August 30.

Sutton, Willis, Jr., and Jiri Kolaja. 1960. "Elements of Community Action." *Social Force* 38: 325–331.

Swanepoel, Hennie, and Frik De Beer. 2006. *Community Development: Breaking the Cycle of Poverty*, 2nd ed. Landowne, South Africa: Juta Press.

Tabb, William K. 1999. *Reconstructing Political Economy: The Great Divide in Economic Thought*. New York: Routledge.

———. 2004. *Economic Governance in the Age of Globalization*. New York: Columbia University Press.

Tabb, William K. and Larry Sawers, eds. 1978. *Marxism and the Metropolis*. New York: Oxford University Press.

———. 1984. *Marxism and the Metropolis: New Perspectives in Urban Political Economy*, 2nd ed. New York: Oxford University Press.

Talen, Emily. 1999. "Sense of Community and Neighbourhood Form: An Assessment of the Social Doctrine of New Urbanism." *Urban Studies (UK)* 36(8): 1361–1379.

———. 2002. "The Social Goals of New Urbanism." *Housing Policy Debate* 13(1): 165–188.

Taylor, Brian. 1975. "The Absence of a Sociological and Structural Problem Focus in Community Studies." *Archives Europeens de Sociologie* 16. DOI: 10.1017/S0003975600004963

Theodorson, George. 1961. *Studies in Human Ecology*. New York: Harper & Row.

Thibaut, John W., and Harold H. Kelley. 1959. *The Social Psychology of Groups*. New York: John Wiley & Sons.

Thomas, William I., and Dorothy S. Thomas. 1928. *The Child in America*. New York: Alfred A. Knopf.

Thompson, Leigh, and Janice Nadler. 2002. "Negotiating via Information Technology: Theory and Application." *Journal of Social Issues* 58(1): 109–124.

Thrasher, Frederick M. 1927. *The Gang*. Chicago: The University of Chicago Press.

Tittle, Charles R., and Mark C. Stafford. 1992. "Urban Theory, Urbanism, and Suburban Residence." *Social Forces* 70(3): 725–744.

Toffler, Alvin. 1980. *The Third Wave*. New York: Bantam Books.

Tönnies, Ferdinand. 1887, 1963. *Community and Society*, translated and edited by Charles P. Loomis. New York: Harper & Row.

Tourangeau, R. 2003. "Cognitive Aspects of Survey Measurement and Mismeasurement." *International Journal of Public Opinion Research* 15(1): 3–7.

Troldahl, Verling C., and Roy C. Carter. 1964. "Random Selection of Respondents within Households in Phone Surveys." *Journal of Marketing Research* 1: 71–6.

Trounstine, Philip J., and Terry Christensen. 1982. *Movers and Shakers: The Study of Community Power.* New York: St. Martin's Press.

Tu, C., and M. Eppli. 1999. "Valuing the New Urbanism: The Case of Kentlands." *Real Estate Economics* 27(3): 425–451.

Turk, Herman. 1970. "Interorganizational Networks in Urban Society." *American Sociological Review* 35: 1–18.

Twigg, L., Taylor, J. and Mohan, J. 2010. "Diversity or Disadvantage? Putnam, Goodhart, Ethnic Heterogeneity, and Collective Efficacy." *Environment and Planning A* 42(6): 1421–1438. DOI: 1068/a42287.

Ullman, Edward. 1941. "A Theory of Location for Cities." *American Journal of Sociology* 46: 153–164.

US Bureau of the Census. 1983. *County and City Data Book.* Washington DC: Government Printing Office.

US Department of Commerce. 1973. *Social Indicators.* Washington DC: Government Printing Office.

———. 1976. *Social Indicators.* Washington DC: Government Printing Office.

———. 1980. *Social Indicators.* Washington DC: Government Printing Office.

Valenzuela, S., Park, N., & Kee, K. F. 2008. "Lessons from Facebook: The Effect of Social Network Sites on College Students' Social Capital." Paper submitted to the 9th Symposium on Online Journalism, Austin, TX, April 4–5. Retrieved at http://online.journalism.utexas.edu/2008/papers/Valenzuela.pdf

Van Dijk, J. 2006. *The Network Society: Social Aspects of New Media.* Thousand Oaks, CA: Sage.

Van Poppel, Frans, and Lincoln H. Day. 1996. "A Test of Durkheim's Theory of Suicide—Without Committing the 'Ecological Fallacy.'" *American Sociological Review* 61: 500–507.

Veenhoven, Ruut. 2000. "The Four Qualities of Life: Ordering Concept and Measures of the Good Life." *Journal of Happiness Studies* 1: 1–39.

Vidal, Avis C. 1997. "Can Community Development Re-Invent Itself? The Challenges of Strengthening Neighborhoods in the 21st Century." *Journal of the American Planning Association* 63: 429–438.

Vidal, Avis C., and W. Dennis Keating. 2004. "Community Development: Current Issues and Emerging Challenges." *Journal of Urban Affairs* 26(2): 125–137.

Vidich, Arthur, and Joseph Bensman. 1955. "Participant Observation and the Collection and Interpretation of Data." *American Journal of Sociology* 60(4): 354–360.

———. 1958. *Small Town in Mass Society.* Princeton, NJ: Princeton University Press.

Vidich, Arthur, Joseph Bensman, and Maurice Stein. 1964. *Reflections on Community Studies.* New York: John Wiley & Sons.

Walton, John. 1966. "Discipline, Method, and Community Power." *American Sociological Review* 31: 684–689.

———. 1970. "A Systematic Survey of Community Power Research." In *The Structure of Community Power*, edited by Michael Aiken and Paul E. Mott. New York: Random House.

Warner, Mildred. 1999. "Social Capital Construction and the Role of the Local State." *Rural Sociology* 64(3): 373–393.

Warner, W. Lloyd. 1959. *The Living and the Dead.* New Haven, CT: Yale University Press.

———. 1963. *Yankee City.* New Haven, CT: Yale University Press.

Warner, W. Lloyd, and Josiah O. Low. 1947. *The Social System of the Modern Factory.* New Haven, CT: Yale University Press.

Warner, W. Lloyd, and Paul S. Lunt. 1941. *The Social Life of a Modern Community*. New Haven, CT: Yale University Press.

———. 1942. *The Status System of a Modern Community*. New Haven, CT: Yale University Press.

Warner, W. Lloyd, Marcia Meeker, and Kenneth Eells. 1949. *Social Class in America*. Chicago: Science Research Associates.

Warner, W. Lloyd, and Leo Srole. 1945. *The Social Systems of American Ethnic Groups*. New Haven, CT: Yale University Press.

Warren, Roland L. 1970. "The Good Community—What Would It Be?" *Journal of the Community Development Society* 1(1) (spring): 14–23. Reprinted in *New Perspectives on the American Community* (1983), edited by Roland L. Warren and Larry Lyon. Homewood, IL: Dorsey Press.

———. 1971. "The Sociology of Knowledge and the Problems of the Inner Cities." *Social Science Quarterly* 52(3): 468–485.

———. 1978. *The Community in America*. Chicago: Rand McNally.

———. 1983. "Observations on the State of Community Theory." In *New Perspectives on the American Community*, edited by Roland Warren and Larry Lyon. Homewood, IL: Dorsey Press.

Warren, Roland, and Larry Lyon, eds. 1983. *New Perspectives on the American Community*. Homewood, IL: Dorsey Press.

Wasserman, Stanley, and Katherine Faust. 1989. "Canonical Analysis of the Composition and Structure of Social Networks." *Sociological Methodology* 19: 1–42.

Webber, Melvin M. 1963. "Order in Diversity: Community without Propinquity." In *Cities and Space: The Future Use of Urban Land,* edited by L. Wingo, Jr. Baltimore, MD: Johns Hopkins University Press.

———. 1968. *Economy and Society*. New York: Bedminster Press.

Weber, Max. 1921, 1958. *The Protestant Ethic and the Spirit of Capitalism*. New York: Charles Scribner's Sons.

———. 1920–21, 1959. *Sociology of Religion*, translated by Curt Rosenthal. New York: The Philosophical Library.

Webster, Frank. 2001. "Re-Inventing Place: Birmingham As an Information City?" *City* 5(1): 27–46.

Weeks, John. 2002. *Population: An Introduction to Concepts and Issues*, 8th ed. Belmont, CA: Wadsworth Group.

Weicher, John C. 1972. "The Effect of Metropolitan Political Fragmentation on Central City Budgets." In *Models of Urban Structure*, edited by David Sweet. Lexington, MA: D. C. Heath.

Weinstein, Jay, and Vijayan K. Pillai. 2001. *Demography: The Science of Population*. Boston: Allyn & Bacon.

Wellman, Barry. 1979 "The Community Question: The Intimate Networks of East Yorkers." *American Journal of Sociology* 84(5): 1201–1231.

———. 2001. "Physical Place and Cyberplace: The Rise of Personalized Networking." *International Journal of Urban and Regional Research* 22(2): 227–252.

Wellman, Barry, and Milena Gulia. 1999a. "The Network Basis of Social Support: A Network Is More Than the Sum of Its Ties." Pp. 83–118 in *Networks in the Global Village: Life in Contemporary Communities*, edited by Barry Wellman. Boulder, CO: Westview.

———. 1999b. "Virtual Communities as Communities: Net Surfers Don't Ride Alone." Pp. 167–194 in *Communities in Cyberspace*, edited by M.A. Smith and P. Kollock. New York: Routledge.

Wellman, Barry, and Keith Hampton. 1999. "Living Networked On and Offline." *Contemporary Sociology* 28(6): 642–654.

Wellman, Barry, and B. Leighton. 1979. "Networks, Neighborhoods, and Communities: Approaches to the Study of the Community Question." *Urban Affairs Quarterly* 14(3): 363–390.

Wellman, Barry, and Scot Wortley. 1990. "Different Strokes from Different Folks: Community Ties and Social Support." *American Journal of Sociology* 96(3): 558–588.

West, James. 1945. *Plainville, U.S.A.* New York: Columbia University Press.

White, Charles B., Nancy Bushnell, and Judy L. Regnemer. 1978. "Moral Development in Bahamian School Children." *Developmental Psychology* 14: 58–65.

White, Michael J. 1987. *American Neighborhoods and Residential Differentiation.* New York: Russell Sage Foundation.

Whyte, William Foote. 1955. *Street Corner Society.* Chicago: The University of Chicago Press.

———. 1964. "The Slum: On the Evolution of Street Corner Society." In *Reflections on Community Studies,* edited by Arthur Vidich et al. New York: John Wiley & Sons.

Whyte, William H. 1956. *The Organization Man.* New York: Simon and Schuster.

———. 1989. *City: Rediscovering Its Center.* New York: Doubleday.

Wilkinson, Kenneth P. 1972. "A Field-Theory Perspective for Community Development Research." *Rural Sociology* 37(1): 43–52.

———. 1989. "The Future for Community Development." Pp. 337–354 in *Community Development in Perspective,* edited by James A. Christenson and Jerry W. Robinson, Jr. Ames: Iowa State University Press.

William, Colin C. 2005. "Cultivating Community Self-Help in Deprived Urban Neighborhoods." *City and Community* 4 (June): 171–188.

Williams, Robin M., Jr. 1970. *American Society: A Sociological Interpretation.* New York: Alfred A. Knopf.

Williams, James M. 1973. "The Ecological Approach in Measuring Community Power Concentration." *American Sociological Review* 38: 230–242.

Wilson, James Q. 1983. *Thinking about Crime.* New York: Basic Books.

Wilson, Thomas. 1985. "Urbanism and Tolerance: A Test of Some Hypotheses Drawn from Wirth and Stouffer." *American Sociological Review* 50(1): 117–123.

———. 1986. "Community Population Size and Social Heterogeneity: An Empirical Test." *American Journal of Sociology* 91(5): 1154–1169.

Wilson, William J. 1987. *The Truly Disadvantaged.* Chicago: The University of Chicago Press.

Wirth, Louis. 1928. *The Ghetto.* Chicago: The University of Chicago Press.

———. 1938. "Urbanism as a Way of Life." *American Journal of Sociology* 44: 8–20.

Wolff, Kurt H., ed. 1978. *The Sociology of Georg Simmel.* Toronto: Free Press.

Wolff, Rick. 2010. "In Capitalists Crisis: Rediscovering Marx." *Socialism and Democracy* 24(3): 130–146.

Wolfinger, Raymond E. 1962. "A Plea for Decent Burial." *American Sociological Review* 25: 636–644.

Wolpert, J. 1965. "Behavioral Aspects of the Decision to Migrate." *Papers of the Regional Science Association* 15: 159–169.

Woodbury, Robert M. 1934. "Statistical Practice." In *Encyclopedia of the Social Sciences,* Vol. XIV, edited by Edward Seligman. New York: Macmillan.

Wuthnow, Robert. 1998. *Loose Connections: Joining Together in America's Fragmented Communities.* Cambridge: Harvard University Press.

Zablocki, Benjamin. 1979. "Communes, Encounter Groups, and the Search for Community." In *In Search for Community*, edited by Kurt Black. Boulder, CO: Westview.

Zorbaugh, Harvey. 1926. "The Natural Areas of the City." *Publications of the American Sociological Society* 20.

———. 1929. *The Gold Coast and Slum*. Chicago: The University of Chicago Press.

Zukin, Sharon. 2009. "Changing Landscapes of Power: Opulence and the Crisis of Authenticity." *International Journal of Urban and Regional Research* 33(2) (June): 543–553.

Name Index

Subject Index